May 2007

# CHRISTIAN HISTORY
# MADE EASY

ROSE
PUBLISHING

Torrance, California

Rose Publishing
4455 Torrance Blvd., #259, Torrance, California 90503 U.S.A.
www.rose-publishing.com

*Christian History Made Easy*
Copyright © 1999 Timothy Paul Jones

To schedule one of Timothy Paul Jones's Christian history seminars for your church, home-school group, or civic organization, contact Timothy Paul Jones through the Christian History Made Easy web-site... *http://www.timothypauljones.com* or e-mail him at *timothywashere@timothypauljones.com*

Rose Publishing is in no way liable for any context, change of content, or activity (i.e., if a site is found to be no longer active) for the web-sites listed.

To place orders for this book, see your local Christian bookstore.

Unless otherwise noted, all scripture quotations are from the Holy Bible, New King James Version, copyright © 1982 by Thomas Nelson, Inc.

Unless designated otherwise, all photographs are the property of Rose Publishing, Timothy Paul Jones, Gretchen W. Goldsmith, Dr. Arvel Witte, Carol R. Witte, or Teri A. Moyer. All rights reserved. Some pictures are in the public domain.

Desktop publishing and design by Teri A. Moyer, Communication By Design

ISBN 1-890947-10-5   Paperback
ISBN 1-890947-11-3   Hardcover

*Printed in the United States of America*

03  04  05  06  07 / 20  19  18  17  16

# Contents

Foreword . . . . . . . . . . . . . . . . . . . . . . . . . .2
By Dr. A. Kenneth Curtis, President of Christian History Institute
and Mark Galli, Managing Editor of *Christianity Today* Magazine

Introduction . . . . . . . . . . . . . . . . . . . .3
Why Does Church History Matter?

Chapter One . . . . . . . . . . . . . . . . . . . . . .6
The Gospels, the Apostles, Then . . . What? (AD 64—177)

Chapter Two . . . . . . . . . . . . . . . . . . . . . .16
Balancing the Past With the Present (AD 90—250)

Chapter Three . . . . . . . . . . . . . . . . . . . .26
The Church Wins . . . and Loses (AD 247—420)

Chapter Four . . . . . . . . . . . . . . . . . . . . .36
Servant-Leaders or Leaders of Servants? (AD 376—664)

Chapter Five . . . . . . . . . . . . . . . . . . . . .48
From Multiplication to Division (AD 496—1291)

Chapter Six . . . . . . . . . . . . . . . . . . . . . .60
God Never Stops Working (AD 673—1295)

Chapter Seven . . . . . . . . . . . . . . . . . . . .70
Everything Falls Apart (1294—1517)

Chapter Eight . . . . . . . . . . . . . . . . . . . .80
Wild Pigs in a Dirty Vineyard (1500—1609)

Chapter Nine . . . . . . . . . . . . . . . . . . . . .92
Change Doesn't Always Do You Good (1510—1767)

Chapter Ten . . . . . . . . . . . . . . . . . . . . . .104
Talkin' 'Bout Some Revolutions (1620—1814)

Chapter Eleven . . . . . . . . . . . . . . . . . . .114
Optimism Has Its Limits (1780—1914)

Chapter Twelve . . . . . . . . . . . . . . . . . . .126
From Modern to Post-Modern . . . and Beyond (1900—1999)

Final Reflections . . . . . . . . . . . . . . . . .141

Leader's Guides . . . . . . . . . . . . . . . . . .142

Index . . . . . . . . . . . . . . . . . . . . . . . . . . .164

About the Author . . . . . . . . . . . . . . . . .166

\* People listed were not all Christians (such as Nero, Diocletian, Muhammad) but affected
  Christian history in important ways.

## *Key People and Events

### Chapter One
Emperor Nero
Paul and Peter Martyred
Destruction of Temple
Martyrdom of Polycarp
Justin Martyr

### Chapter Two
Gnosticism
Marcion
Origen
Montanism

### Chapter Three
Emperor Diocletian
Emperor Constantine
Arius
Athanasius of Alexandria
Paula

### Chapter Four
Ambrose of Milan
John Chrysostom
Augustine of Hippo
Cyril of Alexandria
Leo the Great
Patrick

### Chapter Five
Muhammad
Charlemagne
Photius of Constantinople
The Crusades
Pope Leo IX (Bruno)

### Chapter Six
Cluny monasteries
John Damascus
Cyril of Moravia
Hildegard of Bingen
Francis of Assisi
Anselm of Canterbury
Thomas Aquinas
Thomas Becket

### Chapter Seven
Bubonic Plague
John Wycliffe
Thomas A'Kempis
Joan of Arc
Gutenberg Bible

### Chapter Eight
Martin Luther
John Calvin
Anabaptists
King Henry VIII
Ignatius Loyola

### Chapter Nine
Christopher Columbus
Jacob Arminius
Galilei Galileo
King James I
John Bunyan

### Chapter Ten
Anne Hutchinson
Salem Witch Trials
Jonathan Edwards
George Whitefield
American War for Independence

### Chapter Eleven
William Carey
Hudson Taylor
Barton W. Stone
Charles G. Finney
Charles H. Spurgeon
Dwight L. Moody

### Chapter Twelve
Karl Barth
C. S. Lewis
Charles Fox Parham
Dietrich Bonhoeffer
Second Vatican Council
Mother Teresa
Billy Graham

# Foreword

For so many of our fellow evangelical believers, the study of Christian history seems hopelessly intimidating and overwhelming. They have no idea where to begin. So most struggle on without the benefit of our family treasure that shows us how God has faithfully worked among His people over the centuries.

Now, Timothy Paul Jones has given us a resource that makes Christian history accessible. This can be a launching pad to a lifetime of adventure in detecting the footprints of God across the ages. Jones not only gives a valuable overview that is like an airplane ride over the terrain, but he also supplies follow-up connections to websites and other resources, so that you can pursue the themes and times that most interest you.

As one whose life and ministry has been largely occupied in telling the story of our Christian heritage, I warmly welcome this book as a valuable contribution. Get a copy for yourself. You will refer to it often. But also get one to give to a student you care about.

Dr. A. Kenneth Curtis
President, Christian History Institute
Senior Editor, *Christian History* Magazine


Church history is being stolen from us, and I don't think we should stand for it anymore.

It's being stolen by professional historians who have discarded reporting tales of tragedy, valor, and pathos for writing textbooks crammed with dates, social analysis, and political posturing.

It's being shoplifted by television, which lulls us into an entertainment stupor, so that our minds can no longer grasp anything more complicated than *Wheel of Fortune*.

And we're pickpocketed by our own foolishness, our panting after the latest, the new, the "now."

How do we bring church history back? We can write it in a way that shows its relevance. We can follow Augustine's dictum that communication should entertain while it informs. We can be honest about Christian failures (which have been manifold) but refuse to wallow in cynicism. We can make sure we don't produce textbooks but books filled with people and stories we will never forget.

Okay, I'm biased. I admit I'm saying good history should read like *Christian History* magazine, for this is the sort of history we've been trying to produce for years.

And this is precisely what drew me to *Christian History Made Easy*. I know good history when I see it, and I see it here.

The study of church history can do many things for us, to name a few: it gives perspective; it frees us from faddishness; it shows God's working in the world; it gives wisdom; it implants hope deep within us. If you're looking for such things—or perhaps just wondering how you and your fellow believers ended up at this time and place in the larger scheme—reading Christian history, and this book in particular, is one place to begin.

Mark Galli,
Managing Editor, *Christianity Today* Magazine

# Introduction

## WHY DOES CHURCH HISTORY MATTER?

Sally carefully labels her paper, "Church History." As Charlie Brown glances over her shoulder, Sally considers the subject. "When writing about church history," Sally scribbles, "we have to go back to the very beginning. Our pastor was born in 1930."

Charles Schulz's comic strip may be amusing, but it isn't too far from the truth. In sermons and devotional books, we encounter names like Augustine, Calvin, Spurgeon, Moody. Their stories interest us, but we have a tough time fitting the stories together. The average Christian's knowledge of church history ends with the apostles and doesn't begin again until the twentieth century.

Still, Christian history deeply affects every Christian. It affects how we read the Bible. It affects how we view our governments. It affects how we worship. The church's history is our family history. Past Christians are our mothers and fathers, our aunts and uncles, our in-laws and (in some cases) our outlaws!

When a child in Sunday School asks, "How could Jesus be God and still be like me?" she's asking a question that, in AD 325, three hundred church leaders discussed in a little village named Nicaea [ni-SEE-ah] (modern Iznik, Turkey). Somehow, what those leaders decided will influence your answer.

If you wonder, "Why are there so many different churches?" the answer is woven somewhere within 2,000 years of struggles and skirmishes. When you read words like "predestined" or "justified" in Paul's letter to the Romans, it isn't only Paul and your pastor who affect what you believe. Augustine, Aquinas, Martin Luther, and Jonathan Edwards also influence your response, whether you realize it or not. Still, the story of Christianity can seem like a vast, dreary landscape, littered with a few interesting anecdotes and a lot of dull dates.

What we don't recognize sometimes is that church history is a *story*. It's an exciting story about ordinary people that God has used in extraordinary ways. Yet, most church members will never read Justo González's thousand-page *The Story of Christianity*. Only the most committed students will wade through all 1,552 pages of Ken Latourette's *A History of Christianity*. Fewer still will learn to apply church history to their lives.

That's why I've written this book and these leader's guides. *Christian History Made Easy* is a summary of the church's story, written in words that everyone can understand. I haven't loaded *Christian History Made Easy* with abstract facts and figures. Neither have I cluttered the book with tiresome footnotes. (If you're interested in what sources I used, check the Leader's Guides, near the back of the book). *Christian History Made Easy* is a collection of stories. Together, these stories give us a glimpse of 2,000 years of God's work.

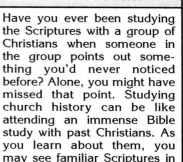

### Think About It...

Have you ever been studying the Scriptures with a group of Christians when someone in the group points out something you'd never noticed before? Alone, you might have missed that point. Studying church history can be like attending an immense Bible study with past Christians. As you learn about them, you may see familiar Scriptures in a new light.

*Jesus Christ, the Beginning and the End of human history (Revelation 1:8).*

## On The Web

Lots of links and teaching helps are available at the Christian History Made Easy web-site . . .

*http://www.
timothypauljones.com*

For more resources, try these sites:

*http://www.gty.org/
~phil/hall.htm*

*http://www.christian
history.net*

*http://www.gospelcom.net/
chi/*

## What Does Your Group Need to Study *Christian History Made Easy*?

The following items are available from Rose Publishing: Each student should have a copy of this book and a *Christian History Time Line* pamphlet (Item #413). Most students will also want *How We Got the Bible* pamphlets (#407). Hang *Christian History Time Line* (#417) and *How We Got the Bible* (#406) wall charts wherever your group meets. A *How We Got the Bible PowerPoint®* (#447) presentation is also available. Samples from the *Christian History Made Easy PowerPoint®* presentation can be downloaded from

*http://www.
timothypauljones.com*

Contact Rose Publishing toll free, at **1-800-53-CHART** or. . .

*http://www.
rose-publishing.com*

Using this book and these Leader's Guides, your group can survey church history in thirteen sessions. (No one in the group, not even the leader, needs to be an expert on church history.) Or, you can simply enjoy the book on your own.

Unlike most church history writers, I am not a professional scholar. I admire people who teach college and university students, but my days aren't spent in the classroom. When I wrote this book, I was the pastor of a small church in rural Missouri. I spent my days among farmers and school-teachers, in hay-fields and hospitals, with lonely widows and life-loving youth. As I wrote, I thought not only about Augustine and Luther and Calvin and Edwards, but also about the people who allowed me to be their pastor, people like Amy Jo and Eric and Leona and Harold—people who are a lot like you. It was for ordinary laypeople that I wrote *Christian History Made Easy*, so that they could grasp what it means to be surrounded by "so great a cloud of witnesses" (Hebrews 12:1).

Special thanks to: Rose Publishing for taking a chance on the manuscript; the many patient members of Green Ridge Baptist Church on whom I tested this material; Jeff Cochran, for remaining single so you could afford so many history books; Robin Sandbothe, Connie Edwards, Daniel Schwartz, Barbara Harrell Brown, Lianna Johns, and Larry Sullivan for proofreading the first draft of the manuscript; Kenny and Brent McCune, and "Princess" Amy Ezell for their help on the Learning Activities; W. T. Stancil for proof-reading above and beyond the call of duty; Stephanie, Heather, Diane, and Christy at the McDonald's on Highway 50 in Sedalia, who fueled this project with copious amounts of cholesterol and Diet Coke; and, my wife, Rayann—if a snowflake fell for each moment I love you, we would live in endless winter.

This book is dedicated to my parents, Darrell and Patricia. By chance, you gave me life. By choice, you gave me love. By wisdom, you let me forge my own path. By grace, you gave me wings to fly. This one is for you.

*Timothy Paul Jones*

# INTRODUCTORY LEARNING ACTIVITY

How much do you know about church history? Fifteen key names from church history are hidden in the word-search. Each name completes one of the sentences below. Feel free to use a hymnal or Bible. If you don't know an answer, guess! To check your answers, look at the Leader's Guides near the back of the book.

```
R  E  F  F  E  O  H  N  O  B
E  L  A  S  C  A  S  A  S  Q
N  S  G  R  A  H  A  M  L  D
I  P  A  U  L  T  B  C  E  R
T  U  T  N  S  R  R  A  F  A
N  R  A  N  I  A  E  L  F  G
A  P  Y  O  M  B  H  V  I  E
T  E  E  E  O  H  T  I  L  D
S  T  L  G  N  O  U  N  C  L
N  E  S  R  S  U  L  L  Y  I
O  R  E  U  U  S  H  A  W  H
C  R  W  P  H  E  G  R  A  H
M  O  T  S  O  S  Y  R  H  C
```

### Notes

1. According to tradition, _____ was crucified upside down.
2. Early Christians met in _____ (Romans 16:5).
3. Emperor _____ claimed that he saw a cross in the sky.
4. John _____ 's nickname meant "Golden-Mouth."
5. One bishop accused _____ of Bingen, a mystic, of heresy.
6. Many Protestants call John _____ "the Morning Star of the Reformation."
7. Martin _____ wrote "A Mighty Fortress Is Our God."
8. John _____ wrote the *Institutes of the Christian Religion.*
9. Menno _____ was an early Anabaptist leader.
10. Bartolome de _____ fought his country's exploitation of Native Americans.
11. Charles _____, who wrote the hymn "And Can It Be", was part of a "Holy Club" at Oxford University.
12. Charles _____ was an English pastor in the mid-1800s.
13. Karl _____ 's commentary on Romans criticized the liberal theology of the 1800s.
14. Hitler had Dietrich _____ executed in 1945.
15. Billy _____ has been called the "best loved American Christian."

# WHAT YOU SHOULD KNOW ABOUT CHRISTIAN HISTORY
## AD 64—AD 177

### Five Events You Should Know

1. *Jerusalem Council* (AD 49-50): Church recognized that the gospel is for Gentiles too (Acts 15).

2. *Fire in Rome* (AD 64): Flames destroyed 70% of the capital city. Emperor Nero blamed and persecuted the Christians.

3. *Destruction of Jerusalem Temple* (AD 70): After a Jewish revolt, Emperor Vespasian ordered his son, Titus, to regain Jerusalem. Titus torched the city and leveled the temple.

4. *Pliny's Letter to Emperor Trajan* (around AD 112): Pliny, governor of Pontus, asked Trajan how to handle Christians. Trajan ordered Pliny not to pursue Christians. Only when people were accused of being Christians were they to be hunted down.

5. *Martyrdom of Polycarp* (AD 155): Polycarp of Smyrna (now Izmir, Turkey) was burned alive because he would not offer incense to the emperor.

### Ten Names You Should Know

1. *Peter* (died between AD 65 and 68): Leading apostle of the early church.

2. *Paul* (died between AD 65 and 68): Early Christian missionary and apostle.

3. *Nero* (AD 37-68): Roman emperor, persecuted Christians after fire in Rome.

4. *Clement of Rome* (died, AD 96): Leading pastor of Rome in the late first century. The fourth pope, according to Roman Catholics. Probably mentioned in Philippians 4:3.

5. *Josephus* (AD 37-100): Jewish writer. His historical works tell about early Christianity and the destruction of the Jewish temple.

6. *Ignatius* (AD 35-117): Apostolic church father and leading pastor in Syrian Antioch. Wrote seven important letters while traveling to Rome to face martyrdom.

7. *Papias* (AD 60-130): Apostolic church father. Wrote about the origins of the Gospels.

8. *Polycarp* (AD 69-155): Apostolic church father. Preserved Ignatius' writings.

9. *Justin Martyr* (AD 100-165): Christian philosopher and apologist. Martyred in Rome.

10. *Blandina* (died, AD 177): Slave-girl. Martyred in Lyons with the city's leading pastor.

### Five Terms You Should Know

1. *Anno Domini*: Latin for "the Lord's Year," usually abbreviated AD. Refers to the number of years since Christ's birth. Dionysius Exiguus, a sixth-century monk, was the first to date history by the life of Christ. His calculations were four years off. So, Jesus was around four years old in AD 1!

2. *Century*: One hundred years. The first century extended from AD 1 to AD 100; the second century, from AD 101 to AD 200; the third, from AD 201 to 300, and so on.

3. *Yahweh*: Hebrew name for God. The name means "I AM" (see Exodus 3:13-14).

4. *Apostolic Fathers*: Influential first-century Christians, such as Ignatius, Polycarp, and Papias. A few later theologians (such as Augustine) are also called church fathers.

5. *Apologists*: Second-century Christian writers who argued that Christianity should be legal.

# Chapter One

## THE GOSPELS, THE APOSTLES, THEN, . . . WHAT?

| In This Chapter AD 64—AD 177 |
|---|
| Emperor Nero |
| Peter and Paul Martyred |
| Destruction of Temple |
| Martyrdom of Polycarp |
| Justin Martyr |

### WHO WERE THE CHRISTIANS, ANYWAY?

Who were the Christians? For you, that may not be a tough question. For thirty years people in the Roman Empire couldn't agree on an answer. According to many Jews, Christians were renegades who had abandoned the ancient Law. Christians, however, claimed that they followed the Jewish Messiah. They even called themselves "the Israel of God" (Galatians 6:16). According to the Romans, the church was simply another Jewish sect (Acts 16:20). Because the Jewish faith was legal throughout the empire, the church's association with the Jews protected the earliest Christian missionaries.

During the last half of the first century AD, the situation shifted completely. By AD 100 the church had endured thirty years of veiled contempt and open violence. Jewish synagogues had excluded Christians. The followers of Christ were a distinct group within the empire. Why? The answer can't be confined to any certain event. Yet two fires—one in Jerusalem, one in Rome—were critically important.

#### Rome Burns, But Nero Doesn't Fiddle—AD 64

In midsummer, AD 64, Rome burned. Flames ravaged the city for six days. When the smoke cleared, blackened rubbish remained in ten of Rome's fourteen districts.

Nero, the Roman emperor, was several miles away when the fire began. When he heard the news, Nero rushed back to Rome. During the fire, he organized fire-fighting efforts. After the fire, thousands of refugees stayed in his gardens. Still, as the rebuilding of Rome began, many citizens blamed Nero for the tragedy.

According to one rumor, Nero had ordered his servants to start the fire. Nero torched Rome—the rumor claimed—so he could rebuild the city according to his own whims. Later rumors insisted that Nero had played his harp while Rome burned. (In fact, the fire probably began by accident in an oil warehouse.)

Nero lavished gifts on the citizens of Rome. Still, nothing slowed the rumors. In desperation, Nero blamed the fire on an unpopular minority group—the Christians. Nero became the first emperor to recognize the Christian faith as a new religion. Nero immediately began to persecute the Christians. One Roman historian wrote, "Some were dressed in furs and killed by dogs. Others were crucified, or burned alive, to light the night."

*Paul's missionary journeys spread Christianity through Asia Minor and the western Roman Empire. Believers were first called Christians in Antioch, in modern Turkey. (The Chora Monastery, Istanbul)*

*Original Bust of Nero*

## On The Web

To take a virtual tour of ancient Rome, log on to the Rome Project...

*http://www.dalton.org/ groups/rome/*

For the dates and historical contexts of New Testament events, check out ...

*http://www.pronetisp.net/ ~diana/wbt6.htm*

Statue of the Roman goddess Diana. Second century AD.

## Words: From The Ones Who Were There

*Anonymous pagan writer who misunderstood the Lord's Supper:* "An infant is covered with dough, to deceive the innocent. The infant is placed before the person who is to be stained with their rites. The young pupil slays the infant. Thirstily, they lick up its blood! Eagerly, they tear apart its limbs. After much feasting, they extinguish [the lights]. Then, the connections of depraved lust involve them in an uncertain fate."
*Quoted by Minucius Felix, Octavius 9.*

The apostle Peter died in Rome during Nero's persecution. According to tradition, Peter didn't believe he was worthy of dying like his Savior. So, the big fisherman asked to be crucified upside down. Roman authorities also arrested the apostle Paul. Since it was illegal to crucify a Roman citizen, Paul probably died by the sword.

In some ways, Nero's false accusation made sense. Christians did think that a great inferno would accompany the end of the world (Revelation 20:9). Some overly eager Christians may have seen a certain sign of Christ's return in Rome's destruction. Yet Christians were (according to a pagan writer) "hated for their abominations" *before* the fire. Why were they so unpopular?

### Christians rejected all other gods

Christians believed in only one God—the God of Israel, revealed in Jesus Christ (Deuteronomy 6:4; 1 Timothy 2:5). This belief seemed arrogant to the Romans. Most Romans covered all spiritual bases by sacrificing to every known god, and sometimes to unknown gods (Acts 17:23). They even offered incense to dead emperors. (As one emperor died, he joked, "I think I'm becoming a god now!") Yet Romans didn't sacrifice simply for their own sakes. They sacrificed for the sake of their empire. Numerous sacrifices, they believed, secured divine assistance for their state. To deny the existence of any divinity was, at best, unpatriotic and, at worst, personally perilous.

### Christian customs were widely misunderstood

When they described their worship, Christians talked about consuming the "body" and "blood" of Christ at their "love-feasts" (John 6:53-56; 1 Corinthians 10:16; 11:23-27; Jude 1:12). Believers called one another "brothers and sisters"—terms used in Egypt to refer to sexual partners.

Alone, either of these practices would have struck the Romans as odd. Together, they convinced many citizens that Christianity was a dangerous cult. Romans couldn't quell their concerns by attending a church service. When early Christians shared the Lord's Supper, they wouldn't let nonbelievers watch. Without firsthand information, Romans began to accuse Christians falsely of cannibalism and incest.

## Christians challenged the social order

Paul had declared, "There is neither Jew nor Greek, there is neither slave nor free, there is neither male nor female" (Galatians 3:28). In other words, every person matters, whatever his or her social status. Early Christians lived out Paul's words. The results offended the Romans.

The church challenged the entire structure of Roman society by welcoming the lower classes and by valuing every human life. Roman law prevented slaves from inheriting property. Ancient custom treated women as lesser beings. Christians welcomed slaves and women as equals. If a Roman father didn't want his child, he left the infant alone in a field, to die. By adopting abandoned infants, Christians defied the Roman father's refusal to raise unwanted children.

## Christianity was a new religion

New and improved products fascinate people today. In Roman society, nothing new was trustworthy. It was better to choose an old, proven product than to fall for a new, improved gimmick. Romans tolerated the Jews' belief in one God partly because the Jewish faith was so ancient. One thousand years before Rome was founded, Abraham had encountered Yahweh [YAH-way] in the desert. Christians claimed that their religion reached back, beyond Abraham (John 8:58). Yet, from the Romans' viewpoint, the church was very new.

Christians also had no sacrifices, no temples, and no sacred city. To many of their neighbors, Christians seemed unusual, unsafe, and unpleasant. Nevertheless, the distinction between Jews and Christians remained unclear in some areas. It was a catastrophe in AD 70 that transformed the situation once and for all.

## Jerusalem Burns and Bleeds—AD 70

In the mid-first century, Romans and Jews were constantly at each other's throats. Around AD 50, thousands of Jews were celebrating the Passover. A Roman fortress towered over the temple. Suddenly, one guard (in the words of Josephus, a Jewish writer) "lifted up his robe and bent over indecently. He turned his backside toward the Jews and made a noise as indecent as his posture." In the riot that followed, as many as 30,000 women and men died.

In AD 64 a new Roman ruler, Florus, arrived in Judea. For two years, Florus flagrantly insulted the Jews. When several Jewish leaders demanded that Florus stop stealing from the temple, Florus sent his soldiers into the market. Their orders? Slaughter and steal. Blood streamed like water through Jerusalem's dusty streets. Before the day ended, 3,600 Jews were dead.

**Think About It...**

Early Christians refused to share in customs that degraded other human beings. What customs should Christians avoid today?

*The silversmiths who made shrines for the goddess Diana rioted in this Ephesus theater when Paul preached the gospel which threatened their business.*

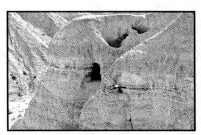

*Many scholars believe that a group of Jews hid their sacred scrolls in these caves near the Dead Sea. When the Dead Sea Scrolls were found in the late 1940s, they confirmed the reliability of the Hebrew Bible.*

# The World of the First Christians

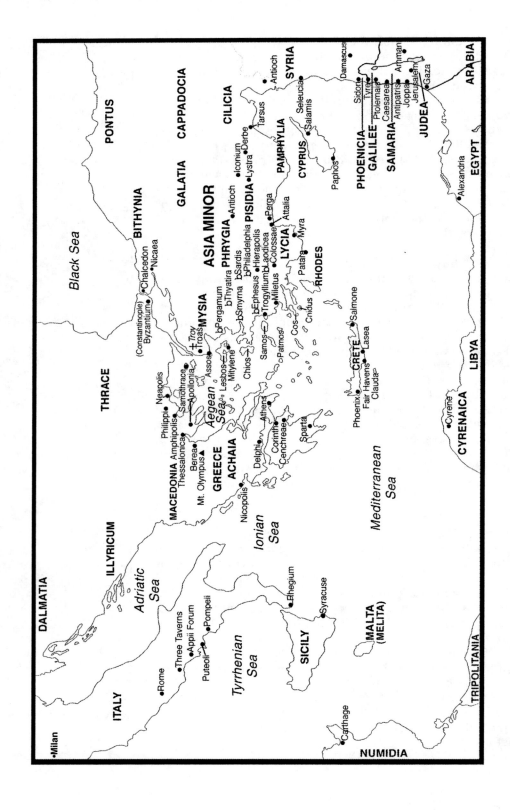

From *Paul's Journeys Then and Now* chart (#304) and *Then and Now Bible Map Book* (#306X), Rose Publishing, Torrance, California.

Seeds of anger toward Rome had germinated for years. Now, they sprouted into open revolt. Bands of Jewish rebels over-whelmed Roman strongholds in Jerusalem and Galilee.

Emperor Nero gave General Vespasian [ves-PAY-see-unn] 60,000 soldiers. Vespasian's task? Regain Galilee and Judea. Vespasian's campaign began in Galilee. Hundreds of Jews fled to Jerusalem in the face of the advancing legions. As Vespasian prepared to attack Jerusalem, he received a message: Nero had committed suicide. Vespasian returned to Rome, planning to take the imperial throne.

General Vespasian did become the emperor, but he didn't forget his previous task. He sent an army to besiege Jerusalem in the spring of AD 70. On August 5, Jerusalem fell. The rebels were massacred. The sacred city was plundered. The survivors were sold as slaves. The temple was burned to the ground. Only one wall of the temple mount (known today as the "Wailing Wall") remained. Within four years, every rebel stronghold had fallen to the Romans. The Jewish defenders of the final fortress —Masada, near the Dead Sea—chose mass-suicide instead of surrender. The revolt was over.

How did the rebellion affect Christianity? After the revolt, many Jewish leaders wanted to avoid another similar tragedy. They excluded all fringe groups, including Christians, from their synagogues. By AD 90 the weekly synagogue prayers included a curse against "the Nazarenes," a reference to Christians who followed Jesus of Nazareth. The division between church and synagogue was complete.

## WHAT SHOULD WE DO WITH ALL THE CHRISTIANS?

### "I Won't Wait to Be a God!"

From AD 69 until AD 81 Roman emperors ignored the church. Then, Vespasian's son, Domitian [do-MEE-shan], became emperor. Domitian didn't want to wait until his death to be declared divine. Domitian demanded the title "Lord and God" throughout his reign.

Domitian also decreed that, since their temple was gone, Jews should send their tithes to Rome. Some Jews refused. Domitian enacted laws against all "Jewish practices." His sweeping sentence included Christian worship. For the first time, persecution spread beyond Italy.

Persecution continued even after a new emperor, Trajan, took the throne. Pliny, a governor in northern Asia Minor (modern Turkey), wrote a letter to Emperor Trajan. Pliny described how he treated Christians. He gave Christians three chances to recant. All who cursed Christ, he released. Roman citizens who refused to curse Christ went to Rome to await their trial. Common persons were killed immediately. Emperor Trajan applauded Pliny's procedures.

*The white triangle in the lower right corner is the siege ramp built by the Roman army at Masada, the Jewish rebels' last stronghold.*

## Think About It...

A few years earlier, Nero had abused the Christians in Rome. Yet Christians refused to partake in the revolt. What does this tell you about the church's relationship to the state? Read 1 Peter 2:13-17.

## On The Web

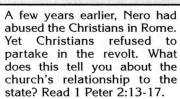

Read Josephus's account of the Jewish rebellion in Book 7 of *The Jewish Wars* ...

*http://www.ccel.org/j /josephus/*

To see a model of the Temple before its destruction, log on to:

*http://www.bible-history.com/jewishtemple/*

Tour Masada at ...

*http://www.mustardseed.net /html/pmasadad.html*

## On The Web

Read Pliny's original letter to Emperor Trajan...

*http://www.tyrannus.com
/pliny_let.html*

*The temple of the Roman goddess Athena frames the temple of Emperor Trajan (AD 98-117) at Pergamum in modern Turkey.*

## On The Web

Do you want to learn more about Justin Martyr?
Surf out to ...

*http://www.earlychristian
writings.com/justin.html*

Pliny had interrogated two women deacons from a nearby church, to find out what Christians believed. He reported that he learned nothing but "outlandish superstitions." Christianity may have looked like an outlandish superstition, but thousands of women and men would die before renouncing their so-called superstition. One of them was Polycarp of Smyrna.

Polycarp [PAW-lee-karp] of Smyrna was a prominent pastor who had known the apostle John. When several Christians were executed at the arena in Smyrna (modern Izmir, Turkey), the crowd began to chant, "Away with the atheists! Find Polycarp!" (Because they rejected Roman gods, Jews and Christians were often called "atheists.") The authorities tortured one of Polycarp's stewards until they learned Polycarp's hiding place. The elderly pastor surrendered peacefully.

At the judgment seat, the governor said, "Have respect for your old age. Say, 'Away with the atheists!'" Polycarp slowly surveyed the throng that surrounded him. Pointing to the crowd, he said, "Away with the atheists! Eighty-six years I have served Christ, and he has done me no wrong. How, then, can I blaspheme my king, who has saved me?" Polycarp was burned alive.

### "Hey, We're Not Outlaws!"

In the mid-100s Christian scholars began to answer the charges that critics hurled at them. These scholars were called "apologists" [a-PAW-lo-jists]. Apologists didn't try to convert the Romans. They only wanted to prove that Christians weren't criminals.

The most famous apologist was Justin. Unlike some Christians, Justin embraced Greek philosophy. Why? According to him, the pagan philosophers had discovered dim shadows of God's cosmic Word. In Jesus, this cosmic order "became flesh" (John 1:14). So, even in pagan philosophy, there was a point of contact with Christian faith.

Justin may have conformed biblical concepts to his own Greek world-view; however, he clearly refused to adapt his faith to paganism. When forced to choose between Christ and the Roman gods, the apologist chose Christ. In AD 165 he was beheaded. He soon became known as "Justin Martyr."

# WHY DID THE CHURCHES GROW?

From AD 64 until the early fourth century the Christian faith could cost people their lives. So, why did they continue to become Christians? Clearly, the church grew because God's Spirit was working. At the same time, God often uses human longings to prepare people for spiritual results. To draw first-century Romans to Christ, God used their longings for moral guidance, for equality, and for a personal relationship with the divine.

## Christianity Provided Moral Guidelines

By the mid-100s, the Roman Empire's depravity didn't repulse only Jews and Christians. It also repulsed Gentiles who had never heard God's moral law. Some Romans turned to the loving-yet-righteous God of Israel. Because of the painful custom of circumcision, Gentile men rarely became Jews. They were content to attend and financially support the synagogues. From the Jews they received a title of respect— "God-fearers" (see Acts 10:2; 13:26). Christianity appealed to these Gentiles. They could experience the God of Israel without submitting to the severe ritual of circumcision.

## Christianity Offered Equality and Respect

The Christian view of women differed deeply from the Roman view. One pagan writer described the role of women with these words: "We have courtesans for pleasurable sex, young female slaves for day-to-day physical usage, and wives to produce legitimate children and to serve us faithfully by managing our houses."

Celsus, an anti-Christian writer, claimed, "Because they admit that ignorant people are worthy of their God, Christians show that they want and can convert only foolish, dishonorable, stupid people, and only slaves, women, and little children."

Not only did Christians accept women; they also refused to treat them as second-class citizens (Galatians 3:28).

Why did Christians treat women with respect? They were following Christ's example! Jesus talked to women. He taught women. It was to women that he first entrusted the news of his resurrection. In the early church, Philip's four daughters were prophets (Acts 21:9). Paul called Junias (a woman) "of note among the apostles" (Romans 16:7). Phoebe was probably a deacon (The word translated "servant" in Romans 16:1 is the word rendered "deacon" in Philippians 1:1).

*Early Christians followed Christ's example by welcoming both women and men.*

*The Celsus Library ruins in Ephesus, south of Smyrna (Izmir, modern Turkey).*

## On The Web

For biographies of hundreds of martyrs (including Blandina) search ...

*http://saints.catholic.org*

## Christianity Offered a Personal Relationship with God

The impersonal gods of ancient times no longer seemed adequate to most Romans. The Jewish and Christian faiths (as well as Eastern mystery cults) offered direct contact with the spiritual realm. Yet Christianity offered more than direct fellowship with the divine. In Jesus Christ, Christianity offered a God who had experienced human suffering, a God who understood (Isaiah 53:3-7; Hebrews 2:17-18).

The knowledge of Christ's sufferings strengthened thousands of early martyrs. In Lyons, Gaul (modern France), nearly fifty Christians died in one bloody massacre. From dawn until evening, Blandina [blann-DEE-nah], a handicapped slave, was tortured. Still, she refused to offer incense to the emperor. In the arena, Blandina's tormentors hanged her naked body on a cross. Wild beasts were released to devour the girl, but they did not touch her. Blandina was stripped from the cross and scourged. Still refusing to offer incense, Blandina was thrown on a red-hot grill. Finally, a bull gored her twisted body and tossed her to the ground. There, she died.

As fellow-Christians watched her, "they saw in the form of their sister"—an eyewitness recalled—"him who was crucified for them." They saw the One who understood their sorrow.

*Heracles, Roman god at Ephesus*

*The knowledge of Christ's suffering strengthened thousands of early martyrs. Christian tomb at Ephesus.*

# CHAPTER ONE LEARNING ACTIVITY

This quiz will help you review what you read in Chapter One.
Try to answer the questions without looking back in the book.

## TRUE OR FALSE

1. ___ Roman citizens rarely served only one god.
2. ___ Nero started the fire in Rome.
3. ___ Peter was probably crucified upside down.
4. ___ Romans loved anything new.
5. ___ Non-Christians often attended Christian worship services.
6. ___ During the first century, the Jewish faith was legal in the Roman empire.
7. ___ Domitian refused to let anyone call him "God."
8. ___ The temple was destroyed in AD 64.
9. ___ After the temple burned, Jewish leaders urged synagogues to accept Christians.
10. ___ Emperor Domitian ignored the Christians.

## FILL IN THE BLANKS
*(Answers to these two questions will vary.)*

11. Name two reasons Christianity was unpopular in the first and second centuries.

    a. _____

    _____

    _____

    b. _____

    _____

    _____

12. God uses social and political factors to produce spiritual results. List two social or political factors that God used to expand the church's mission.

    a. _____

    _____

    _____

    b. _____

    _____

    _____

Notes

# WHAT YOU SHOULD KNOW ABOUT CHRISTIAN HISTORY
## AD 90—AD 250

### Four Events You Should Know

1. *Gnostic Controversy* (AD 90-150): The Gnostics' false teachings first surfaced around AD 60. By AD 140, Gnostics outnumbered Christians in some areas.

2. *Second Jewish Rebellion* (AD 132-135): Simon Bar Kokhba, claiming to be the Messiah, revolted against the Romans. Jerusalem was destroyed again.

3. *Montanist Movement* (AD 156-220): The Montanists (or, New Prophets) tried to return churches to the New Testament's emphasis on dynamic acts of the Spirit. The Montanists' harsh moral standards and false prophecies led most Christians to reject the movement.

4. *Books of the New Testament Recognized* (before AD 190): The Muratorian Canon acknowledged every New Testament book, except Hebrews, James, and the epistles of Peter.

### Ten Names You Should Know

1. *Marcion* (died AD 160): Proponent of Gnostic ideas. Rejected the Old Testament and tried to remove sixteen books from the New Testament.

2. *Montanus* (died AD 175?): Earliest leader of the New Prophets.

3. *Maximilla* (died AD 190?): Leader of the New Prophets.

4. *Prisca* (died AD 190?): Leader of the New Prophets, predicted Christ would return to Phrygia.

5. *Victor* (died AD 198): Overseer of Rome. Excommunicated Christians in the eastern part of the Empire who celebrated Easter during Passover. Fourteenth pope, for Roman Catholics.

6. *Irenaeus* (AD 130-200): Church father. Defended eastern Christians during Easter controversy.

7. *Felicity* (died AD 203): North African slave girl and Christian, probably a Montanist. Martyred with Perpetua, a fellow-Christian. Felicity went into labor in prison. Their guard scoffed, "You're in such pain now! What will you do when you're thrown to the beasts?" She replied, "Now, I suffer alone. Then, there will be another in me. He will suffer for me, for I am about to suffer for him."

8. *Tertullian* (AD 160-225): North African church father. Attacked "modalism" (the belief that the Father, Son, and Spirit are not distinct in any way). Became a Montanist near the end of his life.

9. *Hippolytus* (AD 170-236): Roman theologian. Recorded the *Apostolike Paradosis* (*Apostolic Tradition*), which includes an early form of the Apostles' Creed.

10. *Origen* (AD 185-254): Overseer of Alexandria. Treated difficult Scriptures as allegories.

### Four Terms You Should Know

1. *Heresy*: Any teaching that directly contradicts an essential teaching of Scripture.

2. *Gnosticism*: From the Greek, *gnosis* ("knowledge"), the belief that the physical world is evil and that only secret, spiritual knowledge can free persons from the physical world.

3. *Docetism*: From the Greek, *docein* ("to seem"), the belief that Jesus only seemed to possess a physical body. Most Gnostics were also Docetists.

4. *Rule of Faith*: A series of statements that tested a new believer's understanding of essential Christian doctrines, known today as "the Apostles' Creed."

# Chapter Two

## BALANCING THE PAST WITH THE PRESENT

The Christmas rush had ended. Rayann and I were wandering the supermarket's deserted aisles. We had been married less than six months. Suddenly, Rayann commented, "Of course, we have to buy black-eyed peas." My nose wrinkled, "We have to buy what?" Peas with optical complications have never appealed to me. "Black-eyed peas," Rayann repeated. "You always eat black-eyed peas on New Year's Eve!" About then, she realized I'd never heard of welcoming the new year with a plate of peas. (In the end, I did—against my own more prudent preferences—eat visually-challenged vegetables on New Year's Eve.)

The problem wasn't with Rayann's past or with mine. The problem was, "How do we balance our past traditions with the present situation?" Throughout the second and third centuries, the church dealt with the same sort of question. Christians were forced to ask themselves, "How can we meet our present needs while remaining faithful to God's past works?" As Christians met their present needs, the church's structure shifted. And the issues became far too complex to be solved by a plate of peas.

## CHANGES IN THE EMPIRE, CHANGES IN THE CHURCH

In the first century, "elder" (or, "presbyter") and "overseer" (or, "bishop") had referred to the same role. A group of elders guided each church. Christians gathered in homes. People were baptized whenever they trusted Christ.

By the third century, Christians were organizing themselves above the local level. In most cities, one elder—the overseer—directed the others. Congregations owned their own buildings. New believers received three years of training before baptism. Some elders baptized infants. Others urged parents to wait until their children trusted Christ for themselves. Yet neither group condemned the other.

Why had the church's structure changed? Christians wanted to preserve the truth about Jesus. During the second century a twisted version of Christianity—the Secret Knowledge Movement, also known as "Gnosticism" [NAW-sti-SIZM]—had threatened the church. Powerful overseers, central meeting-places, and careful training arose to help Christians confront the Gnostic [NAW-stik] world-view

---

### In This Chapter
### AD 90—AD 250

Gnosticism
Marcion
Origen
Montanism

### Key Concept

God's people must learn to apply past truths in ways that do not suppress God's present activities.

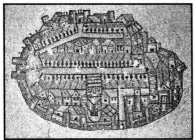

*The Madaba map depicts several rectangular-shaped churches ("basilicas") built by Christians in Jerusalem in the 200s.*

# THE SECRET KNOWLEDGE MOVEMENT

## What Did Gnostics Believe?

For Gnostics, everything physical was corrupt. Only spiritual things were pure. According to the Gnostics, certain persons could achieve secret knowledge about God. This knowledge transported them into a higher realm, beyond ordinary human beings.

Because they detested everything physical, Gnostics rejected verses like John 1:14: "The Word became flesh and dwelt among us." According to many Gnostics, Christ never became flesh; Christ was a spirit that temporarily possessed an ordinary human being named Jesus.

The apostles had, however, repeatedly affirmed Christ's humanity. Paul even commanded Christians to honor God with their bodies—an impossible request for Gnostics! (1 Corinthians 6:19-20). Why? For Christians, salvation isn't a spiritual retreat from the physical realm; it is a renewal that unites and restores both realms.

In the late first century natural disasters began to shake the Roman Empire. A volcano destroyed Pompeii in AD 79. In the mid-80s, an Empire-wide plague killed as many as 10,000 people every day. In this context, Gnosticism's rejection of the physical world appealed to more than a few people.

## A Troublesome Preacher's Kid

One prominent Gnostic sect began with a preacher's kid. His name? Marcion [MARR-see-un]. His father was an overseer on the Black Sea's southern coast. At first Marcion didn't follow in his father's footsteps. He became a ship-owner instead. During his travels, he developed a distaste for the physical world.

Still, Marcion wasn't free from physical desires. Around AD 140, he had sex with an unmarried girl who belonged to his father's church. Marcion was unrepentant, so his father's church excluded him from the church's fellowship. Marcion fled to Rome, where no churches knew about his sin. The Roman church quickly accepted the ship-owner. (Marcion's $2,000,000 gift may have hastened his acceptance!) In Rome, he developed his ideas into a full-fledged system.

Unlike some Gnostics, Marcion didn't search the Scriptures for spiritual secrets. However his heresy did borrow freely from the Gnostic world-view. According to Marcion, Jesus Christ's Father had nothing to do with the wrathful Old Testament God who had created the physical world. The all-loving Father of Christ would never resurrect anyone's body or physically punish anyone. Marcion even reduced the Savior to a spirit. According to Marcion, Christ only *seemed* human. (This belief later became known as *Docetism*.)

## Words: From The Ones Who Were There

*Hymn, written to combat Gnosticism, AD 190:*

"The great Creator of the worlds,

The sovereign God of heav'n,

A holy and immortal truth To us on earth has giv'n.

A holy and immortal truth To us on earth has giv'n!"

"God sent Christ down as sending God;

One man for humankind;

As one with us Christ dwelt with us, And died and lives on high.

As one with us Christ dwelt with us, And died and lives on high!"

"God sent no angel of the host

To bear this mighty Word.

But Christ through whom the worlds were made

The everlasting Lord.

Yes, Christ through whom the worlds were made

The everlasting Lord!"

*Epistle of Diognetus.*

You can sing this song to the tune of "All Hail the Pow'r. . ." (Coronation).

Because they believed the earth was evil, Marcion's followers denied every earthly desire. When they celebrated the Lord's Supper, Marcion's followers drank only water. Why? Drinking the fruit of the vine might incite physical pleasure. They banned all sexual relations—even between spouses.

As he taught, Marcion perceived a problem: The apostles' writings challenged his teachings. His solution was to create the first list of authoritative writings for Christians. Only eleven books made his list—Luke's Gospel and ten of Paul's letters. (In Marcion's Sunday school, learning the books of the Bible was easy!) From Luke, Marcion removed the stories of Jesus' birth. From Paul, he purged every mention of the Hebrew Scriptures. The God of the Hebrew Scriptures was gone.

The new Scriptures may have satisfied Marcion, but they didn't satisfy the Roman church. In 144 the church returned the money Marcion had given. Several Christians—including Polycarp—tried to turn Marcion away from his wayward teachings. In the end, Marcion was removed from the church's fellowship. He responded by forming his own congregations in Italy and Asia Minor.

### On The Web

www

Browse Marcion's writings at...

*http://www.earlychristian writings.com/marcion.html*

## How Did Gnosticism Affect Christianity?

Most Gnostics eventually withdrew from the churches. Yet their beliefs left a mark on the Christian faith, especially through Origen [ORR-i-jenn] of Alexandria. During a local persecution in AD 202, Origen's father died for his faith. Origen begged to offer himself as a martyr, but his mother hid his clothes. The sixteen-year-old was reluctant to become a streaker, and so his life was spared. The Alexandrian church soon noticed Origen's teaching skills. Two years after his father's death, the young man, now fully-clothed, was directing a church-school for new disciples.

Origen preached against Gnosticism. Yet he often slipped into similar views. According to Origen, God's original creation was spiritual. Only after the Fall did God form a physical world. Eventually, Origen taught, God will restore all creation (including Satan) to a sinless, spiritual state.

*Origen of Alexandria*

Like Marcion, Origen renounced all physical comforts. In literal obedience to Matthew 19:12, he castrated himself. He drank only water and wore no shoes. Like many Gnostics, Origen encouraged Christians to search the Scriptures for mystic messages.

Christians had refused to accept the idea that a few believers possessed secret knowledge. Yet many teachers, influenced by Origen, continued to explain difficult texts by looking for hidden, spiritual meanings. First-century Christians had refused to renounce God's gift of sex (see 1 Corinthians 7:3-5). Yet, by the third century many Christians had rejected physical pleasure. Marriage became an acceptable (but less holy) alternative to lifelong virginity.

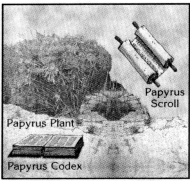

In the first century, papyrus plants were cut into strips and pressed into sheets of writing material. The earliest Christian writings were copied on pieces of papyrus. In the early second century, Christians began to bind pieces of papyrus to form books. Each manuscript volume was called a codex.

## In Case You're Confused

The word "canon" means "measuring stick." For Christians, the word refers to the books that God inspired to form the church's faith. These books are called a canon because they measure the boundaries of the church's beliefs. Look at your New Testament. Does each book conform to the church's three questions? These facts may help: Mark traveled with Peter and translated his accounts of Jesus' life. Luke traveled with Paul. Timothy, Paul's protege, is mentioned in Hebrews 13:23. James and Jude—Jesus' half-brothers—were likely viewed as apostles (Galatians 1:19).

## How Did Christians Respond to the Gnostics?

The Gnostic challenge compelled second-century Christians to ask themselves anew, "What does it mean to be 'Christian'?" Most believers found their answers in a canon of writings, a Rule of Faith, and a priesthood of overseers.

### Which writings do we obey? Three vital questions

Against Marcion, most churches agreed that it was Yahweh—the "I AM" of the Hebrew Scriptures—who Jesus Christ revealed (John 8:58). So, they accepted the Hebrew Scriptures as God's inspired words.

But on which *Christian* writings should God's people rely? Christian teachers frequently quoted oral traditions, handed down by persons who followed Jesus. Then, Gnostic teachers began claiming that they had received secret oral traditions from Jesus. Some Gnostic traditions were probably genuine: In one Gnostic writing, Jesus declares, "Only those who trust in my cross will be saved." However, another Gnostic tract records this exchange: "Simon Peter said, 'Mary should leave us. After all, women aren't worthy of life.' Jesus replied, 'Every woman who makes herself male may enter the kingdom of heaven.'" Surely, the Savior who befriended Martha and encouraged Mary didn't say that!

Without reliable records, Christians couldn't counter Gnosticism. Hundreds of writings were circulating in the Roman Empire. Which works had God inspired to build up the church?

For more than fifty years Christians had relied on twenty or so writings—the four Gospels, Acts, Paul's thirteen letters, 1 Peter, 1 John, and John's Revelation. Many believers also used Hebrews, James, 2 and 3 John, and Jude. A few churches accepted three other works—2 Peter, the Revelation of Peter, and the Shepherd of Hermas. To decide which writings should guide the church, Christians asked three questions:

- Is the book connected to an apostle?
- Do churches throughout the world use the book?
- Does the book agree with what we already know about God?

Eventually, most churches realized that Peter's Revelation and the Shepherd of Hermas (whose author was supposedly mentioned in Romans 16:14) were frauds. Christians argued until the late 300s about who wrote Hebrews, James, 2 Peter, 2 and 3 John, and Jude.

Despite continuing debates about a few books, by AD 200 God had led churches throughout the Empire to recognize one basic canon. Not only did Christians trust in the living Word and Spirit, their faith was also shaped by a book of written words.

## What must Christians believe?

When I baptize a new believer, I ask, "Have you trusted Jesus as your Lord?" Asking questions before baptism isn't a new custom. The tradition is rooted in the Christian Scriptures. Scattered throughout the apostles' writings are statements of faith, like "Jesus Christ is Lord" (Philippians 2:11). These confessions were probably based on questions that Christians were asked before their baptism.

After Marcion left the Roman church, an enlarged series of baptismal questions emerged—"the Rule of Faith." Why? Christians wanted new believers to understand how their faith differed from Marcion's false teachings. Marcion had argued that Christ's Father had nothing to do with the physical world; the Rule of Faith called God "Ruler of all." Marcion claimed that Christ wasn't human; the Rule confirmed Christ's birth and death. Marcion said the human body was beyond redemption; the Rule affirmed "the resurrection of the flesh."

Every Christian could accept the Rule of Faith. Why? Every line was drawn from Scripture. The Rule was the church's answer to the question, "What must a Christian believe?" The Rule is still used today, in a slightly altered form. We call it "the Apostles' Creed."

## Who should protect our teachings?

*From the priesthood of all believers to a priesthood of overseers:* Gnostic teachers often tried to trace their traditions back to an apostle. (No fewer than three Gnostic tracts were supposedly written by Thomas!) How could Christians protect the apostles' true teachings? Some overseers began tracing their beliefs back to an apostle who may have lived in or passed through their cities. By 200 not only were the overseers' *teachings* traced to the apostles, but overseers also traced their *authority* back to the apostles. Overseers became the official trustees of the apostles' teachings. In larger cities, their powers expanded rapidly. Since city overseers nurtured God's children throughout entire regions, they began calling one another "popes"—Latin for "fathers."

In AD 110 Polycarp had urged every believer to protect the apostles' teachings. Eighty years later, one of Polycarp's pupils wrote, "The tradition . . . is protected by the successions of elders." A priesthood of church leaders was replacing the priesthood of all believers.

## On The Web

Examine parts of early New Testament manuscripts at ...

*http://www.xmission.com /~research/gospel/*

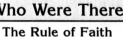

## Words: From The Ones Who Were There

### The Rule of Faith

"Do you believe in God the Father, Ruler of all? Do you believe in Christ Jesus, God's Son, who was born by the Holy Spirit through the virgin Mary, was crucified under Pontius Pilate, died and was buried, and rose again on the third day, alive from the dead, and ascended into heaven, sat at the Father's right hand, and will come again to judge the living and the dead? Do you believe in the Holy Spirit, the holy church, and the resurrection of the flesh?"

*Apostolike Paradosis,* 21

*In AD 110, Polycarp urged every believer to protect the apostles' teaching.*

## In Case You're Confused

Uncertain about how to locate the eastern and western regions of the Empire? The province of Illyricum marked the division between east and west. Locate Illyricum on a map of Paul's journeys.

## Think About It...

Read 1 Corinthians 5:3-13 and 2 Thessalonians 3:14-15. Was Victor's exclusion of Asian Christians a proper use of church discipline? What about how the churches dealt with Marcion?

*Polycarp was the leading pastor here in Smyrna (modern Izmir, Turkey).*

*The rise of the Roman overseer:* The priesthood of overseers did help preserve Christian truth. Increased power can, however, create increased problems.

When Polycarp traveled to Rome to talk with Marcion, Christians were also arguing about when to celebrate Easter. Believers (such as Polycarp) who lived in the eastern regions of the Roman Empire celebrated Christ's resurrection during the Jewish Passover. In the western Empire, Christians waited until the Sunday after Passover.

Both groups celebrated Easter with a pot-luck dinner. So, each spring, some Christians found themselves feasting while others were fasting.

Polycarp and Anicetus [ah-nee-SAY-tuss], the Roman overseer, discussed and disagreed about the Easter issue. Yet Polycarp left Rome at peace with Anicetus. After Polycarp's death, Roman overseers began to secure a more powerful role. Rome was the capital of civilization. As Roman citizens, persons looked to the Roman Empire for direction. It was only normal for Christians to look to the Roman church—which could trace its lineage to two leading apostles, Peter and Paul—for direction.

Thirty years after Polycarp's visit, the Easter dispute arose again. Victor was the new Roman overseer. At Victor's request, churches around Jerusalem began to observe the Roman pattern. Other eastern Christians kept following their own customs. The Roman overseer excluded eastern Christians from fellowship with believers in Rome.

Many church leaders protested Victor's actions. One overseer pled, "The elders who led the Roman church before you, didn't observe the Asian custom. Yet they maintained peace with churches in Asia. The very fact that we can fast at different times proves the unity of our faith!" In a letter to Victor, an eastern elder insisted that the apostles Philip and John had followed the eastern custom of celebrating Easter during the Jewish Passover. Still, Victor would not back down. From his viewpoint, God had cursed the eastern churches. After Victor's death, most Christians ignored his rejection of the eastern churches. Today, churches whose heritage is rooted in the eastern Roman Empire still celebrate Easter during the Jewish Passover.

# THE NEW PROPHECY MOVEMENT

## How Do We Balance the Word with the Spirit?

As their overseers acquired more influence, another question confronted second-century Christians: "What binds the church together? Is it our common traditions, our Scriptures, and our Rule of Faith? Or, is it God's Spirit?" Of course, neither written words alone nor the Spirit alone binds Christians together. The Word and Spirit work together to unite the church. The Word shapes our beliefs, and the Spirit gives them life.

In the western Empire, churches focused on the Word, as understood through the Scriptures, the Rule of Faith, and the Roman overseer. The western system did supply a firm basis for people's beliefs. Yet many Christians were asking, "What about the miraculous acts of the Spirit that saturated the book of Acts? What about God's promise, 'I will pour out my Spirit on all flesh. Your sons and daughters will prophesy'?" (Joel 2:28-29; Acts 2:17-18).

## The New Prophets Call for Renewal

In the mid 100s, a renewed emphasis on the Holy Spirit and personal holiness swept through churches in Asia Minor. The movement began in Phrygia [FRI-jee-yah] (now central Turkey). Around AD 160, three Phrygian believers—two women and one man—began prophesying. Prisca [PRISS-kah], Maximilla [maks-i-MILL-ah], and Montanus [MONT-ah-nuss] called fellow-Christians to embrace radical self-denial.

Church leaders in Rome and Asia Minor denounced the so-called "New Prophets." (Later, when Roman Christians and New Prophets died in the arenas, they died for the same Lord, but they tried to avoid being eaten by the same beasts!) Not everyone agreed with the decision to denounce the New Prophets. One overseer argued that, by denouncing all New Prophets, the church was pushing out both true and false prophets.

Many Christians enjoyed the New Prophets' renewed emphasis on the Holy Spirit. The movement's strict moral standards attracted others. Why, then, were the New Prophets expelled? Some persons claimed that the New Prophets relied on their prophecies instead of Scripture. Whether or not the New Prophets placed their prophecies above Scripture is uncertain.

Two facts are certain:

(1) *The New Prophets made some false predictions*. Montanus and Prisca prophesied that the New Jerusalem would soon arrive in Pepuza, a backwoods village in the Phrygian desert. Because of the false predictions, most Christians concluded that God had not inspired the New Prophets (see Deuteronomy 13:1-5).

(2) *The New Prophets called for stricter moral standards than the Scriptures.* Marriage was banned among New Prophets. Frequent fasts were required. To prepare themselves for Christ's return, the New Prophets tried to focus on a higher, holier realm.

## WHAT MAKES THE CHURCH HOLY?

To guard essential teachings, church leaders had created a chain of command, directed by overseers. Yet some leaders went beyond guarding the church's essential beliefs. Overseers like Victor tried to force unity in nonessential doctrines. For them, unified customs became crucial. As a result, the church's emphasis on personal holiness and the Spirit's dynamic guidance faltered.

Some Christians, especially among the Roman overseers, regarded the overseer as the channel of the Spirit's work. For them, the church's holiness resided in the overseer. The church, like Noah's ark, contained clean and unclean creatures. As long as persons remained united to their overseer, they remained united to God's Spirit.

Other Christians understood that every believer is a channel of God's Spirit. For the New Prophets, the church's holiness resided in individual Christians. They reasoned that, if unholy persons were allowed in the churches, the church could not be Christ's holy bride.

What some people in both groups seem to have missed is that the sacredness of the church flows neither from the church's overseers nor from the church's members. The church is holy because it is the dwelling-place of the Holy Spirit. The church is, the apostle Peter wrote, "made a holy people by [God's] Spirit" (1 Peter 1:2, Good News Bible). It is this Spirit, speaking through Holy Scripture and through the spirits of the saints, who remains our guide as we strive to apply the timeless Word of God amid our human limitations.

## CHAPTER TWO LEARNING ACTIVITY

This quiz will help you review what you read in Chapter 2.
Place the correct letters in the blanks.

1. In the late first century, overseers and elders were _____.
   A. the same position
   B. slightly different positions
   C. nonexistent

2. According to the Gnostics, _____ was evil.
   A. everything spiritual   B. everything physical   C. Christ

3. Marcion created the first _____.
   A. creed       B. church       C. list of authoritative writings

4. The church's responses to Gnosticism included _____,
   and overseers.
   A. a canon, a creed
   B. a canon, a Bible
   C. a cannon, a sword

5. The Rule of Faith is still used, in a slightly altered form.
   Christians call it _____.
   A. the church newsletter
   B. the Baptist Hymnal
   C. the Apostles' Creed

6. Rome's overseer became powerful because _____ and
   because two apostles died in Rome.
   A. Rome was an important city
   B. he was intelligent
   C. of his wife

7. When eastern Christians refused to celebrate Easter on the
   same day as Romans, _____ excluded eastern Christians
   from fellowship with Roman Christians.
   A. Elmo               B. Anicetus               C. Victor

8. The New Prophets made _____ .
   A. fun of the Trinity
   B. some false predictions
   C. love not war

9. Eastern Christians celebrated Easter during the _____.
   A. Jewish Passover       B. winter     C. Super Bowl

10. The church's holiness depends on the _____.
    A. holiness of its members   B. Holy Spirit   C. holy overseers

# WHAT YOU SHOULD KNOW ABOUT CHRISTIAN HISTORY
## AD 247—AD 420

### Five Events You Should Know

1. *Era of Martyrs* (AD 303-305): Emperor Diocletian issued a series of edicts that led to the harshest Roman persecution of the church.

2. *Edict of Milan* (AD 313): Emperors Constantine and Licinius affirmed Galerius' decision to legalize Christianity.

3. *Arian Controversy* (AD 320-364): This heresy remained popular until the late 300's. In AD 350, Arians outnumbered Christians in the Eastern Empire.

4. *The Council of Nicaea* (AD 325): Emperor Constantine invited every overseer in the Roman Empire to deal with the Arian heresy. The Creed of Nicaea confessed the church's belief in the Trinity. The Council of Nicaea was later recognized as the first general council of the church.

5. *Athanasius' Easter Letter* (AD 367): Athanasius' list of authoritative writings included the same books that appear in the New Testament today. In AD 397, the Synod of Carthage confirmed Athanasius' list.

### Eight Names You Should Know

1. *Cyprian* (died AD 258): Overseer of Carthage, North Africa. Allowed Christians who faltered during persecution to return to their churches. Learn more about Cyprian at *http://www.earlychurch.org.uk/cyprian.html.*

2. *Helena* (AD 255-330): Devout Christian and mother of Emperor Constantine. In 326 she visited the Holy Land and had churches built in Bethlehem and on the Mount of Olives.

3. *Eusebius of Caesarea* (AD 263-339): Wrote the first history of Christianity.

4. *Pachomius* (AD 292-346): Founder of cenobitic (communal) monasticism in the Western Empire. His sister Mary founded religious communities for women.

5. *Basil of Caesarea* (AD 329-379): One of the Great Cappadocians, opposed Arianism.

6. *Gregory Nazianzus* (AD 329-389): One of the Great Cappadocians, opposed Arianism.

7. *Gregory Nyssa* (AD 330-394): One of the Great Cappadocians, Basil's brother.

8. *Jerome* (AD 345-420): Monk and scholar, translated the Vulgate.

### Five Terms You Should Know

1. *Eastern and Western Empires:* Diocletian divided the empire into two halves in 292. Rome remained the capital of the Western Empire until AD 476. Constantine placed the capital of the Eastern Empire at Byzantium, later renamed "Constantinople."

2. *The Great Cappadocians:* The Eastern theologians who helped Christians recognize Arianism as a false teaching. All of them were born in the imperial province of Cappadocia.

3. *Donatism:* The belief that—if an overseer had ever faltered under persecution—all ordinances and ceremonies that the overseer performed were invalid. Donatism (named after Donatus, an early leader) split North African churches from AD 311 until the fifth century.

4. *Arianism:* The belief that Jesus is not fully God; Jesus is, rather, God's foremost creation. Arianism (named after the movement's leader) was denounced by the Council of Nicaea.

5. *Vulgate:* From the Latin *vulgaris* ("common"). Jerome's translation of the Bible into ordinary Latin. The Vulgate was the official Bible of the Roman Catholic Church for 1,000 years.

## Chapter Three

# THE CHURCH WINS . . . AND LOSES

When I wrote this book, I was the pastor of a small church—a *really* small church. Some Sundays, I was tempted to join the Society of People Who Count By Two's, just so the attendance would sound better. So, the cards that clogged my mailbox on Monday morning did tempt me: "Double your worship attendance in thirty days!" "You can be the pastor of a mega-church!" Between my mailbox and my wastebasket, I sometimes speculated: *If only I preached more exciting sermons . . .*
*If only our worship services were more appealing . . .*
*If only . . .*

Then, I sometimes thought about second- and third-century Christianity. Quite a few Christians probably thought, *If only we could be free from persecution . . . If only the Roman Empire would listen to us . . .* In the fourth century, the church's "if only's" came true. The churches gained political favor. Congregations grew numerically. Church treasuries expanded exponentially. Yet the outcome wasn't all good.

## THE EMPIRE STRIKES BACK

### The Party the Church Didn't Attend

In AD 247 Rome turned 1,000 years old. Citizens celebrated in the streets for three days and nights. It was New Year's Eve and Mardi Gras mixed into one wild celebration. Most Christians refused to take part in the party. After the party, a plague ravaged Rome. Many Romans wondered if the Christians had angered the gods.

To regain the gods' good will, Emperor Decius [DEE-see-uss] launched an empire-wide persecution. People who sacrificed to the gods received sacrifice certificates. Anyone without a certificate could be imprisoned and tortured. Many prominent overseers, including Origen, died from the injuries they received in prison. (If you don't remember Origen, glance back at Chapter Two.) Emperor Decius died in 251; so, the hardship was short-lived. But the persecution led to problems that lasted for decades.

### How Sorry Do We Have to Be?

When the persecution ended, church members who had sacrificed to the gods wanted to re-enter their churches. However, not everyone who claimed to be repentant was sincerely sorry. How could churches re-admit repentant Christians without also receiving false believers? That was the question that confronted Cyprian [SIPP-ree-yun] of Carthage, a North African overseer. When the persecution

**In This Chapter**
**AD 247—AD 420**

Emperor Diocletian
Emperor Constantine
Arius
Athanasius of Alexandria
Paula

**Words: From The Ones Who Were There**

**Sacrifice Certificate, AD 251**

"To: The Sacrifice Commission
"From: Diogenes, aged 72 years, with a scar over my right eyebrow.

"I've always sacrificed to the gods. Now, in obedience to the emperor, I've sacrificed again, poured out a drink offering, and eaten meat offered to the gods. Please certify this below."

"I, Syrus, saw Diogenes and his son sacrificing."

Paraphrased from *Harvard Theological Review*, 16 (1923): 363-365.

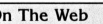

**On The Web**

Christians often met in the catacombs, a series of tunnels beneath Rome—but not to hide from their persecutors! They gathered there to remember deceased Christians who were buried there. Explore the catacombs at...

***http://www.catacombe.roma.it***

## Did You Know?

Valentine, the overseer of Terni, was martyred in 269. People still celebrate his feast-day on February 14.

*One overseer imprisoned during Diocletian's reign was Nicholas of Myra, better known as "Saint Nicholas" or "Santa Claus."*

## On The Web

Download a painting of the real St. Nicholas from ...

*http://www.ocf.org/Orthodox Page/icons/data/nikola.gif*

## Words: From The Ones Who Were There

### Eusebius

"Some had their fingers mangled by sharp reeds. Others had buckets of boiling metal poured on their groins and backs. Others endured agonizing torture of their intestines, so grotesque that we cannot describe them. When the judges were tired of creating new ways to kill us, they were ordered only to tear out our eyes or to cripple us."

*Eusebius,*
*Historia Ecclesiastica, 8:12*

began, Cyprian believed that God wanted him to hide. When Cyprian returned, his congregation was in chaos.

Cyprian urged churches to re-admit Christians who had obtained fake sacrifice certificates. Before being admitted, however, these Christians had to show outward signs of sorrow. How? Prayer and fasting. In Cyprian's mind, true believers would want to show their repentance outwardly.

Not everyone agreed with Cyprian's approach. Many North Africans thought that anyone who had tried to avoid martyrdom was a false believer. At the very least—this group believed—any overseer who cooperated with the persecutors could never confer valid ordination, baptism, or communion. These believers became known as the Donatists [DAW-na-tists], after a prominent leader named Donatus.

Seven years later, another wave of persecution spilled across the Empire. This time, God chose not to spare Cyprian's life. A judge commanded Cyprian to sacrifice. The overseer refused. He died on a Roman chopping-block.

### The Last Roman Persecution

Diocletian [DY-o-KLEE-shan] seized the imperial throne in Rome in AD 284. To avoid spreading his power too thinly, Emperor Diocletian divided his Empire. Diocletian became emperor of the Eastern Empire. A co-emperor governed the Western Empire. To avoid bloody battles over who would succeed the emperors, Diocletian chose two assistants. When an emperor retired, his assistant would replace him. Diocletian was a brilliant ruler in every way . . . except in his treatment of Christians.

Diocletian's assistant was Galerius [gah-LAY-ree-uss]. As an army officer, Galerius had noticed that Christians were more loyal to Christ than to their human commanders. Urged by Galerius, Diocletian lashed out against the church. The torment worsened when Diocletian retired.

Emperor Galerius wanted to rule over his co-emperor's domain. So, he abducted his co-emperor's son, Constantine [KAHN-stann-TEEN]. In 305 Constantine's father became deathly ill. Galerius released Constantine to visit his father, the co-emperor.

When his father died, Constantine demanded the rank of co-emperor. Galerius might have fought Constantine. But a fatal sickness struck Galerius. On his deathbed, Galerius realized his program of persecution had failed. Instead of returning to the Roman gods, church members usually continued to worship Christ or worshiped no god at all. As he died, Galerius issued a decree that allowed persons to profess Christ, "if they don't disturb the public order."

By 312 two power-hungry soldiers, Constantine and Maxentius [maks-ENN-she-uss], were fighting to control the

Empire. Maxentius retreated to Rome, the capital of the Western Empire. As Constantine's army approached Rome, something happened. No one knows exactly what, but the church's relationship with the Empire would never be the same.

## WHAT HAPPENED AT MILVIAN BRIDGE?

### A Sign in the Sky

The day before his battle with Maxentius, Constantine prayed (probably to the Sun-God). As he looked at the sun, Constantine saw a cross. According to one legend, he also saw the words, "By this sign, you will win." That night, Constantine dreamed that Christ commanded him to place a Christian symbol on his shields. In Greek, the first letters of Christ's name look like the English letters *xp*. Constantine's soldiers chalked these letters on their shields the next morning. Constantine even added a cross to his personal battle-flag.

Maxentius was invincible inside Rome's walls, but he was also unpopular. If he stayed in the city, some citizens might revolt during the battle. So, he left the city. To keep Constantine out of Rome, Maxentius cut off the Milvian Bridge. He replaced the bridge with a column of boats, in case he needed to withdraw.

A few miles north of the river, Constantine forced Maxentius to retreat. Maxentius' troops fled across the boat-bridge, back into Rome. As Maxentius crossed the river, the boats broke. Several hundred soldiers, including Maxentius, drowned. Constantine marched triumphantly into Rome, beneath the symbol of the cross. For the first time in history, the cross was smeared with the blood of a battle for human power.

### Christianity's New Corporate Sponsor

The next year, Constantine and his co-emperor, Licinius [ly-SEE-nee-uss], issued "the Edict of Milan" [me-LAWN]. "Our purpose," they decreed, "is to allow Christians and all others to worship as they desire, so that whatever Divinity lives in the heavens will be kind to us."

In Constantine's mind, Christ was now his personal patron. The cross, once an emblem of Christ's death, became a charm, confirming Constantine's power. Constantine granted church leaders (now called "priests") widespread favors. Constantine sincerely believed he was a Christian. Yet he seems to have worshiped Jesus as the Sun-God. In some ways, his confusion made sense. Didn't Christians call Jesus the "sun of righteousness" and the "light of the world"? (Malachi 4:2; John 8:12). They even worshiped on Sun-Day!

A squabble in Africa quickly dashed Constantine's hopes that Christianity would unite his empire. Around 312 the North African Donatists asked Constantine to settle the dispute about who could ordain an overseer. Constantine decided against

*Although many people understood it as a reference to Christ, Constantine's symbol was also a pagan monogram that meant "high quality." Within a century, the pagan meaning had been forgotten, however. Christians today still use the symbol, now known as the "chiron," as an abbreviation for "Christ."*

*The Arch of Constantine was built in honor of his victory over Maxentius.*

### Did You Know?

Constantine moved his capital from Rome to a small village in Asia Minor, called Byzantium. He renamed the village "Constantinople." After Constantine's move, the Empire's strength shifted from the Western Empire to the Eastern (or, Byzantine) Empire.

## On The Web

Read more about Arianism at...

*http://www.monksof adoration.org/arianism.html*

## Words: From The Ones Who Were There

**Council of Nicaea, AD 325**
"We believe in one God, the Father, almighty creator of all things visible and invisible. We believe in one Lord, Jesus Christ, God's Son, begotten from the Father, uniquely begotten from the Father's essence; God from God, Light from Light, very God from very God; begotten not created, of one essence with the Father; through him all things were made, in heaven and earth; for us humans and for our salvation, he came down and was made flesh, was made human, suffered, and rose again the third day; he ascended into heaven and is coming to judge the living and the dead. We believe in the Holy Spirit. The universal apostolic church curses all who say, 'There was a time when he was not' and 'Before he was begotten, he was not' and 'He came out of nothing,' or those who pretend God's Son is of another substance or essence or created or variable or changeable."

*Theodoret,*
*Historia Ecclesiastica, 1:12*

the Donatists. Still, a momentous change had occurred. For nearly 300 years the empire and the churches had remained separate. Now, a church had asked the emperor to sponsor its beliefs. Twelve hundred years would pass before a church completely severed its ties with the state again.

## The Council of Nicea

Constantine's major church squabble began with Arius [AIR-ee-uss], an elder in Alexandria, Egypt. Like many fourth-century Christians, Arius didn't believe God could experience emotions. Yet, if Jesus was fully divine, God did, through Jesus, feel sorrow and pain. Most church members believed that, in some way that transcends human understanding, God the Son had experienced emotions. Arius chose a different option: He taught that Jesus was not God; Jesus was, instead, the first being that God created. "Once," Arius claimed, "the Son did not exist."

Arius knew the power of music. So, he put his theological ideas to a catchy tune. Within weeks Alexandrians were singing in the streets, "Once the Son did not exist!" Church members who rejected Arius' ideas responded with a chorus that Christians still sing: "Glory be to the Father, and to the Son, and to the Holy Ghost; As it was in the beginning, is now, and ever shall be, world without end." (Today, we call this chorus "Gloria Patri.")

Constantine probably didn't care whether Jesus was God, but he did care about a united Empire. To restore unity, he invited every overseer in the known world to Nicaea, a village in northern Asia Minor (now part of Iznik, Turkey). On July 4, 325, three hundred overseers arrived in Nicaea with two thousand elders and deacons. Constantine, having proclaimed himself an overseer and apostle, directed the council.

In the crowded hall, one group denounced Arius in no uncertain terms, because Arius denied the unique deity of Christ. Another group applauded Arius. Most representatives didn't understand Arius. They only wanted peace . . . until an overseer who supported Arius explained the elder's ideas. When the overseer claimed that Christ was created, bedlam broke loose. One overseer screamed, "Blasphemy!" Another overseer ripped Arius' notes into pieces. Suddenly, nearly everyone agreed that the council should condemn Arius.

One overseer suggested a statement of faith that might exclude Arius' ideas. With a few changes, his statement became the Creed of Nicaea. The key change was the added phrase "of one essence with the Father." Even though Eastern Christians worshiped Jesus as God, the phrase "one essence with the Father" bothered many of them. Why? Some Eastern Christians felt the phrase could mean that the Son and the Father were somehow not distinct. Still, only two overseers refused to sign the creed. The council excluded both overseers (as well as Arius) from fellowship in their churches. Constantine wasn't content with the exclusion alone. He exiled everyone who refused to sign the creed.

After the council, the emperor's concern for peace (even at the expense of truth) became clear. By 327 most churches were calmly cooperating again; so, Constantine tried to restore Arius. Few voices protested the emperor's actions. However, one very loud voice came from a surprisingly small man—Athanasius of Alexandria.

## ATHANASIUS OF ALEXANDRIA

Athanasius [AH-tha-NAY-shee-uss] was short and dark-skinned—so short and dark that his enemies called him "Black Dwarf." As a child, he had served the devout Christian hermits (or, "monks") who lived alone in the Egyptian desert. (The word monk means "alone.") As an adult, he retained a deep respect for the monks.

### "I Don't Want to Be an Overseer!"

In 325 Athanasius arrived in Nicaea as a deacon. After the council, the Alexandrian overseer fell fatally ill. The overseer asked Athanasius to replace him, but Athanasius wanted to serve people, not lead them. He fled to his friends, the desert monks. After weeks of running, Athanasius emerged. The church promptly ordained him as an overseer, in spite of his protests.

Athanasius and Constantine quickly clashed. Athanasius refused to restore Arius as a member of the church, because Arius still denied Jesus' unique deity. Constantine threatened Athanasius, "If I hear that you've kept anyone from becoming a church member, I'll banish you." After five years of threats, Constantine exiled Athanasius on a false charge of treason.

In 337 Emperor Constantine died. At Constantine's death-bed, one of Arius' followers baptized him. (In the fourth century, many people believed that God did not forgive sins committed after baptism; so, deathbed baptisms were common among persons who hadn't been baptized as children.) Ironically, Constantine, who did so much to weaken the pagan gods, became a pagan god after his death. The Roman Senate declared Constantine "divine."

### A Pagan Emperor—But No Persecution

By AD 362 Athanasius had returned to Alexandria. The new emperor was Contantine's nephew, Julian. Julian hated Christianity . . . with good reason. When Julian was six years old, Constantine's son had slaughtered Julian's family without a trial. Julian's childhood was spent alone, in constant fear of Constantine's sons.

Athanasius's list of authoritative writings included the same books that appear in the New Testament today. *(Courtesy of the Copic Network)*

Emperor Constantine—AD 337

## Think About It...

Julian should alarm every Christian. Why? He might have been a Christian had it not been for the Christians he knew. People who called themselves Christians killed his family, imprisoned him, and forced him to learn the Scriptures until nothing could relieve his hatred of Christianity.

## On The Web

Intrigued by Athanasius? Learn more about him at...

*http://www.earlychurch.org. uk/athanasius.html*

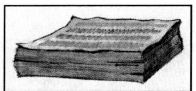

*Fourth century monks copied the oldest known copies of the Christian Scriptures—the Sinaitic Codex and the Vatican Codex—in fine leather (vellum) books.*

When Julian became emperor, Christian clergy lost their civil privileges. Julian also canceled all overseers' exiles, hoping to create turmoil in the churches. How did the churches do without political support? At first, chaos ensued. But, one year into Julian's reign, Eastern and Western churches actually listened to each other.

Athanasius asked both supporters and opponents of the Creed of Nicaea to come to a meeting (or, "synod") in Alexandria. Together, they rejected Arius' ideas. A few Western overseers finally saw why Eastern churches didn't like the phrase "one essence with the Father." Both groups agreed that the Father, Son, and Spirit are three persons who share the same essence.

Emperor Julian feared Athanasius' ability to unite the churches. So, "Black Dwarf" fled to the desert again. When Julian's soldiers found Athanasius, he was sailing up the Nile. The imperial ship drifted behind Athanasius' slower boat. A soldier shouted, "Have you seen Athanasius?" The overseer answered truthfully, "Yes! He is just ahead of you, and if you hurry you shall overtake him." Soon the ship passed by and left Athanasius behind. Desert monks hid Athanasius until Julian's death. A decade later, Athanasius died in Alexandria.

## THE ONES WHO GOT AWAY FROM IT ALL—FOR A LIFETIME

### The Desert Monks

For years Christians—influenced a little by the apostle Paul and a lot by the Gnostics—had revered persons who rejected physical pleasures. Athanasius even wrote a book about a desert monk named Anthony. The biography became the ancient equivalent of a best-seller, and the desert became a refuge for Christians who disliked the church's partnership with political powers. Desert monks lived in extreme poverty, eating only enough to stay alive. Alone for years, many monks endured horrible visions. Extreme sexual urges haunted others.

Some monks began to see the truth behind Genesis 2:18. People weren't created to live alone. So, they founded "monasteries"—communities for monks. Women had already founded their own religious communities. (*Nonnus* is the feminine form of monk; so, these women were called "nuns.") The women's communities became known as "convents" (Latin for "gathering-place"). Some women joined convents because they sensed God calling them to lives of meditation. Others became nuns to avoid distasteful arranged marriages. Others became nuns against their wills. Their fathers forced them to join convents to avoid paying for their weddings.

## Jerome and Paula

Perhaps the most intriguing monk was a guilt-wracked Christian named Jerome. Before retreating to the desert, Jerome felt ashamed because he admired pagan authors. After his retreat, he battled memories of nude dancers in Rome.

Jerome's hatred of everything physical led to some unusual habits and teachings. It was Jerome who first defended the idea that Jesus' mother remained a virgin throughout her life. Jerome also refused to wash his body, claiming that Christ had cleansed him once for all. Still, he could not escape his physical longings. In a final effort to rid his mind of everything but God, he learned Hebrew.

After two tortured years, Jerome realized God had not called him to live alone. He returned to Rome. The overseer of Rome suggested a project to occupy his mind—a reliable, Latin translation of the Scriptures. A wealthy Roman widow named Marcella [marr-SELL-ah] financed the project. Marcella was a brilliant biblical scholar who had committed herself to remain unmarried. Even after he left Rome, Jerome referred pastors who were struggling with unclear texts to Marcella.

In Marcella's mansion, Jerome met the person who would become his closest companion—a woman named Paula. Paula and Marcella had embraced the same sort of self-denial as Jerome, even to the point of refusing to bathe. (That must have been one unique-smelling mansion!) In Paula, Jerome found someone with whom he could discuss his hopes and fears, his questions and dreams. She became an outstanding scholar, quickly surpassing Jerome's abilities in Hebrew.

Jerome completed his Latin translation of the Bible in 405. Deep pain tempered his joy. Paula had died a few months before he completed the project. Jerome died in 420.

## The Great Cappadocians

After Athanasius' death, four Eastern Christians became vocal supporters of the Creed of Nicaea. They were Basil, his sister Macrina [mah-KREEN-ah], their brother Gregory, and a close family friend, also named Gregory. They lived in Cappadocia (in contemporary Turkey). So, they became known as the Great Cappadocians (which certainly sounds better than the Great Turkeys). The Great Cappadocians' support of the Creed of Nicaea helped to unify Christian theology in the Eastern and Western Empires.

Macrina (and later Basil) founded the first Eastern communities for nuns and monks. Persons who joined their communities didn't spend all day meditating. They worked. While they worked, they sang psalms. They sold what they grew and made. All proceeds were used to help the poor. Unlike many nuns and monks, Macrina

*Jerome finished translating the Old and New Testaments into Latin after 22 years of work.*
(Courtesy of Northwind Picture Archives)

### Did You Know?

At first, people didn't like Jerome's Latin translation. Why not? Jerome didn't translate from the old Greek text of the Jewish Scriptures. He translated the Jewish Scriptures directly from Hebrew. Also, his version used easily understood words that some church members didn't like. People called his translation "Vulgate" (Latin for "Common" or "Vulgar"). Even so, within a few years, the Vulgate became everyone's favorite version. Even after people didn't understand its outdated language anymore, churches still used Jerome's Bible.

### On The Web

Want to learn more about Paula, Jerome, Basil, or Macrina? Start your search at ...

*http://www.thesacredheart .com/sts/jerome.htm*

Macrina, Basil and Gregory Nyssa were raised in Cappadocia. The Dark Church (with one small window) in Cappadocia contains many murals of New Testament scenes.

## Key Concept

In God's kingdom, quality matters more than quantity.

Cappadocia (in central Turkey today) was an area of over 400 churches, chapels, and monastaries from AD 300 to 1300, many of them hidden in the caves and underground cities. Rock churches still stand today, full of frescoes portraying subjects from the Bible.

and Basil banned extreme fasting and self-punishment. Instead of withdrawing from the world, they started convents and monasteries in cities. Their nuns and monks taught and doctored thousands of city children.

## IS ALL GROWTH HEALTHY?

Between 300 and 400 Christians gained something they had never possessed before—earthly peace and power. Churches grew more rapidly than ever before. Still, not all growth is good. In God's kingdom, quality matters more than quantity. Many people joined the Christian movement to hedge their spiritual bets by gaining one more deity's good will. Others joined churches to improve their social status. Some believers resisted the church's new status and spent their lives in exile. Others fled to the desert.

Most Christians, however, welcomed their new-found acceptance. (After centuries of persecution, wouldn't you?) One result was that many church members began to identify Christianity with earthly institutions, instead of with the invisible community of all true believers. The institutional aspects of the church became overly important, and the gospel became diluted.

Can changes in individual lives draw believers into vast institutions? Sometimes. Can these changes eventually transform an entire society? Maybe. But God doesn't need vast organizations and mighty nations to accomplish God's work. Most often, God works through ordinary individuals—people like you and me—so that, through human weakness, God's strength can be revealed.

to all the world.

## CHAPTER THREE LEARNING ACTIVITY

Number the following events in the correct order. You will probably need to refer back to Chapter Three. To help you get started, two events are already numbered. Write 2 beside the next earliest event, 3 beside the event that occurred next, and so on.

A. ____ The Donatists ask Constantine to settle a church dispute.
B. ____ Diocletian and Galerius persecute Christians for the last time.
C. ____ Constantine supposedly sees a cross in the sky.
D. ____ Julian, an opponent of Christianity, becomes the emperor.
E. _1_ Constantine restores Arius and exiles Athanasius.
F. _7_ All Romans must obtain sacrifice certificates.
G. ____ The Council of Nicaea agrees that Jesus is one essence with the Father.
H. ____ In Alexandria, Eastern and Western Christians agree that God is three persons with one essence.
I. ____ Cyprian allows persons to reenter their churches if they show outward signs of sorrow.
J. ____ Beneath a cross, Constantine marches into Rome.

Fill in the blanks.

K. Many Eastern Christians disliked the phrase in the Creed of Nicaea that described Jesus as being "of one essence with the Father." Why? _____

_____

Restate the phrase "of one essence with the Father" in your own words. _____

_____

How would you explain the phrase to a sixth-grade Sunday school student? _____

_____

L. Why did many fourth-century Christians flee to the desert?
   1)_____
   2)_____

M. The Cappadocian communities for nuns and monks, founded by Macrina and Basil, weren't like other religious communities. What made their communities different?

_____

N. How do the Council of Nicaea's decisions affect your church today? _____

Notes

© 1999 Rose Publishing

# WHAT YOU SHOULD KNOW ABOUT CHRISTIAN HISTORY
## AD 376—664

### Five Events You Should Know

1. *First Council of Constantinople* (AD 381): The church's second general council denounced Apollinarianism and approved the Nicene Creed.
2. *Emperor Theodosius Declared Christianity the Official Religion of the Empire* (AD 391).
3. *Council of Ephesus* (AD 431): The church's third general council accused Nestorius of teaching that Jesus was two separate persons, one human and one divine.
4. *Council of Chalcedon* (AD 451): At the church's fourth general council more than 500 overseers condemned the One-Nature ("Monophysite") view of Christ. They agreed that, according to Scripture, Christ was one person with two natures (one human, one divine). This became known as the Two-Nature ("Dyophysite") view.
5. *Second Council of Constantinople* (AD 553): Around 542, One-Nature theology became popular again in the East partly through the support of Empress Theodora. Justinian, emperor of the Eastern Empire, convened the church's fifth general council to end the controversy. The council denounced the *Three Chapters*—the writings of three Nestorians (all of whom were dead anyway). The council also declared that Jesus' mother remained a virgin throughout her life.

### Seven Names You Should Know

1. *Pelagius* (died AD 420): Monk who taught that humans have the natural ability to please God. Denounced by a local council in Carthage (AD 418) and by the Council of Ephesus.
2. *Theodore of Mopsuestia* (AD 350-428): Theologian from Antioch who held some Nestorian views. His writings were included in the *Three Chapters*.
3. *Augustine of Hippo* (AD 354-430): North African overseer. Greatest theologian of his era.
4. *Benedict of Nursia* (AD 480-550): Father of Western monasticism. Wrote *The Rule of Benedict*, a manual for monks. Founded religious communities near Monte Cassino, Italy, with his sister Scholastica. Learn more about them at http://www.osb.org/gen/scholast.html.
5. *Columba* (AD 521-597): Irish missionary, founder of Iona monastery. Check out http://members.aol.com/compgeek35/saints.htm#list to learn more about this Irish missionary.
6. *Gregory* (AD 540-604): First Roman bishop to attain the status later linked with the title "pope." The sixty-fourth pope, for Roman Catholics.
7. *Augustine of Canterbury* (died AD 605): Monk, sent by Pope Gregory I to found new churches in England after barbarians destroyed previous missionaries' work.

### Five Terms You Should Know

1. *General Council*: One of seven councils accepted by both Eastern and Western Christians.
2. *Apollinarianism*: The belief that Jesus had no human mind. Named after Apollinarius, an early proponent. The First Council of Constantinople condemned Apollinarianism.
3. *Theotokos*: A Greek word, meaning "God-bearer." Many Christians called Jesus' mother *theotokos*. Nestorius criticized the term, arguing that Mary didn't bear only a divine being; Mary bore the Lord Jesus Christ, who was fully human and fully divine.
4. *Nestorianism*: The belief that Jesus was two separate persons, one human and one divine. Named after Nestorius, who was unfairly accused of teaching this view.
5. *Monophysitism*: From the Greek *monophysis* ("one-nature"). The belief that Jesus' divine nature fully absorbed his human nature. Also called "Eutychianism," after an early proponent.

# Chapter Four

## "SERVANT-LEADERS OR LEADERS OF SERVANTS?"

<table>
<tr><td>

Take a good look at your feet. What do you think? I think I can safely assume that your feet are not your body's most beautiful members, despite the prophet's portrayal of them (Isaiah 52:7). They aren't always clean. And, after a hot day, they don't produce pleasant scents.

In modern times, shoes and sidewalks have removed much of the foot's foulness. In earlier times, feet were far more offensive. Sporadic baths and grimy streets combined to produce uncommonly powerful foot odors. Foot-washing was an act of service reserved for the lowest slaves.

Perhaps that's why Jesus reminded his disciples that no task should be beneath the men and women who lead his people—not even washing feet (John 13:1-17). Or embracing outcasts. Or dying on a cross. "The Son of Man did not come to be served," Jesus said, "but to give His life as a ransom for many" (Mark 10:44-45). That's why God doesn't call ministers who only stand above God's people and tell them how to live. God calls leaders who will also kneel beside God's people and show them how to serve. God calls servant-leaders, not leaders of servants.

</td></tr>
</table>

| In This Chapter AD 376—AD 664 |
| :---: |
| Ambrose of Milan<br>John Chrysostom<br>Augustine of Hippo<br>Cyril of Alexandria<br>Leo the Great<br>Patrick |

### THE CLEFT IN THE CHURCHES

In the 400s leaders of servants replaced servant-leaders in many areas. Church leaders had gained far-reaching powers. Their powers called them to lifestyles that placed them above their people. So, a division between clergy and laypeople slipped into some churches. The gap became more obvious as increasing numbers of church leaders expected priests to remain unmarried.

One Christian who objected to the division was a monk named Jovinian [jo-VIH-nee-ann]. He argued that, since sex wasn't sinful, faithful spouses and lifelong virgins would receive the same eternal reward. He also denied that Jesus' mother remained a virgin throughout her life. Jovinian's ideas did not prevail. Twelve years before he died, church leaders excluded Jovinian from fellowship.

During the fifth century Western church leaders gained more political power, and the gap between clergy and lay-people widened. Why? Masses of migrating "barbarians" were weakening the Empire's ability to manage its provinces. Church leaders found themselves assuming the tasks that had once been shouldered by Roman governors.

| Key Concept |
| :---: |
| God calls servant-leaders—not leaders of servants. |

*Beginning between 400 and 600, monks and priests had the crowns of their heads shaved when they took their vows. This rite became known as the "tonsure." The practice was abolished in 1972 by Pope Paul VI.*

## "SOUTHWARD, HO!"

Who were the so-called barbarians? They were tribes of nomads who had lived on the edges of the Roman Empire. They were dubbed "barbarians" because, to the Romans, their language sounded like someone babbling "bar-BAR-bar." Roman writers accused barbarians of all sorts of savagery. Admittedly, barbarians couldn't comprehend proper table manners. (Then again, neither can many junior high boys, and only their parents call them barbarians.) Yet the Gothic and Vandal tribes were no more savage than the Romans. The Huns—an Oriental tribe that lacked more than table manners and definitely deserved the title "barbarian" —had forced the Goths and Vandals south, in search of farmland.

## THE WESTERN PREDICAMENT

Ambrose was one of the church's most powerful leaders during this turbulent time. In the 370s Ambrose was the governor of Milan, Italy. Even though he had never confessed Christ, Ambrose supported the Creed of Nicaea.

When the overseer of Milan died, tensions erupted between followers of Arius and supporters of the Creed of Nicaea. (If you don't remember Arius, glance back at chapter three.) Each side was willing to fight to choose the new overseer. Riots had recently claimed 137 lives when a new Roman overseer was elected. Would the same thing happen in Milan? In the city cathedral Governor Ambrose raised his voice to support the Nicenes. Suddenly, a child cried, "Ambrose! Overseer!" The crowd took up the chant. Ambrose protested. He was not even a Christian! How could he be an overseer? The mob persisted. A week later, Ambrose the overseer, newly baptized and no longer a governor, began to battle the Arians.

### How Human Was Jesus?

At the same time, Eastern Christians were dealing with their own problems. An Eastern church member named Apollinarius had taught that Jesus had a human body but no human mind. One of the Great Cappadocians—remember them from Chapter Three?—retorted, "If deity took the place of a human mind, how does that help me? Deity joined to flesh alone is not truly human!" (See Hebrews 4:15).

Theodosius [THE-uh-DO-see-us], the emperor of the Eastern Empire, convened a council in AD 381 to settle the dispute. In Constantinople, more than 150 overseers expressed their beliefs in an updated version of the Creed of Nicaea. This creed echoed the truths affirmed at the Council of Nicaea concerning Jesus' unique deity. So, Christians called it "the Nicene Creed."

*Cave church at Cappadocia*

## Ambrose's Challenge

Theodosius had mastered an Empire and united a church. Yet, in Milan, Ambrose the overseer openly defied him. The dispute arose when a mob of church members burned a synagogue. Theodosius justly ordered them to rebuild it. Ambrose protested: "The burning of one building doesn't justify a commotion such as this! . . . It was only a synagogue, an abode of unbelief, a God-damned place." Theodosius backed down . . . sort of. He commanded the church to raise funds to restore the synagogue. This was still too much for Ambrose of Milan. Ambrose threatened to exclude the emperor from communion unless he canceled all charges. Theodosius gave in.

Ambrose also excluded Theodosius from communion when the emperor allowed his guards to slaughter 7,000 citizens after a riot. Only after Theodosius wore sackcloth and ashes for several weeks did Ambrose allow him to partake of the Lord's Supper.

After Theodosius reentered the church, he supported Christianity through the only means he knew—by force. The church and empire grew closer together. Partly through Ambrose's audacity, however, the church remained the stronger partner in the Western Empire.

## THE EASTERN SITUATION

Someone else also defied Emperor Theodosius—but in her own way. Olympias [oh-LIMM-pee-ahs] was her family's only heir. Two years after she married, her wealthy husband died. She became one of the world's richest people when she was only 25.

To the chagrin of nearly everyone, Olympias chose not to remarry. She gave her life to Christ. She used her wealth to buy slaves and set them free. Her church ordained her as a deaconess. At the same time, she attracted scores of suitors, including Theodosius' cousin.

When Olympias rejected his cousin, Theodosius seized her property. Olympias promptly thanked him. "Had I kept my property," she said, "I might have fallen prey to pride." Outfoxed, Theodosius returned her wealth. Again, Olympias gave it away. It was during these years that she met an overseer named John.

John had been a priest in Antioch, Syria. He learned public speaking in the Eastern Empire's finest schools. His eloquent sermons would later earn him the nickname "Chrysostom" [krih-SOSS-tom]— "Golden-Mouth." Unlike Alexandrian preachers, John focused on the original intent of biblical texts.

After Theodosius died, a power-hungry eunuch ruled the Eastern Empire through Theodosius' son. The eunuch had John Chrysostom ordained as Constantinople's overseer. The eunuch

*Inside the Hagia Sophia. The original church, built during Constantine's reign, was burned during the riots after the patriarch John Chrysostom was banished by Emperor Arcadius.*

## In Case You're Confused

Two preaching methods arose in the early church. One method developed in Antioch, Syria; the other emerged in Alexandria, Egypt. Preachers from Antioch (like Chrysostom) searched the Bible for the messages that the authors intended. Alexandrians (like Origen and Ambrose) searched for secret, spiritual truths that were often unrelated to the text's original intent.

## On The Web

Learn more about Olympias and John Chrysostom at ...

*http://www.chrysostom.org/ writings.html*

hoped that, since John owed his power to the eunuch, he could control the church through John. The plan flopped. John the overseer refused to listen to the eunuch. He further enraged the eunuch by living like a monk.

John Chrysostom demanded holiness. Many unmarried priests were living with so-called "spiritual sisters." John sarcastically noted that many "spiritual sisters" were somehow becoming "spiritual mothers." Under his leadership, unmarried priests couldn't live with women. John not only demanded holiness among priests, but he also preached against the empress's sensual lifestyle. To silence him, the empress gave a costly gift to the church. John thanked her and continued preaching, just as he had before.

In 403 the empress exiled John Chrysostom. That night, rioters who supported him burned several buildings. John's foes accused Olympias of arson and had her banished. John and Olympias both died in exile.

## SILVER, GOLD, AND . . . PEPPER?

By the 400s many barbarians were frustrated with Roman rulers. The barbarians wanted to live in the Empire and enjoy its benefits. Yet the Romans treated them as invaders. In 408 Alaric [ah-LAIR-ik] the Goth asked the Western emperor for farmland for his people, 18 tons of gold and silver, and a ton of pepper. (What on earth was he cooking, anyway?) The emperor refused the request for land. So, in 410 Alaric attacked Rome. The Goths pillaged the capital city for three days.

For the first time in eight centuries, Rome—once a symbol of the Empire's invincible power—had fallen. The Empire's ancient glories were gone. The Middle Ages had begun. Even in Africa, Rome's fall shook people's souls. The man who helped them deal with their confusion was a North African who turned to Jesus Christ on a park bench near Milan.

## THE AFRICAN ANGLE

The young man staggered through the park, a dismal void gnawing his spirit. He dropped his book on a bench and stumbled on. "Lord," he sobbed, "how long?" Suddenly, he heard a child singing, "Pick up, read! Pick up, read!" He rushed back to the bench. When he opened his book, one passage seized his eyes: "Let us walk properly, as in the day, not in revelry and drunkeness . . . But put on the Lord Jesus Christ, and make no provisions for the flesh" (Romans 13:13-14). "Instantly," he said, "light . . . entered my heart." The man's name? Augustine [aw-GUSS-tinn].

## Where the Journey to Faith Began

Monica, Augustine's mother, was a Christian, "always in deep travail for [her son's] salvation." As a teen, Augustine had dismissed Christianity as crude and simple. He explored every possible path to find pleasure and truth. He associated himself with the Manichees [MANN-i-kees], a Gnostic-like sect. However, he could not be a full Manichee unless he rejected sex—an impossible request for Augustine. "Lord," he prayed, "make me chaste." "But," he added, "not yet."

Soon, Augustine decided to search for truth in Italy. Monica begged God not to let her son go to Italy. She feared that he would drift further into sin. Little did she know that, in Italy, God would answer her prayers for her son's salvation. It was there that Augustine heard Ambrose of Milan for the first time. Ambrose preached in the Alexandrian style, treating the Bible as a vast allegory. His approach may seem odd to us; but it helped Augustine see that the Bible wasn't simplistic.

One problem lingered. Augustine would not be a halfhearted believer. If he became a Christian, he would become a monk. "But I can't be celibate!" he cried. In the end, the news of two unexpected conversions changed Augustine's outlook.

*Augustine of Hippo*

## Where the Journey to Faith Led

Through a friend, Augustine heard about two powerful officials who read Athanasius's biography of Anthony and became monks. It was too much; Augustine could no longer avoid God's grace. He fled to the park and heard God's voice in the child's song. He then became a monk and headed for the desert. His retreat was short-lived. When he visited a church in Hippo, the church ordained him as an elder. Six years later, he became Hippo's overseer. (No, he didn't become a zoo-keeper. Hippo was a city in North Africa.)

As Hippo's overseer, Augustine struggled against a pious but misguided monk named Pelagius [peh-LAY-jee-uss]. Throughout Rome, Pelagius had seen so-called Christians who were not holy. To promote piety, Pelagius preached that salvation doesn't depend completely on God's grace; people naturally possess the power to be holy. Pelagius also argued that no one is born sinful. (Pelagius obviously never taught preschoolers.)

When Pelagius' teachings reached Hippo, Augustine harshly attacked them. Augustine argued that the first sin corrupted all humanity. This corruption is so radical that no one naturally wants to love Christ. So far, Augustine's ideas conformed to Paul's writings. Still, in some areas, Augustine parted with Paul. According to Augustine, sin was a sexually-transmitted defect. He believed that infant baptism purged the primal sin and prepared persons to receive God's grace.

### Think About It...

It seems as if God denied the request of Monica's lips in order to give her the desire of her heart. Has that ever happened to you?

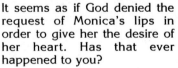

### On The Web

Augustine was the greatest theologian of his era. Read more about him at ...

*http://ccat.sas.upenn.edu/ jod/augustine.html*

## The City of God and the City of Mankind

Augustine also helped Christians deal with the aftermath of Rome's fall. After Rome was pillaged, Christians became targets of criticism. Non-Christians declared, "When we sacrificed to our gods, Rome prospered. Now sacrifices are banned, and look what's happening!" For years, some Christians had argued that Christ fought for Rome. Had Christ changed sides?

In *The City of God*, Augustine responded that two realms exist on the earth—the City of God and the City of Mankind. Even though these cities seem to mingle, God's realm cannot ultimately unite with any human regime. One day, all human regimes will fade. Only God's reign in the hearts of God's people will remain.

## WHAT YOU SAID ISN'T ALWAYS WHAT OTHERS SAY YOU SAID

*Frescoes and mosaics from the Church of Chora in Constantinople. Nestorius became the leading pastor of Constantinople in AD 428.*

Recently, several baseball fans hung their coats on an outfield fence. The announcer immediately asked, "Would the fans along the outfield please remove their clothes?" The announcer said what he meant. But what he said could also mean something that he didn't mean at all. That's what happened to Nestorius [neh-STORR-ee-uss] of Antioch.

In 428 Nestorius moved to Constantinople to become the city's overseer. His tenure began with a blaze of something besides glory. He torched an Arian chapel, to try to force false teachings out of his town. The flames got out of hand and destroyed the whole block. Nestorius' less-than-laudable stunt earned him a nickname—"Fire-Brand."

Nestorius was not only an arsonist. He was also a theologian. His theological talents did (barely) transcend his skills with a torch. Nestorius criticized a common title for Mary—*Theotokos* (or, "God-Bearer"). What he wanted people to understand was that Jesus Christ was not only God; Jesus was also fully human. What some people thought Nestorius meant was that Jesus was two persons (one human, one divine) and that Mary had only borne the human person.

### One-Nature or Two?

Cyril [SI-rill], the overseer of Alexandria, was a brilliant thinker. He was also ruthless and corrupt. In 415 he had even approved the murder of a woman named Hypatia. When Nestorius' teachings reached Alexandria, Cyril accused Nestorius of dividing Jesus into two separate persons. Controversy threatened to split the churches once again.

In 431 the emperor of the Eastern Empire convened a council in Ephesus. Cyril arrived first, condemned Nestorius and his followers, and adjourned the council. When Nestorius' friends arrived, they convened the council (for the second time) and condemned Cyril. When the representatives of the Roman church arrived, they called the council to order (again) and sided with Cyril. In the end, Nestorius was exiled. A confusing chapter in the church's story had ended . . . or had it?

Cyril's successors became known as "One-Nature" ("Monophysite") thinkers. They were eager to forsake the idea that Jesus was two separate persons—so eager that they went to the other extreme. They taught that Christ's divine nature consumed his humanity "like the ocean swallows a drop of wine." One-Nature theology became popular, especially among the Egyptian Copts. Yet it seemed to many Christians that One-Nature thinking ignored Christ's humanity. Again, a council was called.

## Agreement at Last

Leo, the Roman overseer, received his invitation too late to attend the council. Instead, he sent a summary of his teaching, called a *Tome*. Leo, like Nestorius, believed Jesus had two natures, united in one person. The One-Nature party ignored Leo's *Tome* and mortally mauled the opposing spokesperson. Still, the matter did not end.

In 451 a new emperor convened a council in the city of Chalcedon [KAL-se-DAWN]. There, more than 500 overseers combined the Nicene Creed, Cyril's writings, and Leo's *Tome*. The result? A beautiful, biblical portrayal of Christ: "Christ [is] . . . recognized in two natures, without confusion, division, or separation . . . but not as if Christ were parted into two persons." This understanding of Christ became known as the "Two-Nature" view. At last, agreement had been reached. Nestorius (still exiled) said the council confessed what he had always taught.

After the Council of Chalcedon, some Christians in Egypt and Syria still supported One-Nature theology. Both groups eventually divided from the Roman and Eastern churches. Today, the Coptic and Syrian Orthodox Churches remain committed to One-Nature theology. Some native Egyptian churches that accepted the doctrinal statement of the Council of Chalcedon and stayed in communion with churches in the Eastern Empire. These Egyptian churches became known as Melkite (or, Imperial) Churches.

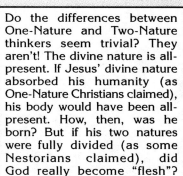

### Think About It...

Do the differences between One-Nature and Two-Nature thinkers seem trivial? They aren't! The divine nature is all-present. If Jesus' divine nature absorbed his humanity (as One-Nature Christians claimed), his body would have been all-present. How, then, was he born? But if his two natures were fully divided (as some Nestorians claimed), did God really become "flesh"? (John 1:14).

*Leo's Tome formed the basis of the Council of Chalcedon's understanding of Jesus Christ.*

### On The Web

Check out the Coptic Church's web site at...

*http://www.coptic.net*

*In the early Middle Ages, God used religious communities like the Saint George monastery in the Judean desert to preserve the Scriptures for future generations.*

*Gregory, overseer of the Roman church*

## ROME FALLS AGAIN . . . AND AGAIN

Leo's *Tome* had helped shape Christian theology. However, survival concerned the citizens of Rome far more than theology. It was Leo's boldness before the barbarians that won him the respect of Rome's citizens.

In 452 Attila the Hun attacked Italy. As the Huns approached Rome, nothing stood in their way. No emperor. No army. No one but Leo, the overseer of Rome. Leo met Attila on the road to Rome. Somehow, Leo persuaded the Huns to retreat. In 455 another barbarian tribe, the "Vandals," besieged Rome. This time, Leo could not convince them to retreat, but he did persuade them not to rape or kill. Instead, they looted and (true to their title) vandalized the city. Finally, in 476, a barbarian named Odovacer deposed the last Western emperor. The Western Empire had ceased to exist. Only the Eastern Empire remained.

## THE CITY OF GOD ENDURES

When I read about the early Middle Ages, I sometimes wonder, "Was anyone really a Christian?" Christian ideas became tools to unite the Empires. Kings claimed to be Christians, yet some of them mercilessly looted and slaughtered. Were people simply ignorant? Was their faith false? I don't know. What I do know is that God preserved a kingdom for God's own glory (the "City of God") amid the darkness of human failure and greed (the "City of Mankind"). One way that God preserved the church was by calling Christians to retreat to religious communities.

### Scholastica and Benedict

Scholastica [sko-LASS-tih-kah] and her twin brother, Benedict [BEH-neh-dikt], were born in Italy. In 520 Benedict organized a religious community in a remote area. Even though Christianity had been the Empire's official religion for more than 100 years, a pagan altar still stood on one hill. Benedict smashed the altar and built a monastery atop it. Scholastica founded a convent near the monastery.

Benedict's greatest gift was the *Rule*, his guide for religious communities. Unlike many communities' rules, the *Rule of Benedict* demanded nothing extreme. The daily routine balanced Bible reading, prayer, and work. In 589 barbarians burned Benedict's monastery. The monks fled to Rome. There, an overseer named Gregory encountered Benedict's *Rule*.

### Gregory

Gregory had grown up in Rome. As a child, he once saw slaves from Angle-Land ("England") being unloaded at the docks. He asked, "Where are they from?" Someone said, "They're Angles." "Angels they may be," Gregory responded, "but who rules them?" "Aella," was the reply. "Alleluia?" Gregory said, "In their land, God's name must be praised!"

God's name had been praised in Britain as early as AD 300. However, in the fifth century, the Anglo-Saxon barbarians had migrated into Britain and destroyed the churches. The burden to see these barbarians turn from their pagan gods followed Gregory throughout his life.

As an adult, Gregory became a powerful politician. In 573 God changed his career plans: Gregory gave everything away and became a monk. Then, a plague ravaged Rome. Unlike many monks, Gregory refused to stay in his monastery. He left his monastery to serve the sick. His kindness earned him an honored place in people's hearts. When the Roman overseer became fatally ill, it was Gregory who succeeded him.

When Benedict's monks arrived in Rome, their *Rule* pleased Gregory. In AD 599 Gregory sent 41 reluctant Benedictine monks to England, to evangelize the Anglo-Saxons. One of the monks would become known as Augustine of Canterbury. By Christmas of 599, ten thousand English—including the king of Kent—had been baptized. Canterbury, Kent's capital, became the center of English Christianity.

As Gregory worked among the citizens of Rome, he wrote about theology and pastoral care. He depended deeply (perhaps too deeply) on Augustine of Hippo. For example, Augustine had wondered if there might be a place where God purged the unconfessed sins of Christians who died. From this, Gregory developed the doctrine of "purgatory," a place between death and heaven where God removes any barriers to total enjoyment of God's presence. Gregory also taught that God's forgiveness sometimes requires works of penance. One of Gregory's most familiar legacies flowed from his concern for the church's music. After his death, one form of Roman plainsong—the "Gregorian chant"—was named after him.

### Hilda of Whitby

The Anglo-Saxon invasions did not reach the Celtic-Irish churches and religious communities. After the invasions, Celtic-Irish Christians found themselves cut off from Roman and Eastern churches. So, they developed their own unique patterns of administration and worship. Celtic-Irish congregations were not ruled by overseers. Monks and nuns led Celtic-Irish churches. Celtic-Irish Christians also didn't observe Easter on the same day as Roman Christians. As Roman Christianity spread throughout the British Isles, tensions emerged between the two groups. In 664 Celtic-Irish and Roman Christians met to resolve their problems. In honor of a English Christian woman named Hilda, they met in Whitby.

After Hilda gave her life to Christ, an overseer noticed her leadership talents and gave her a position of leadership in two religious communities. In 657 Hilda founded a community in Whitby. There, she trained hundreds of monks (five of whom

*This distinct style of cross arose in the Celtic-Irish churches.*

became overseers). At the Synod of Whitby, in 664, only Hilda and one overseer defended the Celtic-Irish Christians' right to follow their traditions. In the end, Celtic-Irish churches became Roman churches. The Roman overseer's power had extended throughout Europe.

## HOW'S YOUR SERVE?

Sometimes, pastors sin. Sometimes, pastors even sin in areas about which they have recently preached. When that happens to me, my wife always reminds me that she was listening to my sermon. "Why are you so worried?" Rayann asks. "On Sunday morning, you said, 'Stop worrying! God has a plan, even when you don't have a clue.'" It sounded so much better when it was me preaching instead of her. Still, I know if my messages are true, I too am obligated to obey them. Servant-leaders cannot stand above God's people and proclaim God's truth unless they also stand among God's people and live God's truth. When ministers stand above God's people, they become administrators and managers instead of shepherds and servants.

That's what seems to have happened in the early Middle Ages. In a society that was falling apart, church leaders found themselves shouldering political power. In the process, many of them became leaders of servants instead of servant-leaders.

Jesus told his followers, "Whoever wants to become great among you must be your servant, and whoever wants to be first must be slave of all" (Mark 10:43-44). If every Christian is a servant, every Christian is equal. If every Christian is equal, every Christian—whether layperson or bishop, pastor or janitor— is equally responsible to reflect God's truth. So, live as if Christ has placed you in your church for a reason. Live as if you are called to be a servant-leader, wherever you are. Then, live as if one servant-leader can change the world. Why? He has, you are, and you can.

# CHAPTER FOUR LEARNING ACTIVITY

This quiz will help you review what you read in Chapter Four. In the word search, locate ten key words from the chapter. Write the words in the blanks.

```
C  H  A  L  C  E  D  O  N  S
Y  I  C  O  O  S  R  L  E  Q
R  L  I  L  P  O  P  E  S  J
I  E  T  Y  S  R  E  M  T  D
S  N  S  M  T  B  Q  O  O  L
C  I  A  P  A  M  U  E  R  I
H  T  L  I  N  A  D  L  I  H
E  S  O  A  T  S  A  N  U  D
V  U  H  S  C  H  O  L  S  L
O  G  C  Y  R  I  E  V  E  I
J  U  S  T  I  N  I  A  N  H
S  A  N  A  I  N  I  V  O  J
```

1. _____ did not like the division between clergy and laypeople.
2. Before he became Milan's bishop,_____ was a governor.
3. _____ used her inheritance to give slaves their freedom.
4. Ambrose's preaching impressed_____.
5. _____ was misunderstood when he criticized a common title for Mary, "God-Bearer."
6. _____ convinced Attila the Hun not to plunder Rome.
7. In AD 451 the Council of _____ used Leo's *Tome*, Cyril's writings, and the Nicene Creed to explain the relationship of Jesus' two natures.
8. _____ convened the Second Council of Constantinople, AD 553.
9. _____ and her twin brother, Benedict, built religious communities in Italy. Their guideline was Benedict's *Rule*.
10. Even though she was English, _____ defended Celtic-Irish traditions at the Synod of Whitby.
11. Gregory is sometimes called "the first _____ ."
12. What person in this chapter would you most like to meet? Why? What questions would you ask her or him? (*Answers will vary.*) _____

_____

## Notes

# WHAT YOU SHOULD KNOW ABOUT CHRISTIAN HISTORY
## AD 496—1291

| Five Events You Should Know |
| --- |

1. *Third Council of Constantinople* (AD 681): The church's sixth general council denounced Monotheletism (see below) and reaffirmed the beliefs of the Council of Chalcedon.
2. *Pepin's Donation* (AD 754): Pepin III, a Frankish battle-chief, gave part of Italy (the "papal states") to the pope. In return, the pope granted Pepin the church's approval and a royal title.
3. *Second Council of Nicaea* (AD 787): The church's seventh and last general council denounced Adoptionism, the idea that Jesus was not God's Son by nature. The council also allowed Christians to revere—but not worship—icons. Learn more about icons at *http://www.unicorne.org/orthodoxy/liens/art.htm.*
4. *Roman Church Excommunicated the Eastern Church* (AD 1054).
5. *Investiture Dispute* (AD 1076—1123): In 1076 Emperor Henry IV claimed the right to invest bishops with their authority; Pope Gregory VII (Hildebrand) forced him to beg forgiveness for three days. In 1122 a concordat signed in Worms, Germany, allowed emperors to be present at bishops' ordinations, but church leaders controlled the selection. The First Lateran Council confirmed the Concordat of Worms in 1123.

| Five Names You Should Know |
| --- |

1. *Clotilde* (AD 474-545): Frankish queen. Led her husband, Clovis, to become a Christian.
2. *Charles Martel* (AD 690-741): Frankish battle-chief. Stopped Muslims from conquering central Europe.
3. *Alcuin of York* (AD 740-804): Monk. Major contributor, with Theodulf of Orleans, to the "Carolingian Renaissance," Charlemagne's effort to decrease illiteracy and preserve ancient texts.
4. *Godfrey of Bouillon* (died AD 1100): First king of Crusaders' Latin (Roman) Kingdom in Palestine which lasted until 1291, when Muslims conquered the port of Acre.
5. *Pope Innocent III* (AD 1161-1216): One of the most powerful bishops of Rome. Claimed power over all secular rulers (1201). Initiated the Fourth Lateran Council (1215).

| Five Terms You Should Know |
| --- |

1. *Monotheletism*: From the Greek *monothelos* ("One-Will"). One-Will thinkers taught that Jesus had two natures, but only his divine nature could make choices. In 681 the Third Council of Constantinople affirmed that Jesus had two wills—one human, one divine. But, they added, his two wills never disagreed.
2. *The Donation of Constantine*: A document, forged around 800, which claimed Constantine gave the pope power over all other bishops, as well as large portions of Italy.
3. *Holy Roman Emperor*: The title which, in theory, made someone the heir of the ancient Roman emperors and the ruler of the Western Empire. In reality, Holy Roman Emperors only ruled portions of central Europe. German kings possessed the title from AD 962 until 1806, when Napoleon abolished it.
4. *Albigensians*: Heretical sect, named after Albi, the French town where they arose. Also called "Cathars" ("Pure Ones"). Condemned by the Fourth Lateran Council for their Gnostic teachings.
5. *Transubstantiation*: Roman Catholic and Eastern Orthodox belief that the Lord's Supper elements become Jesus' body and blood, even though their outer appearance never changes.

# Chapter Five

## FROM MULTIPLICATION TO DIVISION

It is a work of endless insight. Its reflections are unsurpassed. Its wisdom rivals the philosophy of the ancient Greeks. This work is, of course, the comic strip *Calvin and Hobbes*. In one strip Calvin writes "In the Middle Ages lords and vassals lived in a futile system." Hobbes, that feline fountain of facts, remarks, "That's 'feudal' system." Concern clouds Calvin's face. He sighs, "Just when I thought this junk was beginning to make sense."[1]

Even Calvin's errors contain kernels of truth. In the Middle Ages a feudal system did restore some order in Europe, but the attempt ultimately proved futile. So, the heirs of the barbarians fumbled their way toward a new society—a society of countries, united by common cultures, instead of one vast empire. You and I live in that society today.

### THE WOBBLING WEST

Imagine a land with no central government. Imagine cities without police officers. Imagine children without schools. What you've imagined is the former Western Empire in the Middle Ages. With no central government to mint coins, land became the key form of wealth. Landowners ("lords") set up self-sufficient plantations ("manors"). To protect their manors, lords maintained mounted bands of knights. In one area several lords might unite their knights under one king.

Without land of their own, peasants could not provide protection, food, or shelter for themselves. For the promise of provisions, peasants could become a lord's "vassals." They farmed part of their lord's land. In return, they received enough to survive, but nothing more. This was the "feudal system" (or, in Calvin's parlance, the "futile system").

Lords paid priests to serve their manors. Unfortunately, since kings and lords chose their own priests, obedience to earthly lords often supplanted obedience to the heavenly Lord.

Few people could read. Priests relied on statues, stained glass, and plays to teach their people about God. Church buildings became "Bibles in stone" as images and architecture replaced the preached and written Word.

### AN EMPIRE IN SEARCH OF SURVIVAL

Eastern efforts to maintain order didn't take the form of a feudal system. Yet Eastern efforts to preserve order were almost as futile as Western attempts. In the seventh century a "storm" from the south nearly brought the East to its knees.

### In This Chapter
### AD 496—AD 1291

Muhammad
Charlemagne
Photius of Constantinople
The Crusades
Pope Leo IX (Bruno)

### On The Web

Want to learn more about medieval churches? Start your research at...

*http://www.netserf.org*

*A "medieval" manor protected by mounted knights.*

### On The Web

To learn about Islam from a Muslim perspective, log on to...

*http://www.erols.com/ zenithco/muhammad.html*

## The Fire-Storm From the South

Muhammad [mou-HAHM-mahd] lived in Mecca, a small Arabian trading post. In 610 Muhammad claimed that the angel Gabriel had entrusted him with a message from Allah, the only true God. Muhammad, like Moses, preached against idols. At first, no one minded his message. But, around 622, angry idol-peddlers forced Muhammad to flee. When he returned to Mecca, Muhammad had gathered an army of followers. He called his followers Muslims ("those who submit [to Allah]"). Their religion became known as Islam ("submission").

After Muhammad's death, his followers conquered Arabia, Syria, and North Africa. In 638 Jerusalem fell to the Muslims. By 711 Muslim troops had conquered Portugal and Spain. Why did the Muslims make such unbelievable progress?

- Muslims allowed some religious freedom. Yes, they forced Christians to wear distinct clothes and pay higher taxes. In some areas Christians had to wear heavy crosses around their necks. Yet all religions that had holy writings were protected by early Muslims.

- The Eastern church had already rejected North African Christians (especially the Copts) because of their One-Nature theology. So, many North Africans willingly transformed their churches into mosques.

*Muslims believe Muhammad ascended to Allah from the Temple Mount in Jerusalem. Around AD 690, the Dome of the Rock was built over the stone from which Muhammad was said to have ascended.*

## Smashers and Kissers

Paintings of Jesus and the saints had guided Christian worship for many years. But when do these "icons" become idols? That's the question that confronted eighth century Christians. Because Christians used icons in their worship, many Muslims called them "idol-worshipers." As a frontier soldier, one future emperor saw that sometimes the Muslims were right. As pagans, people had worshipped idols. As Christians, some of them seemed to worship images of Jesus and the saints.

A volcano rocked Constantinople in AD 725. Fearing God's fury, the newly crowned emperor of the Eastern Empire acted against the "Icon-Kissers" (or, "iconodules"). The city's grandest icon was a golden image of Christ, set above the palace doors. The emperor sent a crew of soldiers to destroy it. A mob of women, armed with pots and pans, kicked a scaffold out from under the crew. Citizens labeled the emperor an "Icon-Smasher" (or, "iconoclast"). A bloody struggle between "Kissers" and "Smashers" began.

By 780 icon disputes had raged for 61 years. Then, Empress Irene seized the throne. It was she who called the seventh church-wide council. In AD 787 more than 350 overseers gathered in Nicaea to end the icon disputes. The Second Council of Nicaea denounced the "Smashers." Yet the council did not let Christians

*Eastern icons look 'flat' because Eastern Christians strictly observe the Second Council of Nicaea's ban on three-dimensional images.*
(Courtesy of Holy Transfiguration Monastery)

idolize icons. The delegates clearly banned icon-worship, as well as three-dimensional depictions of Jesus and the saints. What they promoted was *icon-reverence*.

What does it mean to revere an icon? Do you own a copy of the Bible that's very special to you? Your special Bible is like an icon. It helps you recall what God has done in your life. You revere your Bible as a channel of God's Word, yet you don't worship your Bible. Furthermore, you know that God's word is not limited to your Bible. Your Bible (like a correctly-used icon) is an earthly tool that focuses your mind on God's glorious works.

## FRANKS BECOME THE TOP DOGS

When the Middle Ages began, the pagan Franks were the prime Western power. The Franks originated in the area now known as western Germany. Around AD 496, Clovis, the Frankish battle-chief, led his people to turn to the Christian God. Clovis even accepted the Nicene Creed. So, when the Franks began their conquest of what was once the Western Empire, few church members resisted them. By 600, the Franks ruled large portions of central Europe. As the Franks' power increased, so did their support of the Roman church. In 754 King Pepin III of the Franks gave all of central Italy to the Roman church.

### How the West Was Won (Or, At Least, Baptized)

Around 780, Pepin III's son, King Charles, launched evangelistic campaigns against his enemies. When Charles mastered a tribe, he forced everyone to be baptized or die. Not surprisingly, more than 90% of his subjects reacted positively to his invitation. Whether or not they really became Christians is another question—one that God alone can answer. When some Germans refused baptism, Charles slashed off 4,500 heads in one day and, then, went to his camp to celebrate Christmas. By the beginning of the ninth century, Charles controlled the lands now known as Germany and France.

### A Frightened Friar Flees to the Franks

During Charles's conquests, a forged decree, *The Donation of Constantine*, arose to bolster the Roman church's political power in central Italy. The results of the church's new possessions were, however, not always pleasant.

In 799 several Italian nobles wanted to control the Roman church. Their candidate for pope was rejected in favor of Leo III. The nobles were, it seems, sore losers. They hired thugs to gouge out Leo III's tongue. Two Franks brought the injured bishop to Charles's palace.

King Charles warmly welcomed Pope Leo III. Yet there was a problem: The nobles who had assaulted Leo III had also sent letters to Charles. The letters charged Leo III with misuse of

### On The Web

To learn more about icons try...

*http://www.ocf.org/ OrthodoxPage/icons/ icons.html*
or
*http://www.unicorne.org/ orthodoxy/liens/art.htm*

### In Case You're Confused

Eastern Christians often kiss icons as they enter their church buildings. Why? They are recognizing that past saints still surround them today (see Hebrews 12:1). By kissing icons, they welcome these saints into their worship.

*Charlemagne, the first Holy Roman Emperor*

## On The Web

Download paintings of the Roman nobles' attack on Leo III from...
*http://www.bnf.fr/ enluminures/manuscrits/ aman5/i1_0022.htm*

The same site also has a painting of Leo III crowning Charlemagne. Get it at...
*http://www.bnf.fr/ enluminures/images/ jpeg/i1_0023.jpg*

## Did You Know?

Many Christians in the 990's believed that in the first year of the new millennium Satan would be "released from his prison" (Revelation 20:7-8). After a time of tribulation, Jesus would—people believed—return to judge to world. When the year 1000 came and went with few disasters, a wave of optimism and hope swept the churches. How does this compare with how some Christians reacted to the year AD 2000?

church funds. Normally, Leo III would have appealed to the emperor, but the West no longer had an emperor. Empress Irene ruled the Eastern Empire. Leo III refused to let a woman judge him. How could he clear his name?

### The Franking Privilege

On December 23, 800, King Charles declared Pope Leo III innocent of all charges. Two days later, amid the candles of the Christmas communion service, Leo III placed a crown on Charles's head and dubbed him "Charles Augustus, crowned by God as supreme and peaceful Emperor." For the first time, the church had created an emperor. Later generations would call this emperor "Charlemagne" [SHARR-le-mayn] ("Charles the Great").

As the newly dubbed 'Holy Roman Emperor,' Charlemagne viewed himself as the guardian of Roman Christianity. He founded monasteries to preserve ancient texts and to increase literacy. He appointed the church's bishops. He ensured the Roman church's control of central Italy.

Even after Emperor Charlemagne's death, the dream of a revived Western Empire refused to die. It lived on under a new name, "the Holy Roman Empire."

## HOLY CHURCH, UNHOLY LEADERS

Between 880 and 980 the Roman bishops office—once held by godly men like Pope Gregory—slipped into the hands of several not-so-noble nobles.

One Italian heiress, Marozia [mah-RO-zee-ah], controlled the bishops of Rome for 60 years. During those years, she was one bishop's mother, another's murderer, and another's mistress. In 955 her grandson, John XII, became the new pope. Before his election, John XII made a toast to the devil. His election did nothing to diminish his devilish lifestyle.

Even after John XII died, corruption continued to disgrace the Roman bishop's place in the church. The Roman church desperately needed reform. Eventually, the reforms came. However, with the reforms, came division.

## THE CHURCH DOES THE SPLITS

Eastern and Roman Christians had quarreled for centuries. Yet, they still viewed themselves as one body. Between the ninth and thirteenth centuries three blows would split Christianity into two separate fellowships.

### Somebody's Messing With My Creed!

Do you recall the Nicene Creed? (If you don't, glance back at Chapter Four.) Ninth-century Christians remembered it too, but there was a problem: Roman and Eastern Christians remembered the creed differently.

A church in Spain had added one Latin word to the Nicene Creed. The original creed confessed, "[The Spirit] proceeds from the Father." The revised creed claimed, "[The Spirit] proceeds from the Father and the Son." The Roman church soon adopted the revised Nicene Creed. Contemporary Christians might respond, "So what? It's only a slight difference!" Why did the addition matter?

- Both Eastern and Roman Christians, led by the Scriptures and the Holy Spirit, had approved the Nicene Creed. At the Councils of Ephesus and Chalcedon, they had vowed never to change the creed.

- Both groups agreed that God is one being in three persons. Yet each group pictured the Trinity differently. Roman theologians believed that the divine being dwelt equally in the Father, Son, and Spirit. According to Eastern thinkers, one being can dwell in only one person. In their view, divinity dwells only in the Father. The Father shares this divine being with the Son and Spirit. This does not, however, decrease the deity of the Son or the Spirit. Eastern Christians could state that "[the Spirit] proceeds from the Father *through* the Son." But they could not confess that the Spirit "proceeds from the Father *and* the Son." If the Spirit arose from "the Father and the Son," the Son would be sharing divine being—which can come only from God the Father—with the Holy Spirit.

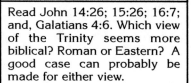

## Think About It...

Read John 14:26; 15:26; 16:7; and, Galatians 4:6. Which view of the Trinity seems more biblical? Roman or Eastern? A good case can probably be made for either view.

In 867 Photius [FO-shee-uss], the bishop of Constantinople in the Eastern Empire, denounced the added phrase. Five years later, the pope offered to drop "and the Son" from the Nicene Creed. But there was a condition: Eastern churches had to accept the pope's supremacy over all churches. Photius declined. A narrow crack pierced the church's unity.

## In Case You're Confused

Ever since the tenth century, popes have assumed new names at their elections.

### A Roman Bull Gores the East

In AD 1048 three shoeless pilgrims—Bruno, Humbert, and Hildebrand [HILL-de-BRAND]—walked through the gates of Rome. Each one would, in his own way, transform the Roman church. In Rome, Bruno was acclaimed as Pope Leo IX.

To prevent priests from passing positions to their children, Bruno banned priests from marrying. Bruno didn't want nobles to exploit the church again. So, he fought to free the Roman church from all outside controls.

Bruno and his successors sincerely believed that God had given the pope authority over all Christians. Their sincere belief contributed to a church-wide split that still exists today.

Michael, the new bishop of Constantinople, refused to recognize Bruno as pope. Then, Michael closed every church

Ruins from the Church of Holy Wisdom (Hagia Sophia) where Humbert laid the bull of excommunication in AD 1054.

## Words: From The Ones Who Were There

*Humbert*
"Let Michael Cerularius and his followers be damned at the Lord's coming, with . . . all other heretics, yes, even with the devil and the devil's angels."

## On The Web

For an Eastern Orthodox perspective on the schism, check out...

*http://www.goarch.org/
en/ourfaith/*

or

*http://www.saintignatius
church.org/timeline.html*

in Constantinople that was loyal to the Roman bishop. Bruno sent envoys to Constantinople to restore peace. Bruno's chief envoy was Humbert. Before he left Rome, Humbert wrote a brash bull. (No, he didn't scrawl on a male bovine's flank. A bull is a notice written in a pope's name. The English word "bulletin" comes from the Latin "bull.")

On July 16, AD 1054, Humbert marched into the Church of Holy Wisdom in Constantinople, during the Lord's Supper. Humbert's notice was a lot like a Texas longhorn—it had a point here, a point there, and lots of bull in between. According to the notice, Eastern Christians:

- allowed priests to marry. (True.)
- re-baptized Roman Christians. (Untrue in most cases.)
- had deleted "and the Son" from the Nicene Creed. (Certainly untrue!)

Humbert flung the bull on the communion table. At the door, he brushed dust from his sandals and bellowed, "Let God look and judge!" An Eastern deacon grabbed the bull and chased Humbert. He begged Humbert to take the bull back. Humbert refused.

Two blows—an altered creed and a brash bull—had divided Roman and Eastern Christians. Had it not been for a third blow, the gash might have healed. The final blow was the Crusades.

## THE CRUSADES

Many medieval people believed they could prove their desire to turn from sin by going on a "pilgrimage." Pilgrims usually traveled to local shrines. The supreme pilgrimage led to Jerusalem. To impede a pilgrim's journey was, from the medieval church's perspective, to imperil that person's salvation. However, Muslims had controlled Jerusalem since AD 638. On the road to Jerusalem, Muslim converts ("Turks") began to force Christian pilgrims to pay vast tariffs.

In 1095 Pope Urban II preached one of history's most influential sermons. "Your Eastern brothers have asked for your help!" he proclaimed in a field in Clermont, France. "Turks and Arabs have conquered their territories. I—or, rather, the Lord—beg you, . . . destroy that vile race from their lands!"

The response astounded Urban II. The crowd began to chant, "God wills it!" Lords and fools, ruffians and serfs, sewed cloth crosses on their tunics. Their campaign would be both a pilgrimage to Jerusalem and a war against "the infidels." The pilgrims agreed to gather in Constantinople. The First Crusade was underway.

Of all the Crusaders, Peter the Hermit probably possessed the strongest scent. The swarthy monk had not bathed in decades. He rode a burro that, according to several eyewitnesses, bore a remarkable resemblance to its rider. Peter's preaching seems to have been even more powerful than his odor. In nine months, he gathered 20,000 European peasants to fight the Muslims.

Peter's peasants caused immediate chaos when they arrived in Constantinople. Complaints of robbery poured into the emperor's office. The emperor knew that the untrained peasants were no match for the Muslims, but he couldn't let them linger in his city. So, the peasants were ferried across the river.

Peter's peasants pillaged Eastern homes for two months. Then, they marched straight into a Muslim ambush. Peter (who was in Constantinople begging for supplies) was the sole survivor. In Huck Finn's words, "As near as I can make it out, most of the folks that shook farming to go crusading had a mighty rocky time of it."[2] Peter the Hermit joined another army, led by European princes and lords. These Crusaders clashed with the Muslims in Antioch and then continued to Jerusalem.

On July 15, 1099, Jerusalem fell to the royal Crusaders. On the Temple Mount, Muslim blood flowed ankle-deep. Newborns were thrown against walls. Crusaders torched a synagogue and burned the Jews inside alive. This wholesale slaughter in Christ's name is one of the major reasons that Jewish and Muslim people today may not trust Christians.

## The Fourth Crusade

In 1198 a noble named Innocent III became the bishop of Rome. It was Pope Innocent III who inspired the Fourth Crusade. However, he didn't inspire the outrages that would finally divide Eastern and Roman Christians.

Innocent III intended to destroy a Muslim army base in Egypt. The merchants of Venice agreed to supply the Crusaders with ships at the cost of 84,000 silver coins. In summer, 1202, the Crusaders arrived in Venice, expecting to sail to Egypt. But there was a problem: Only one-third of the expected number of Crusaders showed up, and they could come up with only 50,000 coins.

An Eastern prince offered to finance the crusade under one condition: The Crusaders had to sail to Constantinople and dethrone the current Eastern emperor. Pope Innocent III forbade the attack, but no one seemed to care.

On July 5, 1203, the Crusaders arrived in the capital city of the Eastern Empire. Not surprisingly, Constantinople's citizens did not relish the intrusion into their affairs. The citizens revolted and installed an anti-Crusader emperor on the Eastern Empire's throne.

The Crusaders were furious. They had set out to destroy the Muslims. Now, they were stranded in Constantinople. The crusade leaders decided to plunder Constantinople. One priest proclaimed (without the pope's approval), "If you rightly intend to conquer this land and bring it under Roman obedience, all who die . . . partake in the pope's indulgence." (To partake in an indulgence was to be freed from enduring the earthly punishment—that is, performing the penance—for one's sins.)

*Reenactment of a Crusade battle.*

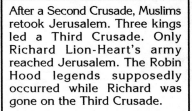

*Until the invention of the crossbow, chain mail protected princes, lords, and knights in battle.*

On Good Friday, 1204, the Crusaders, with red crosses on their tunics, sacked Constantinople. For three days, they raped and killed Christians in the name of Christ. The city's statues were melted down. The Church of Holy Wisdom (the "Hagia Sophia") was stripped of its gold vessels. A harlot danced on the altar, singing obscene songs. One Eastern writer lamented, "Muslims are merciful compared with these men who bear Christ's cross on their shoulders."

Neither the Eastern Empire nor the Eastern church ever recovered from those three days. For 60 years Crusaders ruled what was once the Eastern Empire. The true Eastern emperor established an Empire southeast of Constantinople, in Nicaea. Rather than embrace Roman customs, many Eastern Christians fled to Nicaea. They remained there until 1261, when an Eastern ruler regained Constantinople.

Pope Innocent III had tried to prevent the fall of Constantinople, but no one had listened. Afterward, he attempted to reunite the churches, but it was too late. After the Fourth Crusade, the church was forever divided into two groups—Roman Catholic and Eastern Orthodox.

## SEPARATE CHURCHES, SEPARATE PATHS

### The Shaping of Roman Catholicism

Pope Innocent III's greatest achievement was the council that molded Roman Catholic theology for 300 years. The council convened in the Lateran palace in Rome. Three earlier councils had also gathered at the Lateran palace. In 1215 the Fourth Lateran Council:

- declared that, in the Lord's Supper, the observable features of the bread and wine never change. But, at an unseen level, the elements become Jesus' body and blood. This concept is called *transubstantiation*. The bishops at the council explained transusbstantiation this way: "[Christ's] body and blood are contained in the sacraments under the outward forms of bread and wine; the bread being transubstantiated by God's power into the body, and the wine into the blood."

- formed the groundwork for the Inquisition, a court to uproot ideas that defied the church's understanding of Scripture. Around 1231 the Inquisition became a systematic tool to destroy heretics. At first, the Inquisition focused on the Gnostic-like Albigensians, then expanded to exterminate other groups, including Muslims and Jews.

Chapter 5

## DO YOU UNDERSTAND ME?

Many Christians try to dismiss medieval Christianity as empty and corrupt. However, if we allow ourselves to feel superior to medieval church members, we are guilty of the same misdeed as many people in the Middle Ages. We have become like Charlemagne, celebrating Christmas while 4,500 German widows mourned their spouses . . . like Humbert at an Eastern communion table . . . like a horde of crusaders at the gates of Constantinople. How? We also have condemned before seeking to comprehend.

For every devilish pope or crusader, there were thousands of bishops, priests, and common people who sincerely believed they were following Christ. Some lived out their faith as farmers and merchants. Others lived out their faith as lords and kings. Some were authentic Christians. Others were not.

Nothing can excuse any offense undertaken in Christ's name. However, instead of flinging my own notice of excommunication on the communion tables of the Middle Ages, I must remember that it is not my blameless deeds or my denomination's theology that guards me against the same failures. It is grace and only grace.

*The Hagia Sophia in Constantinople was one target of the Crusaders' greed.*

### Did You Know?

In Latin, the farewell phrase of the communion service is "missa est"—"Go forth." Among Catholics, communion became known as "missa" or "Mass."

### Key Concept

Be critical only after you've tried to comprehend. Even then, speak with compassion.

## How do Roman Catholicism and Eastern Orthodoxy differ?

| Roman Catholicism | Eastern Orthodoxy |
|---|---|
| **Name**<br>"Catholic" means "worldwide" or "universal." | **Name**<br>"Orthodoxy" means "correct glory" and implies faithfulness to the church's ancient teachings and traditions. |
| **Structure**<br>The bishop of Rome is the father ("pope") over all churches. He represents Christ's leadership in the church. Overseers ("bishops") guide each region and are responsible directly to the pope. High overseers ("archbishops") are highly esteemed by other bishops, but they have no power outside their own regions. Since 1150, bishops and archbishops who advise the pope have been called "cardinal" overseers. | **Structure**<br>Today, the Orthodox Church consists of several self-ruling groups of churches. A metropolitan patriarch ("city father") guides each group of churches. Some patriarchs also serve as high overseers ("archbishops"). Orthodox Christians highly esteem the patriarch of Constantinople (modern Istanbul, Turkey). Yet he has little official authority beyond his own churches. |
| **Authority**<br>Scripture as understood through the church councils, church tradition, and bishops in union with the pope. | **Authority**<br>The teachings of the apostles as understood through the Scriptures, the first seven church-wide councils, and the ancient church fathers. |

This timeline summarizes relations between Eastern and Roman Christians from the second century through the thirteenth century.

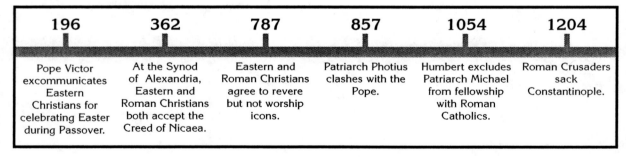

| 196 | 362 | 787 | 857 | 1054 | 1204 |
|---|---|---|---|---|---|
| Pope Victor excommunicates Eastern Christians for celebrating Easter during Passover. | At the Synod of Alexandria, Eastern and Roman Christians both accept the Creed of Nicaea. | Eastern and Roman Christians agree to revere but not worship icons. | Patriarch Photius clashes with the Pope. | Humbert excludes Patriarch Michael from fellowship with Roman Catholics. | Roman Crusaders sack Constantinople. |

# CHAPTER FIVE LEARNING ACTIVITY

This quiz will help you review what you read in Chapter Five. Choose the word or phrase that completes each sentence.

1. Muslims worship _____.
   A. Muhammad          B. Allah          C. idols

2. The Second Council of Nicaea allowed Christians to _____.
   A. worship idols.          B. idolize icons          C. revere icons

3. Pope Leo III crowned King Charles of the Franks as the _____.
   A. Roman emperor     B. Roman bishop     C. Saxon emperor

4. The forged *Donation of Constantine* granted lands to the _____.
   A. Eastern church     B. English church     C. Roman church

5. Pope Leo IX ("Bruno") _____.
   A. promoted priestly celibacy          B. pardoned Henry IV

6. The purpose of the First Crusade was to _____.
   A. sack Constantinople     B. kill Jews     C. conquer Jerusalem

7. Pope Innocent III _____ the attack on Constantinople.
   A. ignored          B. encouraged          C. forbade

Match each statement below with its source.

8. _____ Third Council of Constantinople

9. _____ The Roman Nicene Creed

10. _____ Pope Urban II's sermon

11. _____ Humbert's bull

12. _____ Fourth Lateran Council

A. "If anyone out of devotion sets out for Jerusalem, the journey shall be seen as penance."

B. "Michael Cerularius and his followers be damned."

C. "[The Holy Spirit] proceeds from the Father and the Son."

D. "We glorify two natures and two wills agreeing within [Jesus] for the salvation of humanity."

E. "His body and blood are . . . in the sacraments."

---

1.  Bill Watterson, *Attack of the Deranged Mutant Killer Monster Snow Goons* (Kansas City: Andrews and McMeel, 1992) 56.

2.  Mark Twain, *Tom Sawyer Abroad* (Aerie, [n.d.]) 10.

# WHAT YOU SHOULD KNOW ABOUT CHRISTIAN HISTORY
## AD 673—1295

### Four Events You Should Know

1. *Spread of the Nestorianism* (AD 780-823): Nestorian monks took the gospel into India, Turkestan, China, Persia, and Syria. Nearly 100,000 Nestorians remain in southwest Asia today.

2. *Children's Crusade* (AD 1212): Nearly 20,000 children gathered around a shepherd-boy named Stephen to conquer the Holy Land. A merchant offered them free transportation, but then sold them into slavery.

3. *Second Council of Lyons* (AD 1274): More than 500 bishops tried to unite Roman Catholicism and Eastern Orthodoxy under the pope's authority. Eastern Christians rejected the union.

4. *Kublai Khan's Request* (AD 1266): Marco Polo's father met Kublai in 1266. Christianity so intrigued Kublai that he asked for 100 monks to teach his people. Fewer than eight monks were sent. When the trip became severe, all of them turned back. When monks finally reached Mongolia in the late 1200's, it was too late. Most Mongolians had already converted to Islam.

### Nine Names You Should Know

1. *Caedmon* (died AD 680): Monk. First English Christian poet. Retold Bible stories in song.

2. *Bede the Venerable* (AD 673-735): Christian scholar. Wrote a history of English Christianity.

3. *Anskar* (AD 801-865): "The Apostle of the North." Missionary to Sweden and Denmark.

4. *Alfred the Great* (AD 849-899): English king. Translated parts of the Bible into English.

5. *Odo* (AD 879-942): Succeeded Berno as the abbot (leading monk) of Cluny monastery.

6. *Peter Abelard* (AD 1079-1143): Professor of theology until his affair with a student named Heloise. Heloise's uncle attacked Abelard and had him castrated. Afterward, Abelard retired to a monastery where he wrote several important doctrinal treatises.

7. *Bernard of Clairvaux* (AD 1090-1153): Powerful abbot of Clairvaux monastery. In 1128 he obtained approval for the Knights Templar, an order of crusader monks based at the Temple Mount in Jerusalem.

8. *Bonaventure* (AD 1217-1274): Franciscan theologian. Francis of Assisi's biographer.

9. *Thomas Aquinas* (AD 1225-1274): Scholastic theologian. Applied Aristotle's philosophy to Christian doctrine. "Angelic Doctor" of Roman Catholic Church.

### Four Terms You Should Know

1. *Cistercians*: Roman Catholic monastic order. Also known as "White Monks" (because of their undyed robes) or the "Sacred Order of Citeaux." Named after Cistertium-Citeaux, the French town where Robert Molesme founded the order.

2. *Waldensians*: Group of lay-preachers. Also known as the "Vaudois." Named after Waldo (Valdes), their founder. Condemned at the Third and Fourth Lateran Councils. They survived until the 1600s, when they joined the Protestant movement.

3. *Franciscans*: Roman Catholic monastic order. Also known as the "Order of Friars, Minor." Many leading Scholastic scholars, including William of Ockham, were Franciscans.

4. *Dominicans*: Roman Catholic monastic order. Named after Dominic, their founder. Also known as "Black Friars" (because of their black robes) or the "Order of Friars, Preachers."

# Chapter Six

## GOD NEVER STOPS WORKING

When Protestants read about the Middle Ages, they often ask, "Which church did the real Christians belong to?" Many church members simply can't picture "real Christians" worshiping beside violent crusaders and corrupt clergy. When Christians today disagree with their church, they join another church. Sometimes, they even start their own congregations.

Medieval Christians could not imagine starting their own congregations. To be a Christian was to belong to "one, holy, apostolic church." That's why one medieval church might include customs that one finds spread through several denominations today.

Some church members were vegetarians; some spoke in tongues. Some people believed that their good deeds could earn salvation; others disagreed. Yet, with rare exceptions, they saw themselves as members of the same church.

In this chapter, you will read about a dozen Christians. They—just like Charlemagne and the crusaders—were part of the medieval churches. Yet they lived with their eyes on the cross. They were citizens of Augustine's "City of God." And they were not exceptions. They were part of the rule.

### THE CITY OF GOD AMONG MISSIONARIES AND MONKS

Early medieval monasteries were vital missionary centers, especially among the English and Irish. Monks and nuns started small communities in pagan areas. The communities' farming methods were far ahead of their time. Soon, natives asked about the community's top-quality crops. Conversations about crops led to curiosity about the Christian faith. Curiosity about Christianity often led to authentic conversions. By the late 800's, however, these communities needed revival. Corrupt nobles controlled many monasteries. Vikings had sacked others.

#### The Duke who Lost His Dogs

In 909 Duke William III of Aquitaine, France, founded a new monastery. William, unlike many nobles, didn't want to control his community. He enlisted a godly monk named Berno [BERR-no] to lead the monastery. (Don't confuse *Berno* with *Bruno*, the bishop—also known as Pope Leo IX—who reformed the Roman church in the early 1000s!)

Berno brought Duke William some unwanted news: The best place to build a monastery was Cluny, William's hunting ground. William objected, but Berno reminded him that providing for hunting dogs wouldn't lead to any eternal reward; providing for monks might.

## In This Chapter
## AD 673—AD 1295

Cluny monasteries
John Damascus
Cyril of Moravia
Hildegard of Bingen
Francis of Assisi
Anselm of Canterbury
Thomas Aquinas
Thomas Becket

## Key Concept

Even in the least likely places, God is working.

## Did You Know?

Lioba and Boniface were English missionaries to Germany. According to tradition, Boniface began to chop down a German god's sacred tree. With his ax's first blow, a wind-gust felled the oak. The Germans immediately gave up their old gods. From the tree, Boniface built a chapel. When Boniface needed help, his sister Lioba convinced eleven nuns and monks to follow her across the English Channel. While the monks farmed and preached, Lioba's nuns ran hospitals and trained new converts.

## Words: From The Ones Who Were There

*Duke William III*
"I hand over to the apostles Peter and Paul the possessions that I now control in Cluny... The monks there shall not be subject... to any earthly power."
*Recueil des Chartes de L'Abbaye de Cluny.*

## Think About It...

Only the richest men hunted with dogs. To give up one's dogs was to give up one's status. What prized possession could you release to please God?

## Words: From The Ones Who Were There

*John Damascus*
"To depict God in a shape would be the peak of insanity and impiety. . . . But since God . . . became truly human . . . the Fathers (seeing that not all can read) . . . approved the description of these facts in images."
*On the Orthodox Faith, 4:16.*

*In Orthodox church buildings, an iconostasis (Greek for "icon stand") often divides the altar from the central sanctuary.*

William freed his dogs and deeded his property to Peter, Paul, and the abbot (not to be confused with the much later singing group, Peter, Paul, and Mary). Neither William nor any bishop could meddle in the monastery's affairs. Only Cluny's foremost monk (the "abbot") had any power in the community.

The monks at Cluny stressed perfect obedience to Scripture and to Benedict's *Rule*. Throughout Europe, people began to assess their priests and bishops according to the high ideals of the monks at Cluny. Their hunger for holiness led to Bruno's radical reforms in the Roman bishop's office. And it all started when one duke traded his finest hunting dogs for a monastery full of monks.

### The Maimed Monk

John Damascus inherited a powerful political position in Damascus, Syria. He wasn't only a politician, though. He was the Eastern church's brightest thinker. He remained a committed Christian in the midst of a Muslim government. During the icon disputes, John sided with the iconodules (or, "Icon-Kissers"). It was John who discerned the difference between icon-worship and icon-reverence.

John's political career was, unfortunately, cut short by a lie. An anti-icon Eastern emperor sent a forged document, with John's signature, to a Muslim leader. His letter claimed to expose a plan to hand over the city of Damascus to a Christian army.

The Muslim court convicted John of treason. The first part of John's punishment—lifetime exile in a distant monastery—wasn't too harsh. The second part of his punishment was a bit more brutal; his right hand was to be chopped off.

In the monastery, John and his fellow-monks wove baskets. They sold their baskets to help the poor. John also wrote hundreds of hymns. (John's right hand was still in Damascus, so I assume he wrote them left-handed.) John's genius made his fellow-monks jealous. They sent the one-handed monk back to Damascus. John spent his last days selling baskets in the streets where he once lived as a lord.

### The Magnificent Moravian Failures

In 862 the king of Moravia (now the Czech Republic) asked the Eastern Empire to send missionaries to his people. Photius, Constantinople's patriarch, chose Cyril as his envoy to the Slavic people in Moravia. (Don't confuse Cyril the missionary with the corrupt fifth-century bishop who bore the same name!) Cyril was a Thessalonian Slav. He had moved to Constantinople to study. Now, he taught philosophy in the capital city.

Before he left home, Cyril created a Slavic alphabet, so he could translate the Bible into the Moravian language. Roman and German missionaries opposed Cyril's efforts. The Scriptures and the church's worship should be (they claimed) translated only into "holy languages," like Latin.

In 869 Cyril and his brother, Methodius [meh-THO-dee-uss], traveled to Rome to appeal to the pope. The pope let Cyril translate the Scriptures into common languages under one condition: Cyril had to place his mission under the pope's control. Cyril accepted the pope's terms, bur he died before he could return to Moravia to complete his mission.

Methodius, Cyril's brother, continued to work among the Moravians. Unfortunately, the Moravians could not understand Cyril's translations. In 895 Hungarian invaders forced Cyril's successors to flee to Bulgaria. No trace remained of Cyril's mission. From a human viewpoint, Cyril and Methodius failed miserably in Moravia.

Even though Cyril's efforts failed in Moravia, they began to bear fruit in Bulgaria. Boris, the Bulgar prince, had accepted Christ before Cyril's successors arrived. Through Cyril's successors, Boris' people began to embrace the gospel, too. Cyril's successors refined their master's missionary methods. They adapted Cyril's alphabet to the Bulgarian tongue. They preached and worshiped in the people's language.

By 900 Bulgaria was the center of Slavic Christianity. "Cyrillic" became the common way of writing in southeast Europe and Russia. When Cyril and his brother died, they were fruitless failures. Years later, God transformed their failure into a success.

## THE CITY OF GOD AMONG THE MYSTICS

What image enters your mind when you hear the word "mystic"? Mysterious mantras? Unexplainable enigmas? What may not enter your mind is devotion to Christ. Yet many medieval Christians were mystics. They sought ecstatic encounters with Christ that transported them beyond human logic.

Why did mystics multiply in the Middle Ages? Every source of an encounter with God—the Scriptures, sermons, baptism, communion—was channeled through the churches. Christian faith cannot, however, grow only in the context of the church. It must also flourish on a personal level. Medieval mystics, like Bernard of Clairvaux and Hildegard of Bingen, wanted to reclaim the personal and emotional aspects of their faith.

### St. Bernard—You've Met the Dog; Now, Meet the Monk

The fame of the communities at Cluny had transformed an entire culture. However, the fame that transformed the culture killed the communities. The Cluny communities became so well-known that every noble in France wanted to sponsor them. By 1000 the monks and nuns no longer worked or reached out to the poor. Gold and jewels plastered their chapel walls.

In 1098 twenty-one monks from Cluny decided to return to Benedict's emphasis on poverty and labor. They founded their new community near Cistertium, France. They became known

*Cyril and Methodius of Moravia*
*(Courtesy of Holy Transfiguration Monastery)*

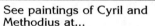

## On The Web

See paintings of Cyril and Methodius at…

*http://www.cybercom.net/ ~htm/images/a-154.jpg*

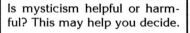

## Think About It…

Is mysticism helpful or harmful? This may help you decide.

### Positively

1. God commands Christians to love God with their whole beings, including their feelings (Mark 12:30).

2. Paul and John described mystical experiences (2 Corinthians 12:1-9; Revelation 1:9-11; 4:1-11).

### Negatively

1. Mystics may give their experiences equal authority with Scripture or with their church's collective wisdom.

2. Christian faith must depend on more than feelings. It must also engage one's mind.

## Did You Know?

In 988 Czar Vladimir of Kiev went shopping for a religion. According to tradition, Vladimir liked to eat, so he rejected the Muslim and Jewish restraints on his diet. Roman Catholicism was okay; but the beauty of Eastern Orthodox worship moved Vladimir and his people to accept Eastern Christianity. Several other tenth-century rulers also turned to Christianity, including King Stephen of Hungary, King Miesko of Poland, and the Viking battle-chief Leif Ericson.

## Think About It...

After Bernard, Roman Christians focused on Jesus' humanity. Devotion to Mary and to Jesus' sufferings increased. Do you think this devotion was wholesome? Why or why not?

## Words: From The Ones Who Were There

*Bernard of Clairvaux*
"Some seek knowledge for the sake of knowledge. That is curiosity. Some seek knowledge to be known by others. That is vanity. Some seek knowledge to serve. That is love."

## On The Web

Learn more about Hildegard at...
> http://music.acu.edu/
> www/iawm/historical/
> hildegard.html

as Cistercian [siss-TAYR-see-ann] monks. So strict was the Cistercian rule that the monks refused to dye their robes to avoid the appearance of wealth. Today, Cistercians still wear white robes.

By 1112 no one was joining the Cistercian community. The lifestyle was simply too strict. The dispirited abbot was preparing to quit when someone knocked at the gate. When the abbot arrived at the gate, he was awestruck. Not one . . . not five . . . not ten . . . but 31 men stood at the gate! All of them wanted to become monks. One of them was Bernard of Clairvaux. Not only would Bernard become the mightiest monk of the Middle Ages, he would also have a breed of dogs named after him!

Bernard never became a bishop. Yet he ruled the Roman church for 30 years. He criticized Cluny's lavish lifestyle. When Anacletus II and Innocent II both claimed to be the pope, it was Bernard who declared Innocent II the true bishop of Rome. How did Bernard become so powerful? His poverty endeared him to peasants. His passion unnerved popes. His focus on God's love touched even the hardest hearts. "The reason for our loving God is God," Bernard once preached. "Yet every soul that seeks God . . . has already been anticipated by him. He sought you before you began to seek him."

According to Bernard, to love God is to be drawn into the love that flows eternally between Father, Son, and Spirit. This encounter mystically unites a Christian with God. Bernard's emphasis on love quickly confronted a barrier. Medieval icons portrayed Jesus as an angry judge. How could people love such fearful images? To help people love God, Bernard stressed Jesus' human weakness. Soon, pictures of the baby Jesus and the crucified Christ replaced the older icons.

### A Renaissance Woman in the Middle Ages

She was a musician and mystic, artist and author, preacher and prophet. Popes and emperors praised her. Only Bernard surpassed her prestige. She was Hildegard [HILL-de-GARD] of Bingen.

When she was five, Hildegard began to experience mystic visions. When she was eight, she entered a religious community. Three decades later, she became the leader (the "abbess") of a convent near Bingen, Germany. In 1151 she published her visions in a book, *Know the Way*.

When Hildegard was nearly 80, the bishop of Mainz denounced her visions. Her convent was excluded from the church's fellowship. But Hildegard's devotion lasted beyond the bishop's condemnation. By 1400 the Roman Catholic Church had forgotten the bishop's charges. Hildegard was officially listed as a saint.

## THE CITY OF GOD AMONG THE MENDICANTS

By the late 1100s the barbarian invasions no longer threatened Europe. People's loyalties were shifting from local lords to larger systems, like shared cultures and kings. In the cities, a class of mobile merchants emerged between serfs and nobles. Members of this "middle class" traded goods and services for cash. Mobile people needed mobile clergy. So, a new type of preacher appeared—the "mendicant" [MENN-dih-kant]. Mendicants traveled from town to town preaching to the merchants and peasants who flocked to the cities.

*Before Bernard of Clairvaux, medieval artists usually portrayed Jesus like this, as a judge.*

### Where's Waldo?

In 1173 a street-corner singer staged a play about a nobleman who gave away his wealth. The play so impressed a French merchant named Waldo (or "Valdes") that he committed himself and his wealth to Christ. He financed a French translation of the Bible and became a mendicant.

Waldo became disturbed as he studied the Scriptures. He found no references to purgatory or to the pope's supreme power. So, he rejected both ideas.

Waldo's fresh focus on Scripture soon attracted a band of followers. They called themselves "the Poor Folk of Lyons." All Poor Folk, including women, learned the Scriptures and preached in the common people's language. Within four years, the so-called "Waldensians" had blanketed France.

Waldo asked the pope to approve his movement. The pope agreed . . . with one condition. Poor Folk could preach only when a bishop asked them to preach. Three years later, Waldo preached in Lyons with no invitation. The Poor Folk were thrown out of Lyons. A few returned to the Roman church. The rest ignored the church's condemnation and kept preaching.

When he died, Waldo remained condemned. At the Fourth Lateran Council, Innocent III restated the excommunication. By the mid 1200s the Inquisition was working to destroy the Waldensians. Hundreds of Poor Folk were executed by Crusaders. The remaining Poor Folk fled to Germany and Spain.

### The Knight Who Stripped for a Bishop

Not every band of mendicants endured condemnation. One mendicant founded a group that would become the Roman Catholic Church's largest religious order.

It all began in 1204. The knights of Assisi, Italy, marched against a rival city. A twenty-two-year-old cloth merchant's son was among them. The young man's name was Francis. He had a vision of the crucified Christ as he traveled. He returned home transformed. Francis rollicked through the city streets. A friend asked, "Why are you so happy?" "Because," Francis exulted, "I have married Lady Poverty!" Francis kissed lepers and sold

### Words: From The Ones Who Were There

*Poor Folk's Confession of Faith*
"We believe . . . the Apostles' Creed . . . and that Christ . . . died for the salvation of all believers . . . . There is no other mediator and advocate beyond God the Father, except Jesus Christ. . . . We have no sacraments other than baptism and the Lord's Supper."

*Francis of Assisi*

some of his father's cloth to repair a chapel. Francis' angry father dragged him to the bishop's office.

Before the bishop, Francis removed his lavish clothes. He handed them to his father. Francis remarked, "Until today, I called you father. Now, I can say honestly, 'Our Father in heaven.' . . . In him alone I place my faith." Francis chalked a cross on a tattered brown tunic. He tied the tunic around his waist with a rope that he took from a farmer's scarecrow. "Grant me, Jesus," he prayed, "that I may never own under heaven anything of my own."

On February 24, 1208, the lectionary text was Matthew 10:8-10. Francis applied Jesus' words directly to himself and his band of followers. A year later, Francis asked Pope Innocent III to approve his movement. Francis didn't want his order to become wealthy, as the order at Cluny had. Each Franciscan "friar" ("brother") could own two tunics—nothing more. The tunics would be simple and brown, like the one Francis took from the scarecrow. Innocent III thought that the rules were too harsh. Still, he approved them.

In 1214 Pope Innocent III allowed a nun named Clare to take up the Franciscan lifestyle. While the friars preached, Clare's nuns nursed the sick. After Francis died, the pope declared that Clare and her nuns could no longer listen to the monks' preaching. Neither could they embrace poverty. Clare was furious. As long as the pope withheld her "spiritual food," Clare refused physical food. In short, she went on a hunger strike. The pope backed down. In 1247 while Clare lay on her deathbed, Pope Gregory IX approved her rules for the community of "Poor Clares."

## THE CITY OF GOD AMONG THE SCHOLASTICS

In the early Middle Ages, survival concerned most folk far more than schooling. When European society stabilized in the late 1100's, merchants and mendicants weren't the only ones who crisscrossed Europe. Scholars also migrated from town to town. In many towns, small groups of scholars instructed circles of promising students. Mendicants and mystics had emphasized practical experiences. The migrant scholars urged people to question their experiences in the light of reason. Yet could reason work together with human experience and with God's revelation? That was the question that confronted the new thinkers—the Scholastics.

### The Scholastics' Exiled Ancestor

In 1093 an abbot from Normandy, France, became the archbishop of Canterbury, England. His name was Anselm [ANN-selm]. Anselm knew that he and the king would clash. Why? King William II of France wanted to control the English churches. Anselm would not conform to the king's agenda.

## Think About It...

Before his conversion, Francis despised lepers. Afterward, he forced himself to greet them with a kiss. God transformed his feelings from loathing to love. What group of people would you prefer to ignore? How can you offer them "a kiss of peace"?

## Did You Know?

Franciscan monks still wear brown robes, tied at the waist with rope.

## On The Web

Learn more about Francis and Clare at ...

*http://www.mgc.org /021.htm* and

*http://members.cox.net /sfobro/page2.html*

As a result, he spent one-third of his career in exile. The works that he wrote before and during his exile earned him the title "Father of the Scholastics."

In the 1000s God's power so obsessed some Christians that they believed God could contradict logic. God could create square circles, change the past, and design a car that lasts until it's paid off. (Okay, so I made up the last one. But it is a contradiction, isn't it?) Anselm affirmed that no one can completely grasp God's actions. Yet he denied that God contradicted logic. "I do not try to understand you so I can trust you," Anselm prayed. "I trust you so I can understand you." To confirm his faith, Anselm composed a logical proof for God's being—the "ontological argument."

Anselm was also a compassionate Christian. Once, an abbot asked Anselm, "What should we do with the boys in the monastery? We whip them constantly and they keep acting worse!" Anselm replied, "If you planted a tree and hemmed it in on all sides, what would result?" "A useless tree," the abbot replied. "So you," Anselm retorted, "have hemmed in the boys. They fill their minds with twisted thoughts because they sense no mercy in you!"

### From Dumb-Ox to Doctor of the Church

"Stupid." "Scum!" "Nerd." Everyone knows the sting of a degrading name. More than anyone else in church history, Thomas Aquinas [ah-KWI-nass] knew what it feels like to endure ridicule.

Thomas was quiet, clumsy, and grossly overweight. When he was 20, he decided to join the Dominicans, a group of black-robed mendicant monks. Thomas' parents had other plans. They wanted him to become an archbishop, not a wandering preacher. So, his brothers kidnaped him. For fifteen months, they tempted Thomas with prostitutes and prestigious positions. Thomas remained unmoved.

In 1245 Thomas escaped his family's castle and fled to the University of Paris. In college, students usually move beyond name-calling. Thomas' classmates didn't. They dubbed the shy Dominican "Dumb-Ox." No one suspected that this ox's bellow would soon resound throughout the world.

Eleven years later, Thomas Aquinas was teaching in the university. Thomas' teachings transformed Christian theology. He integrated the logic of a pagan philosopher named Aristotle with God's revelation. Many monks had treated philosophy and the physical world as Satan's domain. For Thomas, philosophy and the physical world were full of signs that pointed to the Creator.

### Did You Know?

Anselm wasn't the last English archbishop to clash with a king. In 1162 King Henry II made Thomas Becket archbishop. When Becket challenged his power, Henry II cried thoughtlessly, "Won't someone rid me of this bishop?" To please their king, four drunken knights bludgeoned Becket to death on the steps of Canterbury's cathedral.

*This medieval image of Solomon perhaps personifies the Scholastics' search for universal wisdom.*

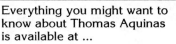

### On The Web

Everything you might want to know about Thomas Aquinas is available at ...

*http://www.niagara.edu/ aquinas/*

## Did You Know?

It wasn't only Scholastics who viewed the physical world as a tool to point to God. Twelfth-century artisans used architecture to point people toward God. They designed lofty cathedrals whose pointed arches and spires seemed to soar into the heavens. These cathedrals added so-called "barbarian" ideals to ancient Roman designs. So, later generations called them "Gothic cathedrals."

Notice the distinctive shape of the Gothic cathedral's windows.

## On The Web

To learn more about Gothic architecture, check out...

*http://www.elore.com/ elore4-2.html*

In 1266 Thomas Aquinas began his masterpiece—the *Summation of Theology*. Thomas worked on the *Summation* for seven years. The English translation of his labors fills over 4,000 pages. Yet Thomas chose not to finish his supreme work.

On December 6, 1273, Thomas attended a communion service. During that worship service, something happened. When he left the chapel, the famed Scholastic said, "All that I have written seems to me nothing but straw, compared to what I have seen and what has been revealed to me." Thomas never wrote another word. Three months later he died. In 1567 he was declared a respected teacher (a "Doctor") of the Roman Catholic Church.

## CAUTION! GOD WORKING AHEAD!

"My Father is always at his work," Jesus once commented (John 5:17). Do you grasp what Jesus was saying? God never stops working! Not when greed corrupts church leaders. Not when the church becomes a political power. Not even when the church loses sight of the cross. Somewhere, there is always a missionary who wants to tell someone about Jesus, a wealthy noble who is willing to give up his prestige, or an ordinary Christian whom God is inviting to join in an extraordinary work.

So, look around your church, your school, your job. Somewhere, Christ is calling someone to join in God's work. Then, get ready. That someone could be you.

# CHAPTER SIX LEARNING ACTIVITY

This crossword puzzle will help you review what you learned as you read Chapter Six. Try to complete the puzzle without looking at the chapter.

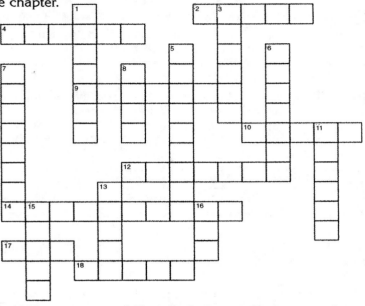

1. In 1112, _____ of Clairvaux became a Cistercian monk.
2. When _____ died, he remained under his church's condemnation.
3. The founder of the Franciscan order was from _____.
4. _____ was an archbishop of Canterbury.
5. _____ preachers traveled throughout medieval towns.
6. _____ wanted to encounter God directly
7. John _____ lost his right hand and his freedom when someone lied about him.
8. English and Irish monks and _____ spread the gospel through self-sufficient religious communities.
9. Thomas _____ combined Aristotle's logic with devout Christian faith.
10. _____ and Boniface were English missionaries to Germany.
11. Hildegard, a mystic, directed a convent near _____, Germany.
12. After his conversion, _____ gave away his possessions and cared for lepers.
13. Duke William gave up his hunting dogs to build a new monastery at _____.
14. _____ scholars, like Anselm and Aquinas, integrated God's revelation with human reason.
15. English and Irish monks used their top-quality _____ to generate interest in the Christian faith.
16. Although he thought Francis' rules were too strict, Pope Innocent _____ approved Francis' movement.
17. In this chapter, you learned that _____ is always working.
18. From a human viewpoint, _____ and Methodius failed as missionaries. Yet God turned their efforts into a success.

# WHAT YOU SHOULD KNOW ABOUT CHRISTIAN HISTORY
## AD 1294—1517

| Three Events You Should Know |
| --- |

1. *Council of Vienne* (1311-1312): Pope Clement V convened this council to disband the Knights Templar (an order of crusader monks) and give their property to the king of France.

2. *Council of Constance* (1414-1418): Pope John XXIII summoned this council to end the Great Schism and reform the Catholic Church. The council forced elected a new pope and declared that a church council "holds its power direct from Christ; everyone ... is bound to obey it." This view became known as *conciliarism*.

3. *Council of Florence* (1438-1445): This council technically reunited Catholic and Orthodox Churches. However, Orthodox laypeople rejected the reunion. The council also claimed (against the Council of Constance) that the pope was superior to church councils. The council recognized seven sacraments to guide Christians from womb to tomb—baptism, communion, confirmation, confession, marriage, ordination, and last rites.

| Seven Names You Should Know |
| --- |

1. *Meister Eckhart* (1260-1328): Dominican monk and mystic. Sought "the unspeakable basis of all reality"—a point at which the soul becomes united with God. Accused of heresy in 1326.

2. *Marsilius (Marsiglio) of Padua* (1275-1342): Wrote that the church derives its power from the state and that church councils are superior to the pope. Condemned as a heretic.

3. *Jan Hus* (1372-1415): Czech priest and reformer. Burned at the Council of Constance. Download paintings of Hus from *http://calvarychapel.com/simivalley/hus.htm*

4. *Julian of Norwich* (1342-1417): English nun and mystic. Focused on Christ's Incarnation.

5. *Valla* (1406-1457): Italian humanist. Proved *The Donation of Constantine* was a forgery.

6. *Girolamo Savonarola* (1452-1498): Dominican preacher. Introduced moral reforms in Florence, Italy. Defended Catholicism but became caught in a political conflict with the pope. Hanged as a heretic in 1498.

7. *Desiderius Erasmus of Rotterdam* (1469?-1536): Renaissance scholar and Catholic priest. Compiled Textus Receptus Greek New Testament.

| Four Terms You Should Know |
| --- |

1. *Conciliarism*: The belief that a church council has authority over all church members, including the pope. The Councils of Constance and Pisa were triumphs for conciliarism.

2. *Ottoman Empire*: Muslim empire, founded by the fourteenth-century warrior, Othman. The Ottoman "Turks" eventually ruled the area now known as Turkey. In 1453, they conquered Constantinople, the Eastern Empire's last stronghold. The Eastern scholars who fled to Europe helped trigger the Renaissance.

3. *Renaissance Humanism*: The Renaissance was a fifteenth-century revival of interest in ancient languages and in the humanities. Renaissance writers were called "humanists" because they focused on practical human actions instead of Scholastic logic.

4. *Spanish Inquisition*: This tribunal—formed in 1479 by King Ferdinand V and Queen Isabella—tortured, burned, and exiled thousands of Jews, Muslims, and heretics. Catholics today condemn the Inquisitors' methods.

# Chapter Seven

## In This Chapter
## AD 1294—AD 1517

Bubonic Plague
John Wycliffe
Jan Hus
Thomas A'Kempis
Joan of Arc
Gutenberg Bible

## EVERYTHING FALLS APART

The lesson was a masterpiece. If you doubted such high praise, you could have asked the meek and modest teacher . . . me. I had presented the finest lesson on God's sovereignty since Paul wrote Romans 9:11. I asked, "Does anyone have any questions?" (How could they? I had explained everything!)

To my surprise, one woman raised her hand. She asked calmly, "If that's true, why did my daughter and son-in-law die last month in a car wreck? How could God let my grandchildren grow up without parents?" I don't recall what I said. But my answer was empty. And everyone knew it.

Paul's teachings about predestination weren't the problem. The problem was that I lost sight of someone's needs. My student needed a soothing awareness of God's sovereign love. I gave her Systematic Theology 101. I spoke the truth, but I failed to speak "the truth in love" (Ephesians 4:15). For love fulfills others' needs (1 Corinthians 13:5).

Between 1200 and 1500 the Middle Ages melted into the past. Church members needed a renewed relationship with the living God. Many church leaders gave them inquisitions, indulgences, and division. The church's answers were empty. And almost everyone knew it.

*Three years before Celestine V became the pope, the Crusaders' last stronghold in Asia, the seaport Acre, fell to Egyptian Muslims.*

## STUMBLING DOWNWARD: THE FATEFUL FOURTEENTH CENTURY

### The Pope Who Quit

In 1294 the cardinal bishops chose Celestine [se-LESS-teen] V, a Franciscan monk, as their pope. Previous popes had ridden into Rome on horses. Celestine V wandered into Rome barefoot, on a donkey.

Celestine V was an aged pastor who loved the common people. Unfortunately, the Roman bishop's duties were no longer common or pastoral. Popes lived in palaces and shaped royal policies. The plain, pious monk simply couldn't play the political games.

After five disastrous months, Pope Celestine V met with the cardinals and shed his rich robes. Clad in his brown tunic, he sat on the floor and resigned.

A ruthless politician named Boniface VIII replaced Celestine V. Pope Boniface VIII believed that the Roman bishop should rule Western society. In 1302 Boniface VIII issued a bull entitled "One Holy Church" (*Unam Sanctum*). The notice claimed that the pope possessed power over all of Europe's kings. The French king disagreed so strongly that he had the pope

## Words: From The Ones Who Were There

*Pope Boniface VIII*
"The true faith compels us to believe that there is one holy, universal, apostolic church . . . Outside of her, there is no salvation . . . . Both swords—the spiritual and the temporal—are in the church's power."
*Unam Sanctum.*

## Think About It...

Some popes and priests failed to help victims of the plague. To what sort of people do today's churches fail to minister? People whose skin is a different color? Prisoners? Unwed mothers? Bedridden elderly? AIDS victims?

kidnaped. One month later, Boniface VIII and his lofty claims of supreme power were dead. Boniface VIII's successor was forced to flee Rome. In exile, he endured a fruitless reign and a very "fruitful" death. Someone served him a plate of poisoned figs.

Never again would popes or emperors rule entire civilizations. That would become the task of kings and lords. (A Holy Roman Emperor—who was neither holy nor Roman—did rule central Europe. But he was little more than a German king.)

Unable to trust bulls, kings, or fruit, the next pope fled to Avignon [AH-veeg-NON], a village on the border of France. For 72 years popes lived it up in Avignon. Bishops openly sold leadership positions. Friars freely hawked indulgences.

Celibate priests became a pious memory. In *The Canterbury Tales*, the indulgence seller sighs to a skeptical woman, "[Your husband] knows that, for a certainty,/You've bedded down a priest, or two, or three." No one challenged his estimate.

This era of political and moral turmoil became known as the church's "Babylonian Captivity." Just as the ancient Israelites were removed from the Promised Land and exiled to Babylon, so the church's dignity was removed from Rome and imprisoned in Avignon. The Babylonian Captivity was, however, not the only source of chaos in fourteenth-century Europe.

In 1337 King Edward III of England—the nephew of a deceased French king—claimed France's throne. Thus began the Hundred Years' War (which actually lasted 116 years). In the midst of a corrupt church and a bloody war, another hardship struck Europe.

### "And No Bells Tolled"

In October, 1347, an unwelcome passenger scurried aboard a cargo ship. It was a rat with a disease-laden flea fixed on its hide. The ship's sailors brought home something more costly than their cargo. Dark spots swelled between their legs and beneath their arms. The blots oozed black blood and putrid pus.

For four years the Black Death ruled Europe and Asia Minor. In Constantinople the plague killed 88 percent of the population. In Paris alone, 800 people died daily. Corpses rotted in the streets, unburied and unblessed. "And no bells tolled," one man wrote, "and nobody wept, no matter what his loss, because almost everyone expected death."

Flushed circles ("rings") formed on victims' cheeks ("rosies"). As victims died, they sneezed. Folk filled their pockets with flowers ("posies") to mask the stench of death around them. So, parents sang to their children: "Ring around the rosie, pockets full of posies./Achoo! Achoo! We all fall down." Popes and priests alike failed to respond to their people's needs.

Some people threw themselves into unbridled parties. Others begged for God's pardon in "penance parades." Against the pope's orders, a few desperate church members butchered and burned entire Jewish communities. Still, the plague didn't stop.

In city squares people flogged themselves and screamed to the heavens, "Spare us! Spare us!" The pope denounced their tactics. Slowly, the mobs faded. Finally, so did the plague.

Between 1347 and 1350 the Black Death killed (according to the pope's estimate) 23,840,000 people—nearly one-third of Europe. And no bells tolled.

## The Church Has Double Vision

Even the plague's end didn't produce peace. The Hundred Years' War dragged on. Corruption reigned in the churches. Catherine of Sienna, an innocent Italian mystic, tried to return the pope to Rome, but even she could not restore the church's place in people's hearts.

When she was 16, Catherine joined a community of Dominicans. After two years of prayer and fasting, Catherine had a vision. She believed that Christ commanded her to help the poor. To avoid doctrinal errors, Catherine surrounded herself with a circle of Dominican scholars. Together, they nurtured the needy and preached to prisoners. Even when the Black Death erupted anew in Sienna, they refused to leave.

In 1370 Catherine experienced another vision. Her new mission? Convince the pope to return to Rome from Avignon. "Sweet papa," she wrote to the Pope, "respond to the Holy Spirit who is calling you!" Throughout Europe Catherine preached against the "stench of sin" in Avignon.

Catherine's dream came true in 1377. Pope Gregory XI rode into Rome. Yet the church's struggle wasn't over. When the pope died, most of the cardinal bishops wanted a French pope. Outside the Vatican, the cardinals could hear the crowd's chant: "Roman! Roman! We want a Roman!" To distract the mob, the cardinals dressed a Roman in the pope's clothes. The trick didn't work. The chant changed to, "Death to the cardinals!" Finally, the cardinals compromised. They elected Pope Urban VI, an Italian (but not a Roman) pope.

When Pope Urban VI didn't support the pro-French cardinals, the cardinals withdrew their former decision. In Avignon, they replaced the Italian pope with a Frenchman. However, Urban VI refused to be deposed. Now, the church wasn't only split between East and West. The "Great Papal Schism" split the Roman Catholic Church between Rome and Avignon.

### In Case You're Confused

By law, church members couldn't charge interest. Many Jews—excluded from the land-based feudal system—became bankers. In the 1300s society shifted from a land-based system to a cash-based system. Jewish bankers became wealthy, and envy arose among church members. Too often, envy erupted into senseless savagery.

Catherine of Sienna, Italian mystic

### Words: From The Ones Who Were There

*Catherine of Sienna*
Once, Catherine wondered if she should minister publicly. According to Catherine, God answered, "Does it not depend on my will where I shall pour out my grace? With me there is no longer male or female, lower and upper classes, but all are equal in my sight." "Catherine of Sienna."
*Christian History* Issue 30 (1991): 9.

*John Wycliffe*
*(Courtesy of Northwind Picture Archives)*

## Words: From The Ones Who Were There

*John Wycliffe*
"The only head of the holy Church is Jesus Christ . . . . So, whatever argument human beings may bring forward . . . it plainly militates against . . . a pope."
*The Church and Her Members,* 2:342-343.

## Triple Trouble at an Italian Pisa Party

In 1409 the cardinals from Avignon and Rome decided that the schism must end. Their council—the Council of Pisa—decreed, "The Church's oneness does not depend on or come from the Pope's oneness." In other words, the church does not need a pope to make a unified decision; a church council can make unified decisions that are binding on the whole church.

The Council of Pisa rejected both the French and the Italian popes and elected a new Roman bishop. Unfortunately, the two previous popes refused to be dismissed. Two popes had been a problem, but three popes . . . that was a catastrophe! Each pope excommunicated the other popes' followers. Priests and laypeople throughout Europe became increasingly unsure about where to find the true church.

## Where Is the Church?

One answer came from an unlikely source—John Wycliffe [WIK-lif], a philosophy professor at Oxford University in England. According to the Roman Catholic Church's teachings, only the true church could correctly understand the Scriptures. Wycliffe agreed, but he applied a new definition to the word "church."

Wycliffe claimed that the church wasn't built on popes, priests, or sacraments. The church was every person called by God to faith in Jesus Christ. How could people know if they had faith in Christ? A godly life proved that a person had trusted Christ (James 2:18).

Every church member should, Wycliffe taught, strive to understand the Bible. That's why Wycliffe's followers translated portions of the Scriptures into easy-to-read English. "Christ . . . taught the people in the language that was best known to them," Wycliffe wrote. "Why should people today not do the same?" Some English people called Wycliffe a hero. Church leaders called him a heretic. Twice, they tried to put him on trial. Political problems and natural disasters prevented the trials. Wycliffe died of a stroke in 1384, still in good standing with his church.

After he died, Wycliffe's followers finished his translation of the Bible. Throughout England, they shared Wycliffe's message of reform. Their friends called them "the Poor Preachers." Their enemies called them "Lollards"—a word that means "mumblers" in Dutch, and "darnel weeds" in Latin.

## Unhushable Hus

Wycliffe's words quickly traveled beyond England. Around 1400 his ideas struck Bohemia (the contemporary Czech Republic). Bohemian bishops banned Wycliffe's writings. But Jan Hus, a brilliant Bohemian professor and priest, had already encountered Wycliffe's words. The encounter would cost Hus his life. Hus echoed Wycliffe's ideas from a pulpit in Prague. In 1407 the church revoked his right to preach. Still, Hus wouldn't hush. He claimed that people should obey the church only when the church agreed with the Bible. He also argued that it was wrong to withhold the cup from laypeople during communion.

At first, the king of Bohemia defended Hus. Then the king needed the pope's support. Hus was forced to flee. In 1415 an imperial herald found Hus and asked him to defend himself at a church council in the German city of Constance. The Holy Roman Emperor promised to protect Hus on the way to and from the council. Hus accepted his offer. Unfortunately, the cardinals didn't keep the emperor's promise. Hus was imprisoned in a castle in Constance. Still, he refused to retract his radical teachings. "I appeal to Jesus Christ," he replied, "since he will not base his judgment on false witnesses and erring councils but on truth and justice."

On July 6, 1415, the cardinals drew demons on a paper hat and jammed it on Hus' head. The church could not kill a heretic. So, the cardinals handed Hus over to the king's soldiers. As soldiers tied him to a pole and prepared to burn him alive, Hus prayed: "Lord Jesus, please, have mercy on my enemies." He died singing psalms. The council also demanded that John Wycliffe's bones be unearthed and burned.

The Council of Constance did do some good. The cardinals imprisoned the pope appointed by the Council of Pisa, deposed the pope in Rome, retired the pope in Avignon, and selected a new pope, Martin V. By 1450 the Great Papal Schism was over, but the movement toward more radical reforms was already underway.

## LOOKING INWARD: THE MYSTICAL ALTERNATIVE

Not only had church leaders lost touch with people's needs; so had the Scholastic theologians. Anselm's use of logic had led him to love God and to serve others. Later Scholastics argued about questions that seemed irrelevant to common people—questions like, "How many angels can dance on a pinhead?" Many theologians wrote treatises about God's power. Yet few of them experienced God's power in their lives.

Around 1374 several Dutch Christians looked past pinheads and empty power. A fresh form of faith arose among them—the Common Life Movement. Members of the Common Life Movement denounced corruption among priests and bishops. Yet they never criticized the church itself. The Sisters and Brothers of the Common Life blended profound scholarship with mystical devotion to Christ. Their focus on personal devotion to Jesus Christ became known as *Devotio Moderna*—the Modern Devotion.

The most famous member of the Common Life movement was Thomas A'Kempis. Kempis organized the movement's ideas in a timeless devotional work, *The Imitation of Christ*. Today, people throughout the world still study Kempis' guide to following Jesus Christ.

*A statue of Czech theologian Jan Hus stands in the center of the square in Prague. Across from the Town Hall is the Tyn Church, once a center of the Hussite movement.*

## Words: From The Ones Who Were There

*Thomas A'Kempis*
"Even if you know the whole Bible by heart and the sayings of the philosophers, what does it profit you unless you also love God? . . . Truly, humble farmers who serve God are greater than proud philosophers who neglect [their need for God] and work to understand how the heavens move."
*Imitatio Christi.*

## On The Web

Read motr of The *Imitation of Christ* at ...

*http://www.ccel.org/k/ kempis/imitation/ imitation.html*

In 1456, Pope Calixtus III admitted that the Inquisition had unjustly condemned Joan. In 1920, Joan of Arc was recognized as a saint.
*(Beverly Hall, Artist)*

Mysticism also flourished outside the Common Life Movement. One young mystic placed her experiences in a political context; her interpretation of her experiences would cost her her life. In 1415 King Henry V of England conquered northern France by defeating the French at the Battle of Agincourt. Ten years later, a French peasant named Joan had a vision. She believed that Michael the archangel and two saints commanded her to throw the English out of France.

In 1428 the peasant girl convinced the French prince to let her lead an attack on the English. United under Joan's command, the prince's troops reclaimed Orleans, France. The French prince was crowned as king. Joan wanted to return home, but the king forced her to continue fighting. Her victories formed an arc across France. So, she became known as "Joan of Arc."

The English desperately needed to disprove Joan's claims about her supernatural visions. Why? The English claimed that God was on their side. If Joan's claims were true, God was fighting for France, not England. In May, 1430, Joan was wounded and captured near the French border. It embarrassed the French king to admit that he owed his crown to a peasant girl. He refused to ransom her. So, a pro-English bishop bought Joan and confined her in a dungeon with male convicts. Even though she recanted once, the bishops returned her to the brutal dungeon. Finally, the Inquisition convicted her of heresy.

In May, 1431, the 19-year-old peasant declared that she had heard the saints' voices again. Soldiers burned Joan of Arc alive. Like thousands of others in France and England, Joan was certain that Christ supported her nation's political pursuits. Her savage death was one sad sidelight within a vast, tragic misunderstanding of God's ways.

## GLANCING BACKWARD: THE HUMANIST ALTERNATIVE

In AD 313 Emperor Constantine had founded Constantinople. By AD 1453 Constantinople was all that remained of the ancient Eastern Empire. On May 28, 1453, the Ottoman Turks prepared to strike the ancient capital city. That evening, the citizens gathered in the Church of Holy Wisdom (the "Hagia Sophia"). Several Roman bishops joined their Eastern Orthodox brothers and sisters amid the flickering candles. For a few moments, Roman and Eastern Christians forgot the ancient schism and shared the Lord's Supper. It was the last service of Christian worship that ever echoed in the church's sacred halls.

On May 29 Muslims conquered the city. When night fell, a Muslim teacher walked slowly into the Church of Holy Wisdom. "There is no God but Allah," he intoned from the altar, "and Muhammad is his prophet." The church building was now a mosque. The building remained a mosque until the 1930's. Today, it is a museum—known as "Aya Sofya"—in Istanbul, Turkey.

Hundreds of Eastern scholars fled west. They carried with them their most precious possessions—ancient Greek manuscripts. For centuries, Roman Christians had neglected ancient authors. The manuscripts from the East caused a rebirth—a Renaissance [REH-na-SONSS]—of interest in ancient Greek rhetoric, art, and writing. Renaissance art, like ancient art, portrayed life from a human perspective. Renaissance scholars, like ancient orators, stressed practical language and actions. Poignant words became more important than precise logic. Because they focused on practical human actions, Renaissance scholars were called 'humanists.'

Christian humanists applied these insights to Scripture. They focused on the original intent and the original language of each biblical text. Their battle cry became, "Back to the sources!" Much of this rebirth was made possible by a printer named Johann Gutenberg. In 1453 Gutenberg discovered how to mold movable metal type. For the first time, printers could mass-produce books. The price of books plummeted. Greek and Roman classics, as well as Bibles, flooded Europe.

The popes supported classic books and Renaissance art. However, most of them neglected the most important aspect of the Renaissance—the renewed focus on Scripture. Roman bishops became increasingly corrupt. Indulgences remained a booming business. The Spanish Inquisition used the church's power to persecute myriads of Muslims, Jews, and heretics. Reform became unavoidable.

*Ruins in the courtyard of the Church of Holy Wisdom (the Hagia Sophia) in Constantinople.*

## LURCHING FORWARD

The first pope of the sixteenth century refused to accept a saint's name at his election. Instead, he took the name of the pagan caesar Julius. Today, people remember Pope Julius II for his support of a young sculptor named Michelangelo. In the sixteenth century few people noticed Julius II's art. No one could, however, ignore his military exploits. In 1507 his army forced every foreign soldier out of the church's lands in central Italy. Pope Julius II rode triumphantly into Bologna, Italy.

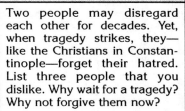

### Julius Caesar or Jesus Christ?

When Julius II rode into the city of Bologna, one young humanist didn't share Julius' joy. "Whose successor is this?" Desiderius Erasmus [eh-RASS-muss] muttered. "Julius Caesar's or Jesus Christ's?" Erasmus was the son of an unwed teenager and a prurient village priest. Erasmus' childhood school-teachers had been Brothers of the Common Life. The Brothers whetted Erasmus' taste for Greek. As a teen, Erasmus longed to study Greek at a university, but he had no money. So, he studied for the priesthood instead. Not only did Erasmus become a priest. He was also such a promising student that his bishop sent him to the University of Paris to study Greek. Soon, the budding

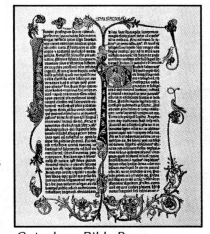

*Gutenberg Bible Page*
*(Courtesy of Northwind Picture Archives)*

*Erasmus 1466-1536*
*His work on the New Testament allowed the Word of God to speak to both simple people and scholars.*

humanist was studying Greek throughout Europe. It was during his travels that Erasmus witnessed Julius II's grand entrance into Bologna. After he saw Christ's representative leading an earthly army, Erasmus demanded changes in his church. He ridiculed Scholastic speculation: "Paul provides the finest example of love (1 Cor. 13). Yet he neither divides it nor defines it according to logical rules!" He attacked the concept of a crusade. "Isn't the Turk also a human being?" he asked.

Despite such scathing charges, Erasmus wanted to transform Christ's body—not split it. Nevertheless, it was this loyal Roman Catholic who created the tool that would lead to radical reforms. In 1516 Erasmus published a Greek New Testament. Now, Christians could read the apostles' words in their original language.

## Calm Before the Storm

In 1517 calm settled on the Roman Catholic Church. Julius II was dead. Pope Leo X began his reign with the pronouncement, "God has given us the papacy—now let us enjoy it!" But it was too late. Wycliffe and Hus had packed a powder keg. Erasmus had woven a fuse. On October 31, 1517, a hotheaded monk lit the fuse and rocked all of Europe.

### In Case You're Confused

What concepts do you connect with humanism? Atheism? Aimless evolution? That's *secular* humanism. Be sure that you know the difference between *secular* humanism and *Renaissance* humanism. Renaissance writers were called "humanists" because they focused on practical human actions and human-oriented arts (the "humanities") instead of Scholastic logic.

### Key Concept

When a church loses sight of people's needs, God raises fresh voices of repentance and reform.

# CHAPTER SEVEN LEARNING ACTIVITY

This learning activity will help you review what you learned as you read Chapter Seven.

1. What sort of pope was Celestine V? _____
   _____

2. For 72 years the popes reigned from _____,
   a village on the French border.

3. Name one way people responded to the Black Death.
   _____

4. How did the Roman Catholic Church end the Great Papal
   Schism? _____

5. Wycliffe believed all Christians were responsible to study
   and understand the Bible for themselves. Why?_____
   _____
   _____

6. Why did many members of the Common Life Movement
   dislike Scholasticism? _____
   _____

7. List two words that might have described Joan of Arc.
   (a) _____     (b) _____

8. Why did many fifteenth-century Christian scholars call
   themselves humanists?     _____
   _____

9. List two words that might have described Erasmus.
   (a) _____     (b) _____

10. God isn't on the side of any human regime. God is on the
    side of his own character. Christ demonstrated God's
    character through a cross—not through military conquests.
    Rent and watch the videos *Joan of Arc* and *Henry V*.
    Each film portrays a battle from the Hundred Years' War.
    When and how did the English (*Henry V*) and the French
    (*Joan of Arc*) both assume God was on their side?
    _____
    _____

11. When and how do Christians today assume that God takes
    political sides?_____
    _____
    _____

## Notes

# WHAT YOU SHOULD KNOW ABOUT CHRISTIAN HISTORY
## AD 1500—1609

### Five Events You Should Know

1. *Moscow Claimed As Center of Orthodoxy* (1500): In 1448, Russian Orthodox Christians protested the Council of Florence by electing their own patriarch. After the Muslim Ottomans conquered Constantinople, Russians claimed that Moscow was the center of Orthodoxy.
2. *Fifth Lateran Council* (1512-1517): Revoked the Council of Pisa's conciliar decrees. (If you can't define "conciliarism," glance back at Chapter Seven.)
3. *Luther's 95 Theses* (1517): Martin Luther, a Roman Catholic monk, protested the sale of indulgences by publishing 95 topics for debate.
4. *Union of Brest-Litovsk* (1596): Several million Ukrainian Orthodox Christians entered into communion with the Roman Catholic Church. These Christians became known as Uniats.
5. *Rheims-Douay Bible Completed* (1609): Scholars from Douay College in England translated the Vulgate into English. The New Testament was published in Rheims, Germany. The Rheims-Douay was the standard Bible for English-speaking Roman Catholics for more than 300 years.

### Ten Names You Should Know

1. *Balthasar Hubmaier* (1485-1528): Anabaptist writer. He and his wife were killed for their faith.
2. *Oecolampadius* (1482-1531): First reformer to support laypeople's participation in church government. Defended Zwingli's view of the Lord's Supper at the Marburg Colloquy.
3. *William Tyndale* (1494-1536): English Bible translator. His Bible formed the basis for the King James Version.
4. *Carlstadt* (1480-1541): First reformer to observe communion in the people's language. Debated Eck at Leipzig.
5. *Johann Maier Eck* (1486-1543): Catholic theologian. Publicly criticized Luther's theology.
6. *Martin Luther* (1483-1546): German reformer. Emphasized justification by grace through faith.
7. *Martin Bucer* (1491-1551): German reformer. Tried to find a middle ground between Luther's and Zwingli's teachings about the Lord's Supper.
8. *John Calvin* (1509-1564): The systematic theologian of the Protestant Reformation.
9. *Heinrich Bullinger* (1504-1575): Swiss reformer. Author of the Second Helvetic Confession, an important Calvinist statement of faith. Influenced the final form of the Heidelberg Catechism.
10. *Theodore Beza* (1519-1605): Succeeded Calvin as leader of the Genevan church.

### Five Terms You Should Know

1. *Sola gratia, sola fide, sola scriptura*: Latin for "grace alone, faith alone, Scripture alone." These words sum up the Protestant belief that justification is received by grace alone through faith alone and that the Bible should be the church's only authority.
2. *Reformed Churches*: Protestant churches, such as the Presbyterians, that were strongly influenced by Calvin and Knox.
3. *Consubstantiation*: Luther's belief that, after the prayer of consecration during communion, the body and blood of Christ coexist with the Lord's Supper elements.
4. *Heidelberg Catechism*: Reformed statement of faith, compiled in 1562. Widely used by Protestants for centuries.
5. *Uniats*: Christians in traditionally Orthodox areas who united with the Roman Catholic Church under the terms of the Union of Brest-Litovsk.

**In This Chapter
AD 1500—AD 1609**

Martin Luther
John Calvin
Anabaptists
King Henry VIII
Ignatius Loyola

## WILD PIGS IN A DIRTY VINEYARD

Shyre was my first love. When I was the Lone Ranger, she was Tonto. When I was Luke Skywalker, she was Princess Leia. But, on June 14, 1979, I had to tell Shyre good-bye. We sat on the edge of her bed and cried together. Another man had stolen her heart, and I was a bit unsure about my role as the ring-bearer in their wedding.

I was six years old. My sister Shyre was 18. For the first time, I realized that division is never desirable. Yet, to build something better, division is sometimes necessary.

Very few (if any) sixteenth-century Roman Catholics wanted division. Yet reform was inevitable. Many people believed they could earn salvation through good works and indulgences. Tradition had displaced Scripture as the church's supreme authority. The church's leadership was corrupt. With the necessary reforms came division. Yet the reformers were striving to build something better, both inside and outside the established church.

### ALL HE WANTED WAS PEACE

#### Lightning Never Strikes Twice (Once is Enough)

A lawyer plodded along the rutted road. Suddenly, a summer shower unfolded into a raging thunderstorm. A lightning bolt knocked the traveler to the ground. As he struggled to stand, he screamed, "Saint Anne, save me! I will become a monk!" The lawyer kept his promise, but the shadow of God's wrath followed him to his monastery and beyond. The year was 1505. The lawyer was a German Saxon named Martin Luther.

By 1511 Martin's deep awareness of his own sin and of God's holiness drove him to the confessional for six hours at a time. The guilt remained. "Love God?" the monk once wept, "I hate him!" Martin's monastery sent him to Wittenberg University to study. Yet no amount of study could drive away Martin's anguish.

*Martin Luther*
*(Courtesy of Billy Graham Center Archives)*

One man who did try to understand Martin was John Staupitz, Wittenberg University's Bible professor. Staupitz was an aged, godly mystic who was able to look beyond his church's corruption. "Perhaps," Staupitz seems to have thought, "if Martin explores the Scriptures more deeply, he will find peace." Beneath a pear tree, Staupitz told Martin his decision: Martin Luther would replace him as the university's Bible professor.

Still, one question haunted Martin Luther: How can anyone please a righteous God? When he considered the phrase "the righteousness of God" (Romans 1:17), the question tormented him even more deeply. Martin found his answer in Erasmus's Greek New Testament.

*Saint Peter's Basilica*

While reading Paul's epistles, Martin realized that the word "righteousness" means not only the *condition of being righteous*, but also the *act of declaring someone to be righteous*. God not only is righteous. God can also give righteousness to sinners! This righteousness is God's gift, given to every person who trusts Jesus Christ.

"The righteousness of God is," the apostle Paul had written, "from faith to faith. As it is written, 'The just shall live by faith'" (Romans 1:17). For years Martin had searched for peace. In the end, peace found him. In 1517, Martin's peace in the truth became an explosive passion for the truth. The trigger was a Dominican monk named Tetzel.

## Prince Albert Indulges the Pope

Martin Luther was the pastor of a village church near the German region of Mainz. Albert was both the archbishop and the ruling prince of Mainz. Pope Leo X needed cash to finish St. Peter's Basilica; so, he made a deal with Prince Albert: The German prince could sell indulgences in Mainz if he gave the pope half of his profits.

One of Prince Albert's peddlers was Tetzel. "As soon as the coin in the coffer rings," Tetzel claimed, "the soul from purgatory springs." Tetzel's misuse of the church's power enraged Martin Luther. Martin decided he wanted to debate the indulgence peddler. So, he angrily scribbled a list of 95 topics to debate ("theses"). All Martin wanted to do was challenge Tetzel's teachings about indulgences. What he did was shake the world.

## A Wild Pig, a Broiled Bull, and a Diet of Worms

A few years ago, a Lutheran group rented the Roman Catholic cathedral in St. Louis, Missouri. The priest greeted them with this comment: "We are pleased to provide the cathedral. Please don't nail anything to the doors this time." The crowd roared.

On October 31, 1517, Martin Luther nailed his theses on the chapel door in Wittenberg. That time, no one laughed. At first, the theses upset only a few scholars. Pope Leo X muttered, "Luther is a drunk German. He'll recant when he's sober."

Three years later, Leo X realized that if Luther were still drunk, his intoxicated condition must be permanent. The pope published a bull entitled, "Arise, O Lord" (*Ex Surge Domine*). "A wild pig," Leo lamented, "has invaded the Lord's vineyard!" The "wild pig" was Luther; the "vineyard" was the church. Martin Luther broiled Leo's bull in a bonfire.

Two months later, Luther received a letter from the Holy Roman Emperor. The letter read, "Come under safe conduct, to answer with regard to your books." The Latin word for an imperial meeting is "diet." The meeting would occur in the German city of Worms. So, the meeting was called—I'm not making this up!—"the Diet of Worms."

Martin expected to die at the diet. A century earlier, an emperor had promised safe conduct to Jan Hus. Hus was burned at the stake. How could Luther escape the same fate?

The diet began on April 15. A bishop pointed to a heap of books on the floor. He asked Martin, "Did you write these?" "They are all mine," Martin answered. "Do you defend them?" the bishop demanded. This time, Martin did not reply with his typical boldness. Instead, he whispered, "Give me time to think it over."

The next day, the bishop posed the same question. As sweat flowed from Martin's face, he replied: "My conscience is captive to the Word of God. I cannot and I will not recant anything, for to go against conscience is neither right nor safe. God, help me."

Martin would have suffered the same fate as Hus, but the ruler of Saxony secretly sent soldiers to safeguard him. As Martin headed home, five men attacked his wagon. They blindfolded him and took him to an abandoned castle. Martin had been kidnaped to save his life.

### "Other Women Have Even Worse Faults"

Ten months later, Martin emerged from hiding. A dozen Cistercian nuns had recently embraced his ideas and wanted to leave their convent. Because it was a capital crime to remove a nun from her convent, one of Martin's friends spirited the nuns away in herring barrels. Eight nuns married; three returned to their homes. Only Katherine von Bora, a feisty, red-haired 26-year-old, remained.

In April, 1525, Katherine commented that she might marry Martin. She was probably joking. (Martin was 42 years old, and marriage did not seem to interest him.) Yet he decided to marry "Kaetie" for three very romantic reasons: It would please his father, provoke the pope, and pass on his name. While preparing for his marriage, Martin wrote, "I would not exchange Kaetie for France . . . because God gave her to me and other women have even worse faults."

Despite his doubtful reasons for marriage, Martin grew to love and enjoy his "lord Kaetie" and their six children. He nick-named Galatians (his favorite book of the Bible) "my Katherine." When the neighbors saw the great reformer hanging diapers on the clothesline, Martin quipped, "Let them laugh. God and the angels smile."

### How Is Christ Among Us? Or, Is He?

Soon after Martin nailed his theses on the chapel door, the citizens of Zurich, Switzerland, also defied their church's teachings. During Lent, Ulrich Zwingli [ZWEEN-glee], their priest, led them to go on a diet of sausages (which certainly sounds better than Luther's Diet of Worms).

*Kaetie Luther*

Now, two reformers were working to renew the church. One German Lutheran realized that, if Luther and Zwingli united their movements, their chances for survival would increase. So, he asked them to meet in the German city of Marburg.

One issue kept the Zwinglian and Lutheran movements apart: How is Christ present in the Lord's Supper? Luther and Zwingli agreed that transubstantiation missed the point, but what was the biblical alternative? (If you can't define transubstantiation, glance back at Chapter Five.)

According to Luther, the communion elements never change. Yet, in the bread and cup, Christ's body is present with the visible elements. Christ's bodily presence conveys grace to persons who are at peace with God. Nothing less could explain Jesus' words, "This is my body." (This belief became known as *consubstantiation*.) Zwingli, on the other hand, taught that Jesus' words merely meant, "This symbolizes my body."

When he faced Zwingli at Marburg, Luther pulled a chunk of chalk from his pocket. He scrawled his central thesis on the banquet table: "This is my body." Five days later, neither side had budged. The rift remained. The last words of the Marburg Colloquy were, "We have been unable to agree on the issue as to whether the true vine and blood of Christ are corporally present in the bread and wine. Still, each party will prove toward the other its spirit of Christian love, insofar as conscience permits." In 1530 Luther's followers published their own statement of faith, the Augsburg Confession.

## ALL HE WANTED WAS A PLACE TO STUDY

### The Reforming Refugee

In 1534 another lawyer traveled along another rutted road. His life had been shaken, but not by lightning. He was a Renaissance humanist fleeing the University of Paris. His name? John Calvin.

A few months earlier Calvin had helped a friend write a speech. They peppered the address with quotes from Luther and Erasmus. The speech angered the French government and forced Calvin to flee. Soon afterward, Calvin became a Protestant and a Christian.

Calvin fled first to Noyon, France, his home-town. From Noyon, Calvin turned toward Switzerland. There, he wrote the first systematic summary of Protestant theology, *Institutes of the Christian Religion*.

### The Long Detour Home

After the *Institutes* were published, Calvin decided to move to the Protestant city of Strasbourg, Switzerland. On the way, a war forced him to veer east, through Geneva. He intended to stay in Geneva for one night, concealed by the alias "Espeville." That night stretched into a lifetime.

A preacher named Farel had already promoted Protestant ideas in Geneva. One of Calvin's companions told Farel that "Espeville" was actually the well-known author of the *Institutes*. That evening, Farel confronted Calvin at the inn.

"Stay here!" Farel begged, "Geneva needs someone with your gifts." "But I need a rest," Calvin countered. Farel exploded, "May God damn your rest and the calm you seek for study, if you leave behind such a great need!" Calvin chose to stay. Within a year, Geneva agreed to Calvin's vision for the Reformation.

Two years later, the Geneva city council forced Calvin to leave the city after a series of political and religious quarrels. Calvin found refuge in Strasbourg, his original destination. There, Calvin cared for French Protestants ("Huguenots") who, like Calvin, had fled because of persecution. He found the life of study that he always wanted. In 1539 Geneva needed someone to debate a Roman Catholic thinker. The city council swallowed its pride and asked Calvin to return.

When Calvin returned to his pulpit, everyone in Geneva expected a severe rebuke. Calvin did not preach the expected sermon. Instead, he began to preach precisely where he had stopped three years earlier, without a trace of spite.

*John Calvin (1509-1564)*
*French reformer and theologian*

## ALL THEY WANTED WAS TO BE OBEDIENT

Calvin (as well as Luther and Zwingli) never escaped the idea that the church and the government could mingle. The Genevan government enforced the Genevan church's beliefs. In 1553 the Genevan council burned Michael Servetus, a theologian who denied the Trinity.

It was in Zwingli's Zurich that a movement arose with the radical idea that no government should enforce theological truths. Priests in Zurich still conducted communion in Latin. Some of Zwingli's best students, including Felix Manz, urged them to lead the Lord's Supper in the people's language. "When he introduced the Lord's Supper," one student argued, "Christ didn't speak nonsense! He used understandable words." Zwingli referred the matter to the city government. For Felix and his friends, this was not a question for the government. This was a question of submission to Scripture. Felix Manz decided to start a weekly Bible study in his home. There, Felix and his "Swiss Brothers" came to an unexpected conclusion: The New Testament never commanded infant baptism. In 1524 the Swiss Brothers openly criticized infant baptism.

In January, 1525, one Swiss Brother asked one of his friends, "Baptize me with true Christian baptism, upon my faith." Water was poured over his head in the name of the threefold God. One by one, all of the Swiss Brothers, including Felix, received believers' baptism. Their revolutionary act earned them the name "Again-Baptizers," or "Anabaptists." That night, the city council of Zurich banished the Anabaptists.

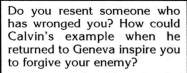

### Think About It...

Do you resent someone who has wronged you? How could Calvin's example when he returned to Geneva inspire you to forgive your enemy?

### Did You Know?

Missions deeply concerned Calvin. He sent missionaries to Scotland, France, and Brazil. A dishonest guide forced the missionaries to Brazil to turn back.

## Think About It...

Read Acts 16:30-33 and Colossians 2:11-12. Which does the Bible teach—believers' baptism or infant baptism? Find two Bible verses to support your belief.

## In Case You're Confused

Sixteenth century baptism was not simply a consequence of one's faith. Nor was it only an entrance into church membership. Through baptism, people became citizens of a (supposedly) Christian society. Anabaptists did the unthinkable: They separated the community of faith from the civil society.

## On The Web

To learn more about the Anabaptists, begin at . . .

*http://www.gty.org/ ~phil/anabapt.htm*

*An Anabaptist preacher*

Most Anabaptists fled to nearby villages. Still, they could not escape. Felix Manz was seized and sentenced to life in prison. After five months in a dungeon, he escaped. He was recaptured in October, 1526. The Zurich city council sentenced Manz to death. The charge? "He wanted to gather those who wanted to accept Christ . . . and unite with them through baptism."

In a cruel mockery of his beliefs, it was by water that Felix Manz died. The executioner tied Manz's arms behind his back and shoved him into an icy river. Manz died singing, "Into your hands, Lord, I commit my spirit."

Felix Manz was the first non-Catholic to be martyred by a Protestant, but he wasn't the last. The persecution of Anabaptist leaders spread rapidly. This loss of reliable teachers and leaders allowed a series of heresies to spread unchecked among the Anabaptists. These heresies led to a tragic twist in Anabaptist history.

### The Munster Massacre

Imagine with me: A self-appointed biblical scholar preaches an apocalyptic message. He and his followers create a compound where they can follow their fanatical beliefs. An army cuts off the sect's food and communications. After a tense siege, troops swarm into the compound. The leaders are killed, and the movement wanes.

Sound familiar? Probably. Yet the date wasn't 1993. And the place wasn't Waco, Texas. The year was 1535. The place was Munster, in the German province of Westphalia. The rebels were a heretical group of Anabaptists. After the Munster massacre, Protestant and Roman Catholic princes brutally oppressed all Anabaptists. Even Calvin urged rulers to destroy the Anabaptists. "It is far better that two or three burn now," Calvin wrote, "than to have thousands perish in Hell." Only Erasmus defended the Anabaptists' right to follow their beliefs. By 1600 the Anabaptist death toll would reach 10,000. It was a Dutch preacher named Menno Simons who saved the Anabaptists from extinction.

### Peace Amid Persecution

Menno Simons became a priest in 1524. He performed his duties and accepted his paychecks. But he spent most evenings at a local bar with a mug of beer in one hand and a deck of cards in the other. Two years after his ordination, Menno wanted to impress other pastors. So, he began to study his Bible for the first time. Despite his mixed motives, Menno couldn't escape the truths that he read. Ten years later, he left his comfortable lifestyle and joined the Anabaptists. He knew that the name "Anabaptist" could be fatal. "The Anabaptist minister's only payments," he later wrote, "are fire, sword, and death."

Menno salvaged two beliefs from the jumble of heresies that had marred Anabaptist thought after the Munster massacre: (1) The church should baptize only believers. And, (2) no government should enforce religious beliefs. In the process, Menno became the Anabaptists' most esteemed leader.

Menno Simons strictly observed New Testament patterns. During the Last Supper, Jesus had washed his disciples' feet; during communion, Menno washed his followers' feet. In literal obedience to Scripture, Menno's followers refused to fight or to swear oaths (Matthew 5:33-39).

In 1542 Menno's radical ideas landed his name on the Empire's "most wanted criminals" list. Menno and his family escaped capture for 19 years, but the stress took a heavy toll. Menno's wife and two of their children preceded him in death. Menno became severely crippled.

Menno Simons died a natural death in 1561—a privilege that few sixteenth-century Anabaptists shared. So profound was Menno's influence on the Anabaptists that they soon became known as "Menno's people" or "Mennonites."

## ALL HE WANTED WAS A BIBLE THAT EVERYONE COULD READ

College students frequently fall into (and out of) love, but few fall in love with their studies. At Cambridge University in England, however, one student fell in love with Greek and with Renaissance humanism. William Tyndale's two loves would cost him his life.

Tyndale became a wealthy family's chaplain. At a banquet, Tyndale and a priest debated the meaning of a Scripture. The priest remarked, "It would be better to be without God's law than the pope's." "If God spares my life," Tyndale retorted, "I will cause the plow-boy to know more about Scripture than you do!" But Tyndale's bishop refused to let him translate the Greek New Testament into simple English. Tyndale fled to the German provinces to publish his New Testament without the bishop's interference. In 1526 a printer in Worms, Germany, published 6,000 copies of Tyndale's New Testament. Three months later, the testaments poured into England.

English bishops bought and burned thousands of Tyndale's testaments. But ecclesiastical arsonists didn't bother Tyndale. He used the money to finance a revision of his New Testament. The revised testaments were smuggled into England in flour sacks. It wasn't, however, just Bibles that cost Tyndale his life.

*William Tyndale*

*King Henry VIII*

**www**

## On The Web

Dig deeper into the English Reformation at . . .

*http://www.geocities.com/ SoHo/Studios/1344/ henryviii.html*

For more about Thomas More, try . . .

*http://www.luminarium.org/ renlit/tmore.htm*

Foxe's *Book of Martyrs* records the deaths of many English Protestants; check it out at . . .

*http://www.luminarium.org/ renlit/foxe.htm*

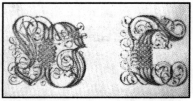
*The editor of the Matthew's Bible placed William Tyndale's initials on the last page of the Old Testament, to honor Tyndale's contribution to the translation.*

## ALL HE WANTED WAS A SON

Before the Reformation, English monarchs usually supported the pope. In 1520 a tract that attacked Martin Luther sported King Henry VIII's name on the front cover (even though Henry's chancellor, Thomas More, probably wrote it). Pope Leo X rewarded Henry's zeal with the title "Defender of the Church." Little did Leo X know that the Defender of the Church would soon be damned by the church.

### "Henry the Eighth, I am, I am; the Head of the Church, I am"

Henry's current queen, Catherine of Aragon, had not produced a son to succeed Henry as king. Catherine had been Henry's sister-in-law, and Henry was already enchanted with an attractive 25-year-old named Anne Boleyn. So, Henry claimed, based on Leviticus 20:21, that God would never let Catherine have a son and his marriage should be annulled. In 1529 Henry asked Pope Clement VII to revoke his vows to "that Spanish cow." But there was one problem with Henry's request: the Holy Roman Emperor Charles V currently controlled the pope, and Charles V was Catherine's nephew. The pope could not afford to anger Charles V.

Thomas Cranmer, a professor at Cambridge, suggested a solution. Cranmer would ask the lawyers at Europe's universities to overturn the pope's decision. In 1533, newly ordained as England's archbishop, Cranmer repealed Henry's vows. Henry married Anne Boleyn and declared himself head of the English church. Chancellor Thomas More refused to recognize Henry's rule over the English church. So, in the words of one English jester, "Chancellor More became chancellor no more." After More's resignation, one of Henry's advisors, Thomas Cromwell, had him beheaded.

### "Lord! Open the king of England's eyes!"

How did Henry's marriage problems affect William Tyndale? In 1530 one of Tyndale's tracts denounced Henry's attempt to dispose of Catherine. William Tyndale was captured, strangled, and burned by the king's soldiers. Tyndale's last words were, "Lord! Open the king of England's eyes!"

God answered Tyndale's prayer. In 1538 Henry approved the Matthew's Bible, a completed edition of Tyndale's work. The next year, the king placed a "Great Bible" (a revised Matthew's Bible) in every English church.

Still, the English Reformation was far from complete. In 1541 Jane Seymour, Henry's third queen, finally had a son. Under Henry's son, Thomas Cranmer edited *The Book of Common Prayer*. This common order of worship replaced elaborate Latin liturgies with simpler English versions. Cranmer's *Book of Common Prayer* led the English churches away from Roman Catholicism.

Henry's son died as a teen in 1553. Mary Tudor, Henry's daughter by Catherine, took the throne. She propelled England back toward Roman Catholicism. She earned the title "Bloody Mary" by executing more than 300 Protestants for their faith. Among those killed during her reign were Archbishop Thomas Cranmer and Bishop Hugh Latimer. As soldiers prepared to burn Latimer, he declared, "We shall this day light such a candle by God's grace as I trust shall never be put out."

It was Queen Elizabeth, Henry's daughter by Anne Boleyn, who placed England on a middle route between Catholicism and Protestantism. She refused the title "Supreme Head of the Church," yet she rejected the pope's power. Her revised *Book of Common Prayer* included Protestant and Catholic ideas. Today, it is still Elizabeth's middle way that shapes the Church of England (or, the Anglican Church).

## ALL THEY WANTED WAS RENEWAL

Martin Luther wasn't the only sixteenth century Roman Catholic who wanted to see the church reformed. Catholic leaders had been planning reforms several years before Luther nailed his theses to the chapel door.

The Protestant Reformation forced the Roman Catholic reformers to rethink their original plans. At first, the Catholic reformers tried to reunite with the Protestants. In 1541 several Protestants—including Luther's aide, Philip Melanchthon [me-LANK-thawn]—met with Roman Catholic leaders in Ratisbon-Regensburg, Germany. Their goal? Reunion.

It was not the issue of justification that prevented reunion. Both sides agreed that God's grace justifies the sinner by faith and that saving faith produces good works. The Roman Catholic delegates, however, demanded agreement on the pope's power and on the Lord's Supper. The Ratisbon-Regensburg Conference quickly dissolved. From that moment onward, Roman Catholics forged their own distinct road to reform. A soldier named Ignatius Loyola [loy-OH-lah] represented the new face of Catholic faith.

Ignatius Loyola was wounded in battle in 1521. While his wound healed, he read Thomas A'Kempis's *Imitation of Christ*. Kempis's emphasis on direct knowledge of Jesus Christ transformed Loyola's life. Loyola and six friends committed themselves to poverty, chastity, and obedience to the pope. In 1540, Pope Paul III approved Loyola's "Society of Jesus," and the Jesuit order was formed.

The Jesuits became the Roman Catholic Church's greatest missionary force. One Jesuit priest, Francis Xavier, preached in India and Japan 150 years before Protestants sent missionaries to either country. It was the reforming spirits of people like the Jesuits that pointed the Roman Catholic Church toward renewal.

*The Rack: The Duke of Exeter introduced this instrument of torture in 1447. Sir Thomas Wyatt was racked for heresy in 1581 during Queen Elizabeth's reign.*

### Did You Know?

Tyndale's New Testaments ignited a Protestant movement in Scotland. John Knox led the Scottish Parliament to deny the pope's power in Scotland. Elders ("presbyters") directed Scottish Reformed churches. So, Scottish Protestants became known as Presbyterians.

*People chained the Great Bibles to their church's pillars to prevent theft.*

### On The Web

Learn more about Ignatius Loyola at . . .

*http://www.jesuit.org/ resources/*

Francis Xavier, a Jesuit priest and missionary, took the message of Christ to southeast Asia.

## Key Concept

Division is never desirable, but sometimes it is necessary.

The council of Trent met in Austria and responded to many of the Reformers' criticisms of the Roman Catholic church.

## Being Catholic in a Post-Reformation World

Pope Paul III called for a reforming council in 1538. The delegates met in Trent, Austria. Between 1545 and 1563 the Council of Trent transformed the Roman Catholic Church. The marketing of indulgences and church offices ended. Priestly celibacy was enforced again.

The Council of Trent also made doctrinal decisions. Scripture and church tradition were given equal authority. Both faith and works were viewed as necessary for salvation. And, the Mass had to be said in Latin. These decisions defined for more than 400 years what it meant to be Roman Catholic.

## THE AFTERMATH

Medieval Europe had been, in the eyes of many citizens, a Christian society, united under the Roman bishop. The Reformation forced folk to ask themselves, "How can we remain unified if every person follows a different form of Christianity?"

In the German provinces, the Peace of Augsburg tried to help Protestants and Catholics coexist peacefully. The prince of each province chose his people's confession of faith. If a Protestant found oneself ruled by a Catholic prince, the Protestant could move unhindered to a Protestant prince's province and vice-versa. Yet the Peace of Augsburg only allowed Lutheran Protestants. What about Calvinists, Zwinglians, and Anabaptists? From a religious perspective, Europe was in fragments at the end of the sixteenth century. Could anyone pick up the pieces?

## BUILDING SOMETHING BETTER

Were the divisions that shattered sixteenth-century Christianity desirable? No. Were they necessary? Probably, yes. The divisions returned millions of people to a renewed awareness of God's sovereignty, of the Bible's authority, and of salvation by grace through faith. Division is never desirable, but sometimes it is necessary. So, like a certain six-year-old ring-bearer at his sister's wedding, I accept the division. I believe that God preserves a people for God's own glory, despite the divisions that tear apart God's church. And I work to build something better on the foundation that remains.

# CHAPTER EIGHT LEARNING ACTIVITY

In each blank, write words from the list that relate to the name beside the blank. Most words in the list will be used more than once. After you finish the learning activity, add one word of your own in each blank.

| | | | |
|---|---|---|---|
| Anabaptist | Dutch | Jesuit | Studious |
| Barrel | English | Monk | Swiss |
| Cambridge | French | Nun | Theses |
| Catherine | Fled | Priest | Translator |
| Catholic | Geneva | Soldier | Wife |
| Council | German | Spanish | Wittenberg |
| Drowned | Institutes | Strangled | Zurich |

1. Ignatius Loyola _____

2. John Calvin _____

3. Henry VIII _____

4. Kaetie Luther _____

5. Martin Luther _____

6. Felix Manz _____

7. Menno Simons _____

8. Trent _____

9. William Tyndale _____

10. Ulrich Zwingli _____

## Notes

# WHAT YOU SHOULD KNOW ABOUT CHRISTIAN HISTORY
## AD 1510—1767

### Three Events You Should Know

1. *Persecution of Japanese Christians* (1596-1643): In 1597, the Japanese government crucified 26 native Christians for their faith. Persecution continued until 1643. In 1859 and 1890, the Japanese government issued agreements that legalized Christianity again.

2. *Chinese Rites Controversy* (1704): Dominican monks taught Chinese Christians not to venerate their ancestors or partake in Confucian rites. Jesuit monks allowed both practices. The pope decided the Dominicans were correct. Severe oppression erupted against Catholics in China.

3. *Suppression of the Jesuits* (1759-1767): Theological and political disputes led to the removal of Jesuit priests from Portugal, Spain, and the Americas.

### Eight Names You Should Know

1. *John I of the Cross* (1542-1591): Mystical Doctor of the Roman Catholic Church.

2. *Matteo Ricci* (1552-1610): Jesuit missionary to China. Believed the Confucian Supreme One was also the threefold God of Christianity.

3. *Rene Descartes* (1596-1650): French philosopher. To find a firm basis for thought, he decided to doubt everything. He concluded that everything could be doubted except his own existence (hence his famous maxim, "I think, therefore I am"). He reasoned all other truths from that basis.

4. *Blaise Pascal* (1623-1662): French scientist and Catholic thinker. Supported Jansenism. Fragments of his defense of Christian faith were published after his death as the *Pensees*.

5. *Johannes Amos Comenius* (1592-1670): Bohemian educator. For him, the final goal of education was not learning, but the development of Christian character.

6. *John Milton* (1608-1674): English Christian poet. Argued for the separation of church and state. Wrote *Paradise Lost*.

7. *Sor Juana Ines de la Cruz* (1651-1695): Latina nun and Catholic theologian. Her bishop disallowed her studies, but she kept studying until a mystic experience fulfilled her longings.

8. *Antonio Vieyra* (1608-1697): Portuguese priest. Worked to convert and protect Native Americans. Clashed with Sor Juana over theological issues.

### Three Terms You Should Know

1. *Dissenters*: English church members who agreed with the link between church and state but who disagreed with the Anglican Church's theology. This group included Puritans and Catholics.

2. *Nonconformists*: English church members who disagreed with the entire concept of linking the church with the state. This title included Independents, Separatists, Congregationalists, English Presbyterians, Methodists, Quakers, and Baptists.

3. *Jansenism*: Jansen, a Catholic theologian, asserted that humans can do nothing good apart from God's grace. Jansen derived his teachings from Augustine of Hippo. Jansenism was condemned by the pope in 1653.

# Chapter Nine

## In This Chapter
### AD 1510—AD 1767

Christopher Columbus
Jacob Arminius
Galilei Galileo
King James I
John Bunyan

## CHANGE DOESN'T ALWAYS DO YOU GOOD

My mind requires two fuels—Diet Coke and constant change. That's why I can't write at a library or in my office. My most worthwhile words are written at Western society's grandest institution, at a focal point of excitement and change. I write at McDonald's!

This morning, two buses pulled into the parking lot. A horde of uncouth creatures swarmed into the lobby. The front-line crew donned steel helmets. The manager began to hyperventilate. Innocent customers reviewed their life insurance policies. It was—horror of horrors!—a sixth grade field trip.

Three food fights are currently threatening my notebook computer's survival. (I never knew a Chicken McNugget could fly *that* far!) I am questioning the sanity of the person who put noisemakers in Happy Meals. (Don't kids make enough noise without help from their Happy Meals?) This morning, I got more change than I wanted.

Reformation Christians wanted change—and they got it. Yet some of the changes brought conflict, disunion, and chaos. People got more change than they wanted. More than a few church members wondered whether reform was really what they needed after all.

### Key Concept

**Change doesn't solve everything.**

### CHANGING VIEWPOINTS

Post-Reformation Europe was an untidy blend of Lutherans, Calvinists, Anglicans, Catholics, and Anabaptists. But people could follow their own consciences. So, peace would settle across the continent. Right? Wrong.

#### "We'll Always Have Paris"—Whether We Want It Or Not

In 1572 the queen of France convinced her husband that the "Huguenots" (French Protestants) were plotting to rebel against him. On the evening of St. Bartholemew's Day, the king's soldiers swept through Paris. The next day, Protestant blood still trickled down the steps of the Louvre. Ten thousand Protestants died in the St. Bartholemew's Day massacre. Not until the Edict of Nantes in 1598 did Protestantism become legal in France.

Internal battles afflicted the Protestant movements, too. The Lutherans argued for 20 years about whether humans are fully or partly depraved. (Their own inability to get along should have given them a hint.) In 1577 the Formula of Concord unified the Lutherans again. Calvin's followers should have been predestined to fare better than the Lutherans. They didn't.

### Words: From The Ones Who Were There

*De Thou*
Describing the St. Bartholomew's Day Massacre . . .
"One woman was about to deliver a baby. . . They ripped her open and threw her infant against the wall. . . Old men were thrown into the river. A pack of boys dragged one infant through the streets with a rope around its neck."
*Histoire des choses arrivees de son temps.*

## Predestination—On What Does It Depend?

Jacob Arminius [arr-MIH-nee-uss] was a popular Dutch pastor. In the late 1500's, another pastor argued that Calvin had been wrong about predestination. Arminius agreed to defend Calvin's views. Arminius lost the debate before it began. As he studied both sides, he became convinced that his opponent was correct.

Arminius' conclusions split the Calvinist movement. Arminius died in 1609, but the conflict about predestination didn't. The next year, the followers of Arminius published the *Remonstrance*, a statement that outlined five beliefs about salvation:

1) On their own, humans can do nothing good.
2) Before the foundation of the world, God chose to save everyone who would freely choose to trust Christ.
3) Jesus died for everyone, but his death only redeems believers.
4) People can choose to reject God's attempts to save them.
5) Scripture doesn't clearly state whether Christians can forfeit their salvation.

"These Articles," the Arminians' *Remonstrance* concluded, "set out what is . . . sufficient for salvation. It is unnecessary to look higher or lower."

A Dutch prince tried to end the conflict in 1618. Prince Maurice despised the Arminians for political and religious reasons. So, he invited Calvinist pastors throughout Europe to gather at the city of Dort. Their task? Denounce the Arminians.

Despite the council's political overtones, the Synod of Dort tried to draft a balanced declaration of Calvinist beliefs. The Calvinists responded to each of the Arminians' five statements. From the Calvinists' response, we get the five points of Calvinism:

1) Human beings are by nature spiritually dead. No one naturally desires to seek Christ (Romans 3:10-12; Ephesians 2:1-3).
2) If someone trusts Christ, it is because God chose to regenerate that person. God's choice is unconditional; it isn't based on any human decision (John 6:44; Romans 9:10-16).
3) Christ's death atoned only for those who would believe in him (John 3:16).
4) When God regenerates someone, that person will neither resist nor reject God's grace (John 6:37, 44).
5) Every Christian will persevere in faith until the end (John 10:27-28; Romans 8:29-39).

## On The Web

Read the proceedings of the Synod of Dort at . . .

*http://www.gty.org/~phil/ creeds/dort.htm*

## Think About It...

Study the Scriptures listed with the five points of Calvinism. Do you agree with the Synod of Dort? Why or why not?

## Did You Know?

A flower can help you recall the five points of Calvinism. The points are T-U-L-I-P:

1) Total depravity of mankind (absence of desire for Christ)
2) Unconditional election (unconditional choice by God)
3) Limited atonement
4) Irresistible grace
5) Perseverance of the saints (Christians will never forfeit their salvation)

Predestination had been only one part of Calvin's theology. Its purpose was to assure Christians of God's love. After the Synod of Dort, predestination became the center of Calvinist theology. Among some Calvinists, strict confessions of faith displaced a dynamic faith-relationship with Christ.

### How Many Poles Does It Take to Change the World?

When sixteenth century Europeans looked at the stars, they knew humanity was special. After all, didn't everything—sun, moon, stars—spin in perfect circles around humanity?

In the mid-1500s Nicolas Copernicus [ko-PER-ni-kuss] of Poland challenged the common world-view. Several ancient Greeks had suggested that the earth rotated around the sun. Copernicus realized that, mathematically, a sun-centered universe made more sense than an earth-centered universe.

The Pole knew his ideas would turn the galaxy inside out (literally). He refused to release his manuscript until he was on his deathbed. A Protestant pastor's preface presented Copernicus's ideas as speculations to simplify math, not as scientific theories. Copernicus was dying, and few people were interested in a book about math anyway. So, his views remained unchallenged.

Another scientist, Galileo [GAH-lee-LAY-oh], didn't wait until he was on his deathbed to publish his papers. His impatience almost sent him to his death. Galileo carried the ideas of Copernicus from speculation to science. One year after Galileo published his ideas, the Inquisition condemned his assertion that the earth moved around the sun. After all, didn't Scripture clearly teach that the sun, not the earth, moves? (See Josh. 10:12-13.)

Under the threat of death, Galileo reduced his ideas from theories to speculations. He spent the rest of his life under house arrest. But he had started a revolution that no wall could confine. (In 1992, the Roman Catholic Church closed the case in Galileo's favor. I'm sure Galileo felt much better afterward.)

*Galileo*
*(Courtesy of Northwind Picture Archives)*

Once, the world had been a vast puzzle. The church explained the puzzle, and people trusted the church's explanation. After Galileo, the world was still puzzling, but never again would the church alone choose how people viewed their physical world. That would become the task of scientists.

## CHANGING COUNTRIES

### Well, That's One Way to End a Business Meeting

Not only did the churches lose a voice in matters of science. The Roman Catholic Church also lost its place in politics. In 1618 several Bohemian Protestants met their Catholic king's envoys in Prague. The Catholic envoys refused to listen to the Protestants' complaints. So, a mob adjourned the meeting with a violent motion (which no one seconded). They threw the envoys through a second story window.

As he plunged out the window, one envoy screamed, "Mary of Jesus! Help!" A Protestant yelled through the window, "Let's see if your Mary helps you now!" Then, he saw movement below. "By God," he murmured, "his Mary has helped."

Fortunately, the envoys survived. Unfortunately, they survived because they landed in a heap of horse manure. The Holy Roman Emperor immediately declared war on the Protestants. Historians have named this foul-smelling event "the Defenestration of Prague." The resulting conflict would become known as the "Thirty Years' War" (although, obviously, they didn't call it that then, because they didn't know how long it was going to last).

At first, the conflict was a war for religious toleration. However, it quickly faded into a series of political skirmishes and senseless pillaging. Before the conflict ended, it had enmeshed France, Denmark, and the entire Holy Roman Empire. In the Empire alone, soldiers slaughtered 10 million citizens. In 1648 the Peace of Westphalia ended the Thirty Years' War.

Before the Peace of Westphalia, Roman Catholic leaders had presided over international treaties. Yet the pope didn't even appear at Westphalia in 1648. Sickened by religious conflict, Europeans began to search for something beyond Christianity to cement their societies together.

## Puritans—They Weren't What You May Think

England endured its own religious struggle during the Thirty Years' War. A band of English reformers had met with King James I at Hampton Court in 1604. Unlike the Bohemians, these reformers didn't throw anyone through the window. Their desire was simply to purify the Church of England. So, they became known as "Puritans."

Who were these "Puritans?" A social critic once commented, "Puritanism is the haunting fear that someone, somewhere, may be happy." His perception was dead wrong. When Puritans worshiped, they wore dull clothing—but not to be gloomy. They wanted to turn their thoughts away from one another and toward God. Otherwise, they wore both vivid and plain colors.

Puritans enjoyed beer and complained bitterly when it ran out. They expected spouses to sustain mutually satisfying sexual relations. They swam and skated, hunted and bowled. They expressed their faith through lively relationships with one another and with God.

For Puritans, the Bible was vital. Why? They wanted to purify the church of all practices not required by Scripture. "The Church ought not," the Puritans wrote to King James, "to be governed by . . . any human invention, but by the laws and rules which Christ hath appointed in his Testament." Their preferred translation was the Geneva Bible.

*King James I*

### On The Web

Explore Puritan theology at . . .
*http://www.puritansermons.com*

King James disliked the Geneva Bible's Calvinist study notes. So, when one Puritan at the 1604 Hampton Court Conference suggested a new translation, James quickly agreed. Forty-seven scholars worked for 33 months on King James' version. In 1611 the first King James Version of the Bible rolled off the presses.

It would, however, take more than a new Bible to solve England's problems. After the Hampton Court Conference, some Puritans separated from the Anglican church. In 1607 two so-called "Separatist" churches fled to Holland. For safety's sake, one of those congregations divided. Each half would, in its own way, change the world.

One group would sail west, to a New World. They would settle on the coast of Massachusetts. We know them as the Pilgrims. In Holland, the other group's understanding of the church would change radically. Their heirs would include John Bunyan, Charles Spurgeon, Martin Luther King, Jr., and Billy Graham. We know them as the Baptists.

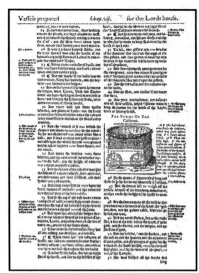

*Page from Geneva Bible*

### The First English Baptists

The leader of the second group was an uncommon man with a common name, John Smyth. In Amsterdam, Smyth embraced the radical idea that only believers' baptism was valid.

Smyth and his followers wanted to receive believers' baptism. But there was a problem: If infant baptism were invalid, no one in Smyth's church was correctly baptized. Could an unbaptized person baptize anyone? Smyth wasn't sure. In 1609 John Smyth took a chance. He "cast water on himself." Smyth's self-baptism spawned a new congregation—"the Brothers of the Separation of the Second English Church in Amsterdam." Later, they became known by a name that can actually fit in a church bulletin— "the Baptists."

The Brothers of the Separation embraced Arminian theology, with its emphasis on the general (or, universal) extent of Christ's atonement. For this reason, they became known as "General Baptists."

*Page from the King James Bible*

In 1610 Smyth questioned whether self-baptism was valid. He tried to join the Mennonites, but he died before they accepted him. The next year, Smyth's closest friend, Thomas Helwys, led the congregation home. Near London, they founded England's first Baptist church.

### John Bunyan Wasn't a Lumberjack

One of the most famous English Baptists was John Bunyan. When John was nine, King James' son, Charles, commanded every church in Britain to follow the Anglican church's rituals. This church dispute quickly turned into a political dispute, and chaos spewed across England. Oliver Cromwell, a member of Parliament, formed a pro-Puritan army. Within five years,

## Think About It...

With whom should Christians share the Lord's Supper? Only members of their church? Only members of their denomination? All believers?

*John Bunyan (1628-1688)*

Cromwell controlled Britain. His troops beheaded King Charles and his archbishop. Cromwell's army drafted John Bunyan on Bunyan's sixteenth birthday. After two uneventful years, Bunyan's unit disbanded. "Lord Protector" Cromwell was already growing unpopular.

Around 1648 Bunyan married. He built his bride a thatched hut. Unfortunately, he had nothing to put in it. The entire dowry of his wife, Mary, consisted of two Puritan books! "We had not so much household stuff," Bunyan remarked, "as a dish or spoon."

Whether the Bunyans ever bought any flatware, no one knows. What is certain is that Bunyan read Mary's books, as well as John Foxe's *Book of Martyrs*. (Without a bed or dishes, what else was there to do?) The books changed Bunyan's life. He realized that he had never truly trusted Christ. After an intense struggle, he gave his life to Christ. "Down fell I," he wrote, "as a bird shot from a tree."

In 1653 Bunyan was immersed by a Baptist pastor in Bedford. The Bedford Baptist Church seems to have been one of the first Baptist churches to baptize by immersion instead of pouring. Bunyan quickly became one of the Baptists' most popular traveling preachers.

Unlike other Baptists, Bunyan shared the Lord's Supper with all Christians, regardless of their denomination. "The Church," Bunyan argued, "hath not warrant to keep out of their communion [any] Christian."

In 1660 Cromwell's Commonwealth ended. King Charles's son suppressed all non-Anglican churches. A few months later John Bunyan was jailed in Bedford for preaching without the Anglican Church's permission.

In prison, Bunyan wrote his most famous work—an allegory entitled *Pilgrim's Progress*. John Bunyan died in 1688, only a few months before a new ruler returned religious toleration to England.

In 1688 William of Orange and King James's daughter Mary became the rulers of England. Their "Glorious Revolution" returned England to Queen Elizabeth's "middle way." The Toleration Act allowed anyone who agreed to a list of 39 doctrines—*The Thirty-Nine Articles*—to worship without fear.

The Puritan movement in England was over, but the Puritan ideal would persist for centuries among Presbyterians and Baptists. And, for a few years, in an unruly band of American colonies, the Puritan dream would thrive.

## CHANGING CULTURES

While religious wars transformed Europe, another conflict was changing another hemisphere. The clash began in 1492. Christopher Columbus wasn't only looking for a passage to the Indies when he collided with Central America. He was looking for gold. Why? He wanted Spain to finance a crusade that would crush the Muslims. Columbus lacked one thing to sail across the ocean—money. Columbus used the Bible to convince kings to finance his quest. He claimed that his journey would fulfill Isaiah 11:11-12.

In 1492 Columbus' boats landed in the Bahamas. Eventually, he also landed on the coast of Honduras. When Columbus died, he still believed that he had found an eastern route to India. What he had actually found was more marvelous than India. He had found a new world.

*Christopher Columbus*

### The Trust-Jesus-Or-Else Campaign

Spain and Portugal were quick to send soldiers to subdue the Americas. The Spanish and Portuguese were not (they claimed) conquering the Native Americans. They were evangelizing them. Soldiers read aloud (in Spanish!) a summary of Christian beliefs before each battle. If no one responded to their evangelistic invitation, they gave a new meaning to "Evangelism Explosion": They slaughtered the natives. In the settlers' minds, the natives were going to Hell anyway. Why did it matter whether they went sooner or later? The settlers even found a Scripture to excuse their violence: Didn't Jesus command his people to "compel them to come in"? (Luke 14:23, King James Version).

### Slaves of Sugar

Until the 1500s only honey could indulge Europe's sweet tooth. In the Americas, Europeans found a whole new way to gain weight—sugar. Spain and Portugal could make vast profits if they overcame one problem: It was illegal to enslave a native.

*On his fourth trip to the New World, Columbus landed here, near Trujillo, Honduras.*

The Spanish solved their problem with the *encomienda* [en-KOM-ee EN-dah] system. This system "entrusted" natives to Spanish settlers. The settlers were supposed to teach their natives about Christ. The result was worse than slavery. Because the settlers received natives without making any financial investment in them, the native workers were often treated worse than slaves.

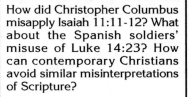

### Think About It...

How did Christopher Columbus misapply Isaiah 11:11-12? What about the Spanish soldiers' misuse of Luke 14:23? How can contemporary Christians avoid similar misinterpretations of Scripture?

## Words: From The Ones Who Were There

*Bartolome de Las Casas*
"The Indians are our brothers; Christ has given his life for them. Why do we treat them with such inhuman savagery? . . . They aren't stupid or savage! . . . I do not know of any other people more ready to receive the gospel."
*Defense Against the Persecutors and Slanderers.*

## Did You Know?

One seventeenth-century Aztec claimed that he saw a vision of a Native American Virgin Mary. Eventually, a bishop was compelled built a shrine at the site of the vision. Since then, the Virgin of Guadalupe has been a symbol of Mexican self-rule.

*These structures in modern Copan, Honduras, were built by the Mayan natives. The ancient Mayan culture disintegrated in the ninth century AD. In the seventeenth and eighteenth centuries, European diseases probably destroyed many of the remaining Mayans.*

### Bartolome's barren battle

In 1510 Bartolome de Las Casas became the first priest to perform his first Mass in the New World. The Spanish priest acquired an encomienda in Haiti to enhance his income. For four years, his plantation produced a healthy profit. Then, on Pentecost Sunday, 1514, something happened to Las Casas. He released his natives, closed his encomienda, and declared that no true Christian could exploit the natives.

Las Casas returned to Spain to campaign for natives' rights. Five years later, the Holy Roman Emperor actually did something holy. He approved Las Casas' *New Laws of the Indies*—a law-code that limited Spain's power over the natives. Most settlers ignored the New Laws. The Inquisition listed Las Casas' writings in the Index of Forbidden Books. Until the day he died, Bartolome de Las Casas tried to curb his country's cruelty with no success.

### A new source of slaves, a new curse on the Americas

The natives might have survived European brutality, but they couldn't survive European diseases. In Mexico alone, European diseases and cruelty killed 17 million of the 18 million natives.

The Spanish and Portuguese settlers were troubled—but not because they had destroyed an entire culture. They were upset because their plantations could not make a profit without workers. The settlers' solution would curse the Americas for centuries. They enslaved and imported Africans.

One ancient philosopher had suggested that some races were intended for slavery. Settlers assumed that African people fit the philosopher's suggestion. Some even used Scripture to defend their actions. They connected the Africans with "Canaan" in Genesis 9:25.

### The slave of the slaves

Imagine yourself as a seventeenth-century African. Light-skinned men with tremendous weapons have ripped you from your native land. They cram you and hundreds of others into the dank belly of a ship. You receive little food, little water, no light. You are naked. Several of your fellow-slaves die. The living and the dead lay together on a solid sheet of human waste. With the stench comes sickness. Day after day, you vomit bile. Bitter gall congeals on your chin and chest.

Your captors' destination is Colombia. A furlong from the beach, light skinned men drag you from the ship's hold. Flies swarm around you as you collapse at the dock.

You glimpse a man running toward you. He wears a robe. He pours water into your mouth. He is not like other light-skinned men. Several Africans surround him. They speak to you . . . in your language. You do not quite understand their words. You do recognize one phrase . . . "living water." The light-skinned man points to himself. His name feels strange on your swollen tongue. "Pedro . . . Claver."

When Pedro Claver took his priestly vows, he committed himself to helping slaves. He even added a phrase to his name, "always a slave of Africans." In other words, "always a slave of the slaves." In 1622 Pedro became a Jesuit missionary in Colombia. He didn't know any African languages; so, he convinced his monastery to buy some Africans. Pedro demanded that the African translators be treated as brothers— not as slaves.

When a slave ship neared the coast, Pedro ran to meet the ship. He gave each slave a drink of water. He grouped the Africans according to their native languages. In each group, he shared the good news about Jesus Christ, "the living water." Pedro showed each slave a snake's skin. Just as a snake leaves behind its skin, Pedro said, so a person who receives baptism must leave behind one's old life. Pedro baptized anyone who wanted to trust Christ.

After decades of service, Pedro became paralyzed. His fellow-priests refused to nurse him. Instead, they hired an African slave to care for the priest. Years of abuse had taught the slave to hate white men. He treated Pedro Claver like his owners had treated him. Pedro lay in the same cot for months, until his own waste seeped into his bedsores.

Nearly everyone despised Pedro Claver. However, several slave-owners realized that Claver might be declared a saint. If this happened, his possessions would be priceless. They invaded his cell and stole everything he owned—even his clothing and the cross that he had carried most of his life. In 1654 Pedro Claver died, naked and alone, "always a slave of the slaves." Two hundred years later, he was officially listed as a saint.

Pedro Claver wasn't the only Jesuit who defended the oppressed. In Paraguay, Jesuit priests built settlements for the Native Americans who had survived slavery and disease. Everyone was equal in the Jesuit missions.

In 1628 Portuguese and Spanish plantation owners attacked the Jesuit missions and enslaved their natives. The Jesuits moved their missions farther inland, but the slave traders pursued them. In 1640 the Jesuits armed the missions and allowed the natives to defend themselves. At first, the experiment worked. By 1731 nearly 150,000 Native Americans were living safely within Jesuit missions. In the end, the slaveowners' greed and superior weapons won. In 1767 Spain forced the Jesuits to leave the New World. By 1800 slavery, disease, and greed had destroyed the Jesuit missions.

*This Spanish fort was built in 1585 to defend Spanish settlers from British pirates.*

## On The Web

Does Pedro Claver's story inspire you? Learn more about him at . . .

*http://www.cin.org/ petclavr.html*

## Think About It...

Read Mark 10:42-45. To what group of people could you be "a slave?"

## IT TAKES MORE THAN CHANGE

Christians put a lot of faith in change. Is Sunday school stumbling? "We need different literature." Is the church's income plunging? "We need a new pastor." Do the people fail to catch the pastor's vision? "I think I'll look for another place to serve." Is the songleader homely? "We need new lights in the sanctuary." (Okay, so I made the last one up.)

Change isn't necessarily bad. But change can't solve every problem. Remember New Coke? The Edsel? Certain aspects of post-Reformation Christianity? Before Christians try to change something, perhaps they should ask themselves, "What is God doing here that we may be missing?" Maybe God is preparing the church for a new spurt of growth. Maybe the pastor's vision isn't the Holy Spirit's vision. Maybe people's hearts simply are not open to the Bible's teachings. Maybe post-Reformation Christians were still looking for earthly power when God's power was all that they needed. And maybe contemporary Christians sometimes follow the same path. "Savior, like a shepherd lead us; Much we need thy tender care."

**Key Concept**

Change doesn't solve everything.

# CHAPTER NINE LEARNING ACTIVITY

This quiz will help you review what you read in Chapter Nine. Match the statements with the people or events.

1. _____ Jacob Arminius
2. _____ Galileo
3. _____ Huguenots
4. _____ Bohemian Protestants
5. _____ Puritans
6. _____ King James
7. _____ John Smyth
8. _____ John Bunyan
9. _____ Westminster Assembly
10. _____ Bartolome de Las Casas
11. _____ Pedro Claver

A. "Always a slave of Africans."

B. People must choose to cooperate with God.

C. "The chief end of man is to glorify God . . . ."

D. "The Indians are our brothers."

E. "Am I not free to dissent from Vieyra's opinion?"

F. Brothers of the Separation of the Second English Church in Amsterdam.

G. Mathematically, a sun- centered universe makes the most sense.

H. Threw two Catholic envoys through a window, marking the beginning of the Thirty Years' War.

I. Wrote Pilgrims' Progress.

J. Wanted earthly joy to lead them to glorify God.

K. Disliked the Puritans' Geneva Bible.

L. Were slaughtered on St. Bartholomew's Day.

12. The movie *The Mission* portrays the demise of one Jesuit mission. Check out the movie from your library or video store. After you watch the movie, reread the stories about the sugar plantations, Las Casas, and Claver. How did the movie help you understand the Jesuit missions?

_____

_____

_____

_____

_____

_____

# WHAT YOU SHOULD KNOW ABOUT CHRISTIAN HISTORY
## AD 1620—1814

### Five Events You Should Know

1. *Cyril Lucar Befriended Protestants* (1623-1637): Lucar, the Orthodox patriarch of Constantinople, embraced Calvinism and gave the king of England the earliest known copy of the New Testament, the Alexandrian Codex. Four Orthodox synods denounced Lucar's Calvinist views.
2. *Czar Peter Placed the Russian Orthodox Church Under the Government's Control* (1721).
3. *The Great Awakening* (1720's-1750's): This religious revival began in the Congregational and Reformed churches of Massachusetts and New Jersey. It emphasized outward signs of conversion.
4. *Methodist Conference Formed Within the Anglican Church* (1784). The formation of the Methodist Conference paved the way for the Methodists to become a separate denomination.
5. *Pope Pius VII Restored the Jesuit Order* (1814).

### Six Names You Should Know

1. *Roger Williams* (1603-1683): Upheld religious liberty in his booklet The *Bloody Tenent of Persecution*. Founded Providence (Rhode Island) after being expelled from Massachusetts.
2. *George Fox* (1624-1691): Founder of Friends Society. Fox removed all human elements (including baptism and communion) from worship, because he believed God guides Christians through an "inner light." The Friends were harshly persecuted for their beliefs. One Friend told a judge he should "quake" before God's wrath. So, the Friends also became known as "Quakers."
3. *Margaret Fell* (1614-1702): Leader of the Friends Society. In 1666, wrote *Women's Speaking Justified by the Scriptures*, a defense of women preaching.
4. *Nikolaus Zinzendorf* (1700-1760): Wealthy Pietist leader. Sheltered the Moravian Brethren and founded Herrnhut, a Moravian community.
5. *John Wesley* (1703-1791): Founder of the Methodist movement. Emphasized the pursuit of holiness and the achievement of "Christian perfection."
6. *Francis Asbury* (1745-1816): Methodist circuit-riding preacher. He and Thomas Coke were the first Methodist superintendents in America.

### Five Terms You Should Know

1. *Separatists*: English church members who separated from the Anglican Church over several issues, including the degree of adornment in the church's worship. (Separatists preferred simple worship; Anglican worship tended to be ornate.) Most Separatists became Congregationalists.
2. *Moravian Brethren*: Pietist descendants of the Bohemian Protestants, who derived from Jan Hus' followers. Today, they are known as the United Brethren.
3. *Pietists*. Eighteenth-century Christians who emphasized experiencing God's presence through intense, personal prayer and Bible study.
4. *The Enlightenment*: An intellectual movement in the eighteenth and nineteenth centuries that focused on human reason, words, science, natural law, and the created order.
5. *Deism*: From the Latin *deus* ("deity"). A movement that searched for a universal foundation on which all religions could agree. Most deists believed that a divine being had created the universe and natural laws. However, they also believed that this divine being was revealed to humanity primarily through the created order.

# Chapter Ten

## TALKIN' 'BOUT SOME REVOLUTIONS

When I tell people I'm a writer, one question always surfaces: "How do you get your ideas?" I hate that question. It's not that I don't have an answer. It's just that the answer sounds so . . . stupid. I call my method "creative scenery changes." (Warning! To most people, my method looks suspiciously like loafing.) I sit for awhile in one spot. If that spot does not inspire me, I go somewhere else. I keep moving until I'm inspired. (Nothing, I might add, is more inspiring than an editorial deadline.) After inspiration strikes, a revolution begins within my brain. That's how I get my ideas.

In the 1600s and 1700s, many people found that their parents' faith no longer inspired them. So, they performed a series of creative scenery changes. Puritans and patriots found their inspiration in new societies. Pietists searched for religious revival. Rationalists created a new vision of the divine. The result was a series of revolutions that still shape our world today.

## TALKIN' 'BOUT SOCIAL REVOLUTION

In 1620 one hundred English Separatists and their military escort left their native land. Every American knows the rest of the story: The "Pilgrims" founded a colony where everyone could worship freely. Right? Wrong.

The Mayflower excursion was a bit like the first episode of *Gilligan's Island*. The Pilgrims wanted to land in Virginia—not Massachusetts. Storms and faulty steering sent them far north of their goal. The Pilgrims named their landing point "Plymouth."

Several years later, the Puritans' Massachusetts Bay Colony absorbed the Plymouth settlement. Neither group wanted religious freedom for everyone. What they wanted was freedom to form a society based on their own beliefs. For a few years, the Puritan experiment worked. To become voting citizens, residents had to confirm that Christ had saved them. So, their church and their society were firmly linked. The arrangement didn't last.

### Roger Williams' Providential Experiment

It was a Separatist named Roger Williams who first challenged the colony's alliance with the church. When Roger arrived in Massachusetts, the Puritans' Congregationalist Church offered him the position of pastor teacher. Roger, unlike the Puritans, believed that civil judges should not enforce religious beliefs. So, he refused the position; he preached among the Native Americans instead. Few people cared about Roger's beliefs until he made a political claim that the colony's leaders couldn't allow. He declared, "The Natives are the true owners of [this land]."

### In This Chapter
### AD 1620—AD 1814

Anne Hutchinson
Salem Witch Trials
Jonathan Edwards
George Whitefield
American War for Independence

## Key Concept

When former forms of faith fail to inspire them, folk forge fresh—and, sometimes, false—forms of faith.

## On The Web

Learn more about the Pilgrims' beliefs at . . .

*http://pilgrims.net/ plymouth/history/*

and . . .

*http://www.seanet.com/ Users/pamur/colo.html*

*This ship, the* Susan Constant, *was the largest of three ships that brought the first permanent English settlers to America.*

The Massachusetts court banished Roger in 1635. His daughter was two years old. His wife was pregnant. Winter was approaching quickly. Roger had no horse. Yet he had to leave. He trekked alone through the icy eastern landscape for 14 weeks. Finally, a native tribe gave him shelter.

The next year, Roger Williams paid a Native American tribe a fair price for a small bay to the south of Massachusetts. His wife, children, and several friends joined him there. Roger named his patch of earth "Providence." Every faith was welcome in Providence. Roger's charter declared, "No person within said colony shall be called in question for any opinion in matters of religion. Persons may enjoy their own judgments in matters of religious concernment."

Three years after he founded Providence, Roger became the first Baptist in the New World. He even founded the first Baptist church in the colonies. Eight months later, he questioned his new beliefs and became the first *former* Baptist in the colonies.

One of the first folk to flee to Providence was Anne Hutchinson. On Wednesday nights, the 44-year-old midwife and six other women discussed their pastor's Sunday sermon in Anne's Boston home. Soon, sixty women and men were attending Anne's classes. Such meetings were common in the Massachusetts Bay Colony. What was uncommon was that Anne was "a woman of ready wit and bold spirit."

Anne's boldness led her to make a risky claim: Christians aren't bound to obey any human laws. Anne was trying to echo Paul's doctrine of grace (Romans 3:24-28), yet she neglected another truth—real faith leads to good works, including obedience to civil authorities (Romans 13:1-7; James 2:14). The leaders of the Massachusetts Bay Colony accused Anne Hutchinson of promoting treasonous ideas.

During the trial, it became clear that Anne knew more about the Bible than her judges. When the governor denounced the idea of a woman teaching, Anne quoted Acts 18:26 ("Priscilla . . . explained to [Apollos] the way of God") and Titus 2:3-5 ("older women . . . [should] admonish the younger women"). "But neither of them will suit your practice," a judge replied. "Must I," Anne countered, "show my name written therein?"

No one could prove any charges against Anne. Then, she made a mortal mistake (at least from the Puritans' perspective): She appealed to a personal experience in which she believed God spoke to her. The governor challenged her: "How did [you] know that it was God that did reveal these things?" "How," Anne retorted, "did Abraham know that it was God that did bid him offer his son?" "By an immediate voice." "So to me," Anne said, "by immediate revelation." This was too much. The court banished Anne Hutchinson. She and her family fled to Providence (now known as Rhode Island).

Rhode Island would remain America's smallest colony. Yet, in that bay, a radical idea was birthed—a civil government that refused to favor any religious faith. That idea transformed our world.

## Reclaiming the Colony

A generation after their arrival, a perennial problem confronted the Puritans: Christian parents don't always produce Christian children. Most of the first-generation settlers had professed a personal relationship with Christ. Yet about half of their children never trusted Christ. If not everyone in the colony had trusted Christ, could Christian principles still govern their society?

The first answer was a "Halfway Covenant." For years, pastors had baptized only the children of Christians. Hoping to retain a bond between the children and the church, pastors began to baptize the children of non-Christian parents.

The new approach didn't work. Fewer and fewer children trusted Christ as their personal Savior. To many Puritans, it seemed like an evil presence was fragmenting their colony. In Salem, Massachusetts, in 1692, veiled fears erupted into open fury. Someone caught a 12-year-old girl practicing magic. The girl and her friends falsely charged several older women with witchcraft. Righteous anger turned into mass hysteria. Fifty citizens admitted, under pressure from the colony's leaders, that they had practiced magic. All 50 were freed. Nineteen citizens refused to confess. All 19 were hanged. One man was tortured to death because he refused to testify against his wife.

This event became known as "the Salem witch-hunt." It lasted less than a year. In Europe, witch-hunts were longer, bloodier, and far more frequent. One judge later confessed "the blame and shame" of the Salem trials. Still, a blot had forever blackened the Puritan experiment.

After the witch-hunt, the Massachusetts Bay Colony endured several political conflicts with England. By the early 1700s a spiritual stupor had replaced the early Puritans' fiery faith. "There hath been a vital Decay," one pastor wrote. "There is already a great Death upon Religion, little more than a name left to live."

## TALKIN' 'BOUT A REVOLUTION IN HUMAN REASON

If you attend Sunday school, you have probably asked yourself at least once, "How can two people read the same Scripture and arrive at two different conclusions?" Here's a key to the answer: Throughout your life, you collect certain experiences and assumptions, some true, some false. You read the Bible through the lens of these assumptions. Different experiences and assumptions lead to different understandings of a text.

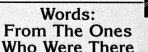

### Words: From The Ones Who Were There

*John Cotton, Puritan Pastor*
"[Anne] did much good in our Town . . . . She was not only skillful [as a midwife] . . ., but readily fell into good discourse with the women about their spiritual estates. . . . Many of the women and their husbands were . . . brought to inquire more seriously after the Lord."

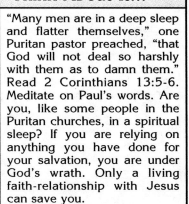

### Think About It...

"Many men are in a deep sleep and flatter themselves," one Puritan pastor preached, "that God will not deal so harshly with them as to damn them." Read 2 Corinthians 13:5-6. Meditate on Paul's words. Are you, like some people in the Puritan churches, in a spiritual sleep? If you are relying on anything you have done for your salvation, you are under God's wrath. Only a living faith-relationship with Jesus can save you.

## Think About It...

Look up "[the] Enlightenment" in an encyclopedia. Define the Enlightenment in your own words.

Before the Reformation, Christians looked at their world through the lens of church tradition. In their eagerness to return to Scripture alone, sixteenth-century Protestants discarded many church traditions. In the 1600s and 1700s what replaced church tradition as the primary way to understand the world was an internal power shared by all humans (except tired two-year-old's)—*reason*.

This emphasis on human reason was a chief feature of the eighteenth century movement that became known as "the Enlightenment." Before the Enlightenment, people looked to past traditions for guidance. The Enlightenment focused people on a new future, in which human reason would reign supreme.

**The Universe—From Cosmic Puzzle to Reasonable Machine**

The astronomer Copernicus had realized that the planets moved around the sun. Yet he couldn't explain why. Perhaps angels pushed them in their places. Or, maybe the universe itself was alive. Isaac Newton, a quiet professor from England, shattered such assumptions. Through scientific reasoning, Newton proved that gravity could explain the mystery of the planets' movements.

When Newton published his ideas, people throughout the world gasped. It seemed that one man had solved an infinite mystery! And the explanation was so simple! One Enlightenment poet exulted, "Nature and Nature's Law lay hidden in Night;/God said, Let Newton be: and all was light."

## Think About It...

"The results of [Deism were] not all of the best. If God is first and last a Maker, then what happened after? Certainly nothing much which involved God. He might have gone off to a retirement cottage once his contract was completed, and for some Christians he did just that."
*Gavin White, How the Churches Got to Be the Way They Are (London: S.C.M. Press, 1990) 1.*

**God—From Personal Savior to Distant Creator**

Newton's discoveries provided the foundation that Enlightenment thinkers would use to construct a new way of thinking. The old world of unseen spirits and unruly fate was gone. In its place, Enlightenment thinkers molded a new vision: The universe was a self-maintaining machine, endowed by a Divine Creator with forces that forever followed the unvarying laws of nature.

Skeptics soon asked, "If human reason can grasp nature's inner workings, why does humanity need the Bible? or religious creeds? or redemption?" Perhaps reason and nature were enough. In this context, a new vision of God arose— *"Deism."* Deists rejected every belief that reason could not confirm. Miracles? Impossible. The Trinity? Absurd. Jesus? A human Messiah. God's mystery? Gone. For them, to be Christian was simply to live according to Christ's ethics. Creation was the first and last meaningful act for the Deists' so-called "God."

## In Case You're Confused

Freemasonry arose in the 1100s to guard the secrets of building stone structures. After the Renaissance, the "Masonic brotherhoods" became clubs dedicated to charity, peace, and education. Their focus on education and peace led them to support Deism in the 1700s.

Masonic brotherhoods spread Deist ideas in Europe. In 1738 Pope Clement XII denounced Deism and forbade Catholics from becoming Masons. Still, Deism remained popular. Influenced by Deism, many churches embraced "Unitarianism" (the belief that God is not a Trinity). In the 1600s narrow religious views had only brought bloodshed. "Maybe," people reasoned, "all religions can unite beneath the banner of Deism and end religious war." In this way, the false religion of Deism wove itself into the fabric of European and American religious life.

## TALKIN' 'BOUT RELIGIOUS REVOLUTION

### Revival in the Colonies—The Northampton Awakening

When he was 18, an American colonist named Jonathan Edwards wrote in his diary, "Resolved: That all men should live to the glory of God. Resolved, secondly: That whether or not anyone else does, I will." And he did.

Yet Jonathan Edwards was not the type who could move people's souls. In his day it was stylish to be short. Edwards was tall. He was a staunch Calvinist. He read his messages in a squeaky monotone. His sermons sometimes lasted two hours. He served as the pastor of Northampton Congregational Church for five years with few visible results. Nothing but the Holy Spirit's power can explain how the people of Northampton, Massachusetts, responded to Edwards' words in 1734.

In 1734 flashes of revival pierced the Northampton church's spiritual darkness. The Holy Spirit convicted and converted 300 church members. What they once believed in their heads became embedded in their hearts. "The Town," Jonathan Edwards wrote, "was never so full of Love, nor of Joy, and yet so full of distress, as it was then." This first wave of revival lasted only three years. Had it not been for a new movement in Europe, the Northampton revival would never have become known as "the Great Awakening."

### Revival in Europe—Pietism

In the late 1600s European Christianity wasn't in any better shape than American Christianity. God used a European movement known as *Pietism* [PI-eh-TIZM] to bring about a spiritual awakening that would reach around the world. Pietism began with a booklet entitled *Pious Desires* by Jacob Spener. The book urged Christians to pursue a personal relationship with Christ through intense meditation on the Scriptures.

Count Nikolaus Zinzendorf was a wealthy noble who lived on a spacious estate near Dresden, Germany, but most importantly, he was an ardent Pietist. Several nearby Catholic princes were still persecuting the Moravian Brethren, a small group of Bohemian Protestants known as the Moravians. One rainy evening in 1722 a Moravian refugee knocked on Zinzendorf's front door. He asked if Nikolaus Zinzendorf might shelter the flourishing Moravian movement. Nikolaus agreed. He helped the Moravians found a Christian community on his lands. They called their community "the Lord's watch" (or, "Herrnhut"). By 1725 nearly 100 Moravians had made Herrnhut their home.

### On The Web

Intrigued by Edwards? Check out . . .

*http://www. JonathanEdwards.com*

*Jonathan Edwards preached the most famous sermon of the Great Awakening, "Sinners in the hands of an Angry God."*

### Words: From The Ones Who Were There

*Jonathan Edwards*
"God seems now to be hastily gathering in his elect in all parts of the land. . . . Everyone that is out of Christ, awake and fly from the wrath to come. The wrath of Almighty God is now undoubtedly hanging over a great part of this congregation."
*Sermons, "Sinners in the Hands of an Angry God."*

## On The Web

Download pictures of Herrnhut from . . .

*http://www.mun.ca/rels/
morav/pics/pics.html*

## Think About It...

A few years after Herrnhut's prayer meetings began, the Great Awakening began in the American colonies. Coincidence or Providence? You decide.

## Did You Know?

Before Pietism, most churches sang only psalms. Nikolaus Zinzendorf, Charles Wesley, and Isaac Watts wrote Pietist hymns that remain popular today. Their hymns—like their theology—focused on the individual's relationship with Christ. In your church's hymnal, locate several songs written by Zinzendorf, Wesley, or Watts. Find one phrase in each song that reflects its Pietist origin.

*John Wesley*

(Courtesy of General Commission and
Archives of the United Methodist Church)

Count Zinzendorf joined the Moravians in 1727. His Pietism infused the Moravians with a passion for prayer. Under Zinzendorf's guidance, the Moravians began round-the-clock prayer meetings. "The sacred fire was never permitted to go out on the altar (Lev. 6:13)," the community declared, "so, the intercession of the saints should incessantly rise up to God." The Moravians at Herrnhut continued to meet for 24-hour prayer meetings for more than 100 years.

In 1731 Count Zinzendorf traveled to Denmark for an imperial meeting. There, he met an African slave and a group of Christian Eskimos. Hans Egede, a Lutheran missionary, had led the Eskimos to Christ. God used the African and the Eskimos to infuse Zinzendorf with a passion for missions. In less than a century, the pietist Moravians would send 300 missionaries throughout the world and baptize more than 3,000 converts.

So, how did Pietism affect the Great Awakening? In 1736 an Anglican priest was sailing to the colony of Georgia to witness to Native Americans. Suddenly, a storm struck the ship. Most passengers screamed in terror. But a band of Moravian Pietists calmly sang psalms. The priest was amazed. "This was," he wrote, "the most glorious day which I have hitherto seen." The priest's name? John Wesley.

A Moravian later asked John, "Do you know Jesus Christ?" John answered, "I know he is the Savior of the world." "But do you know he has saved you?" John stammered, "I hope he has saved me." "I went to America to convert the Indians," John wept, "but, oh, who shall convert me?" After two fruitless years in the American colonies, John Wesley returned to England.

When John Wesley was a child, his mother, Susanna, had preached "awakening sermons" in the Wesleys' home. "One Sunday," Susanna remarked, "we had above 200. Many went away, for want of room." Yet neither John nor his brother, Charles, trusted Christ alone for salvation.

In 1738 Charles Wesley trusted Christ as his Savior. Three days later, his brother John visited Aldersgate Street in London. He heard someone teaching from Martin Luther's commentary on Romans and began to listen intently. "About a quarter before nine," John wrote, "I felt my heart strangely warmed. I felt I did trust in Christ alone for salvation: And an assurance was given me, that he had taken away my sins, even mine, and saved me." This wasn't a case of heartburn. This was an awakening of the soul. This was conversion.

John and Charles Wesley had already organized Pietist societies (which they dubbed "Holy Clubs") within the Church of England. John urged members to seek God's presence through intense meditation on Scripture, fasting, and frequent participation in the Lord's Supper. John's well-ordered methods earned him the nickname "Methodist." The name stuck.

After John's conversion, his "Methodist" followers encouraged outdoor preaching crusades. One Methodist preacher was Sarah Crosby. Sarah crisscrossed England, preaching the gospel, for 20 years. When her health no longer allowed her to preach, Sarah established the "female brethren," a fellowship of women evangelists.

The most popular Methodist preacher, George Whitefield [WHITT-feeld], had been a servant at Oxford University, working to pay his tuition. When Charles Wesley recruited the cross-eyed young servant, Whitefield showed little promise. However, when the former servant arrived in America, no one could ignore him. By the time his preaching tours throughout the colonies ended, eight out of every ten American colonists had listened to George Whitefield. Thousands of people responded positively to his emotional pleas to accept Christ. When Whitefield preached in Northampton, Jonathan Edwards wept for joy. The response to Whitefield's messages was so amazing that people dubbed it the "Great Awakening."

For a few years, Whitefield and the Wesleys split over the doctrine of predestination. Whitefield was a Calvinist. The Wesleys' theology was closer to Arminianism than Calvinism. (If you can't define "Arminian" and "Calvinist," glance back at Chapter Nine.) Around 1749, Whitefield and the Wesleys agreed to disagree. Charles—always the poet—wrote, "Come, my Whitefield! (the strife is past)/And friends at first are friends at last."

Sadly, George Whitefield—unlike John Wesley—refused to condemn slavery. Whitefield did, however, preach to the African slaves. When Whitefield died, Phyllis Wheatley, an African-American poet, recalled: "He freely offer'd to the num'rous throng,/That on his lips with list'ning pleasure hung. . . . 'Take [Christ], ye Africans, he longs for you,/Impartial Savior is his title due.'"

Revival continued in the colonies until the 1750's. In frontier areas and among the lower classes, Baptist and Methodist congregations blossomed. However, as the colonies began their struggle for independence, decline pierced the churches again.

## TALKIN' 'BOUT POLITICAL REVOLUTIONS

### Revolution in the Churches, Churches in the Revolution

Religious rhetoric pervaded every stage of the colonial struggle for independence. If you don't believe me, pull a dollar bill from your purse or pocket. Assuming that three of your nation's initials are "U.S.A.," I can predict some of the words that appear on the back of your bill: "*Annuit Coeptis—Novus Ordo Seclorum.*" Or, "He has favored our enterprise—a new order now begins."

John Wesley strongly opposed the independence movement. He wrote, "I have no representation in Parliament, I am taxed, yet I am no slave. . . . Who then is a slave? . . . See the Negro,

*George Whitefield's preaching set the colonies ablaze with revival.*

*Some Methodist church leaders refused to ordain African-Americans as bishops. In 1816, Richard Allen formed the African Methodist Episcopal Church to give African-Americans freedom to serve as bishops.*

*(Courtesy of the Billy Graham Center Archives)*

## Think About It...

Many early Christians wanted to resist the Roman Empire—a pagan state in which they were taxed without representation. Read Matthew 22:17-21 and Romans 13:1-7. Should Christians ever revolt against their government? Why or why not?

## Did You Know?

After the War for Independence, the Anglican Church in America became known as the Episcopal—or, "Bishop-Guided" —Church.

fainting under the load . . . . You and I, and the English in general, go where we will and enjoy the fruit of our labors: this is liberty. The Negro does not: this is slavery." Anglicans, Mennonites, and Quakers also refused to support the war. They suffered dearly for their reluctance. Patriots "tarred and feathered" Americans who objected to the war. Many objectors lost their property. Several lost their lives.

Most church members, however, supported the revolution. Many American pastors deserted their emphasis on revival and focused on revolution instead. They used Israel's biblical battles as calls to fight the British. One pastor even proclaimed, "The cause of America is the cause of Christ."

Despite the patriotism in many pulpits, the religion of most of the founders of the United States was Deism, not Christianity. Thomas Jefferson called Jesus' miracles, "Vulgar ignorance . . . and fabrications." Benjamin Franklin remarked, "I have some doubts as to [Jesus'] divinity . . . and think it needless to busy myself with it." The Declaration of Independence refers to "Nature's God," a clear Deist title.

Still, Deists and Christians could agree on one issue: Religious faith is a personal issue. So, when the new nation molded a Bill of Rights, the third article declared, "Congress shall make no law respecting an establishment of religion, or prohibiting the free exercise thereof." Roger Williams' dream had finally been realized. A government had refused to tie itself to any religious faith.

## WHAT IS TRUTH?

A Roman ruler once muttered, "What is truth?" (John 18:38). It's still a popular question. One of today's most popular answers is, "The truth is whatever works for me." If something doesn't work for me, it must not be true. Or, at least, it must not be relevant.

That's what a lot of eighteenth-century people believed too. Ancient truths did not seem to be working. So, many people forged a new faith—and a false vision of God. They placed their trust in human reason and called themselves "Deists."

A few people, however, tried to let God's Word stand above every human idea and institution. Roger Williams and William Penn refused to tie the Christian faith to any human society. The Moravians begged for God's guidance, even when God seemed silent. Edwards and Whitefield continued to proclaim God's Word, even when it seemed uninspiring and irrelevant. When God's Word reigned supreme, people no longer needed to look for truth. "The way, the truth, and the life" revealed himself to them and revived their searching souls (John 14:6, 17).

# CHAPTER TEN LEARNING ACTIVITY

This quiz will help you review what you read in Chapter Ten. Fill in the blanks.

1. Under_____, Rhode Island became a haven for religious refugees.

2. The Massachusetts Bay Colony exiled _____ because of her unpopular views.

3. By contemporary standards, _____ would have been a boring speaker.

4. Count _____ started round-the-clock prayer meetings which the Moravian Brethren continued for more than 100 years.

5. Hundreds of people came to _____'s home, to hear her speak. One of her sons wrote more than 5,000 hymns.

6. _____ disagreed with the Wesleys about predestination.

7. _____ , the founder of the Methodist movement, opposed the Revolutionary War.

8. During the Great Awakening, _____ preached throughout England. Her preaching tours continued for 20 years.

9. Review the section entitled, "Talkin' 'Bout a Revolution in Human Reason." Look up "[the] Enlightenment" in an encyclopedia. Define the Enlightenment in your own words.

   _____
   _____
   _____

10. Review the sections that explain Deism. Name two ways that Deism differs from biblical Christianity. Find a Scripture that gives God's view of each difference. List the differences and the Scriptures below.

    A. _____
       _____

    B. _____
       _____

**Notes**

# WHAT YOU SHOULD KNOW ABOUT CHRISTIAN HISTORY
## AD 1780—1914

### Four Events You Should Know

1. *Publication of* **Critique of Pure Reason** (1781): According to Immanuel Kant's *Critique*, human reason can neither prove nor deny any spiritual reality, including the being of God.
2. *Formation of African Methodist Episcopal Church* (1816). Richard Allen, a free Black, formed the AME because some American Methodists refused to ordain African-American bishops.
3. *Five Fundamentals Declared* (1895): At a conference in Niagara the Evangelical Alliance, an association of conservative Christians, set forth five beliefs that they viewed as fundamental to their faith—the inerrancy of Scripture, and Jesus Christ's unique deity, virgin birth, substitutionary atonement, and future return.
4. *Boxer Rebellion* (1901): A Chinese political party reacted violently against foreign interference in China's national and cultural affairs. Many missionaries were murdered.

### Seven Names You Should Know

1. *G.W.F. Hegel* (1770-1831): German thinker. Taught that all ideas (theses), opposing opinions (antitheses), and debates (dialectics) are part of an upward process of intellectual evolution.
2. *Soren Kierkegaard* (1813-1855): Danish thinker. Emphasized subjectively experiencing God's revelation. Criticized coupling Christianity with any nation or culture.
3. *J. Nelson Darby* (1800-1882): Leader of the Plymouth Brethren, a Christian sect that stressed piety and simplicity. Taught a dispensational view of Scripture.
4. *Ralph Waldo Emerson* (1803-1882): Liberal philosopher and poet. Taught that "the highest revelation is that God is in every man."
5. *George Mueller* (1805-1898): Plymouth Brethren pastor and English social reformer. Founded orphanages that relied on Christians' gifts for support.
6. *Walter Rauschenbusch* (1861-1918): As a Baptist pastor in a New York slum, Rauschenbusch struggled to deal with social evils. He became the foremost proponent of the Social Gospel.
7. *Cyrus I. Scofield* (1843-1921): American lawyer. Wrote the study notes in the Scofield Reference Bible, which popularized dispensationalism among conservative Christians.

### Four Terms You Should Know

1. *Dispensationalism*: The belief that God's work can be divided into distinct eras (dispensations). Dispensationalism treats all biblical references to "Israel" as references to the earthly nation. Most dispensationalists also believe that Christians will be removed from the world ("raptured") before God judges the world. J.N. Darby and C.I. Scofield popularized this view.
2. *Covenantalism*: The belief that God's covenants with Israel are fulfilled in the church. Covenantalism treats most New Testament references to "Israel" as references to the church (see Rom. 9:6-7; Gal. 6:16). B.B. Warfield and J. Gresham Machen defended this view.
3. *Social Gospel*: A Protestant movement that stressed social reforms more than personal salvation.
4. *Holiness Movement*: A movement within Methodism that stressed a spiritual experience (a "second blessing") that leads to "entire sanctification" and "Christian perfection." Charles Finney spread Holiness ideas in America. A convention in Keswick, England, popularized the movement in Europe. In 1908 several Holiness groups merged to form the Nazarene Church. Modern Pentecostalism arose among Holiness Christians.

# Chapter Eleven

## OPTIMISM HAS ITS LIMITS

Every human heart longs for eternal satisfaction. The author of Ecclesiastes put it like this, "God has put eternity in their hearts" (Ecclesiastes 3:11). People try to satisfy their eternal longing with more possessions, more pleasure, more knowledge, more power—with everything except the living God. All that they find is more restlessness. For only God can satisfy their longings. "O Lord, you have made us for yourself," Augustine of Hippo wrote, "and our heart is restless until it finds its rest in you."

In the nineteenth century, humanity's restless longings drove society to a new level of progress. With the progress came optimism. In some ways, the optimism of the Modern Age made sense. Europe did not suffer a major war from 1815 until the beginning of the twentieth century. Mass production enabled people to purchase more possessions more cheaply. The train and the steamship conquered distance. Advances in farming diminished hunger. Medical discoveries reduced disease.

Yet the progress did not come cheaply. "It was," Charles Dickens observed, "the best of times, it was the worst of times." People became commodities, consumed in the name of modern progress. European and American settlers shoved the white man's burden into every corner of the globe. The dismal working conditions of the Industrial Revolution drove many people to despair. Still, people pressed on, optimistically believing that their efforts could calm humanity's restless heart.

## MODERN OPTIMISM AND THE MODERN MISSIONS MOVEMENT

### The Movement that Began in a Snuff Box

A few Christians turned the optimism of the Modern Age into a passion for missions. One of them was an Englishman named William Carey. When William was seven, a skin disease forced him to find indoor employment. He became a shoemaker.

William's cobbling skills were second-rate, but he had learned five languages. So, he opened a language school. Unfortunately, his teaching skills were third-rate.

Then, God called him to be a Particular Baptist pastor. But his preaching skills were worse than his teaching skills. Two years passed before his sermons reached the minimum acceptable level for ordination.

When he was 26, Carey chose an unthinkable challenge—changing the Particular Baptists' view of missions. He was abiding by words he would later preach: "Expect great things from God! Attempt great things for God!"

| In This Chapter AD 1780—AD 1914 |
| --- |

William Carey
Hudson Taylor
Barton W. Stone
Charles G. Finney
Charles H. Spurgeon
Dwight L. Moody

## Key Concept

Only God can heal humanity's restless heart.

## In Case You're Confused

The Modern Age lasted from end of the Enlightenment in the late 1700s until the mid-1900s. In the Modern Age, people emphasized human potential, progress, and the material world.

## In Case You're Confused

Because of their emphasis on the limited—or "particular"—extent of Christ's redemption, Calvinist Baptists were known as "Particular Baptists." In the 1700s many Particular Baptists decided if God had predestined who would be saved, evangelism was unnecessary. Particular Baptist churches declined sharply until Carey helped them recover their passion for missions.

*William Carey*
(Courtesy of Billy Graham Center Archives)

## Think About It...

Read 1 Samuel 3:11-14 and 1 Timothy 3:1-5. Is God pleased when ministers neglect their spouses or families for the church's sake? Does your church provide enough money and time for your missionaries' family lives? How about your ministers' needs?

*Damien, missionary to Molokai in the Hawaiian Islands, ministered to the spiritual and physical needs of 600 lepers and eventually contracted leprosy (Hansen's Disease) himself.*

Again, failure flagged Carey's footsteps. A fellow pastor bellowed, "When God pleases to convert the heathen, he'll do it without consulting you or me!" Carey's written reply argued that Calvinism and evangelism go hand-in-hand.

Finally, Carey succeeded. A dozen Particular Baptist ministers formed a cross-cultural missions society "according to [Carey's] recommendations." Each one made a pledge to support the missions society financially. They placed their pledges in a snuff box.

### "I can plod."

William Carey and a doctor volunteered to go to India. William's wife, Dorothy, and their children arrived the next year. Again, failure dogged William. The doctor pilfered their funds. Two of the Careys' children died. While William focused on missions, depression seized his wife. After seven years, William had baptized only one person in India.

Nevertheless, the cobbler's vision engulfed the world. What was his secret? "I can plod," he said. "I can persevere in any definite pursuit." Eventually, William Carey did translate and publish New Testaments in 24 of India's native languages. His work laid the foundation for thousands of future missionaries.

After William's death in 1834, Christian missionaries were sent into every corner of the world. Ann and Adoniram Judson continued William's work in India. John Veniaminou, an Orthodox priest, preached in Alaska. Damien, a Roman Catholic priest, cared for lepers in Hawaii and died of leprosy there. Another priest, Allemand Lavigerie, campaigned against slavery in Africa.

In 1860 Hudson and Maria Taylor founded the China Inland Mission. Both of them became "Chinese" to reach the Chinese. Hudson donned a black pigtail and baggy pantaloons. He also allowed single women to be missionaries. Hudson's fresh outlook opened doors for women like Lottie Moon and Amy Carmichael to spread the gospel in China and India.

Seventy-six years after William Carey's death, more than 1,200 missionaries from 160 mission boards met in Edinburgh, England. By that time, the number of Christians living outside Europe and the Americas had increased 1,000 percent. Not bad for a movement that started in a snuff box. ·

## MODERN OPTIMISM AND THE AMERICAN FRONTIER

People on the American frontier also embraced the optimism of the Modern Age. Some folk were so optimistic that they embraced *universalism*—the belief that God will never condemn anyone. The result was spiritual darkness. Around 1800 many American Christians began to seek a renewed vision of the true God. The Presbyterians set aside days for prayer. They begged God to redeem their nation from darkness. In 1801 in Kentucky, God began to answer their prayers.

## The Cane Ridge Revival

Last weekend, I risked my life for Christ's sake. I spent three days at a youth retreat. (If you've ever driven a van full of eighth-graders, you know what I'm talking about.) The singers and speakers at Young Christians' Weekend were contemporary. The retreat was, however, rooted firmly in the "camp meetings" of the 1800s.

When nineteenth century folk gathered for a camp meeting, they set up tents near a church on Thursday or Friday. For two days, they sang and listened to speakers. On Sunday, anyone with a communion token—granted by one's church—could share the Lord's Supper. The camp meetings were intended to provide Christian fellowship and spiritual renewal for frontier church members.

In 1801 all heaven broke loose at a camp meeting in Cane Ridge, Kentucky. Rev. Barton W. Stone expected fewer than 10,000 campers; 20,000 Presbyterians, Baptists, and Methodists arrived. On Saturday someone fell to the ground during a sermon and began to beg for God's grace. Other campers lurched and laughed hysterically. (Critics claimed that they "barked.") Hundreds of pioneers dropped to their knees and asked for God's mercy. The Second Great Awakening had begun. For 30 years, revival fires glimmered across America.

What happened at Cane Ridge, Kentucky? Critics called it a mass emotional outburst. "As many souls were conceived at the camp meetings," one person quipped, "as were saved." Were some antics bogus? Maybe. Yet what would cause hundreds of hardened pioneers to fall on their faces, weeping in repentance? What . . . besides that Spirit who bursts into human self-satisfaction to convey God's word of judgment and grace?

*By the 1800s missionaries were building missions throughout the American West. This Kansas mission was a center for Baptist work among the Pottowatomi Native Americans.*

## On The Web

Intrigued by the Restoration Movement? Check out . . .

http://www.mun.ca/ rels/restmov/

## Do We Really Need Denominations?

After the Cane Ridge camp meeting, Barton W. Stone took nineteenth century optimism to a new level. He became convinced if Christians forsook everything but the Bible, they could restore New Testament Christianity. Stone joined a band of former Baptists, led by Alexander Campbell. The Stone-Campbell Restorationists urged believers to call themselves only "Christians" or "Disciples." "Where the Scriptures speak," they claimed, "we speak. Where the Scriptures are silent, we are silent."

The Restorationists' goal was to fulfill Jesus' prayer that all believers would be brought to complete unity (John 17:23). They urged Christians to forsake all denominational loyalties and to unite on the basis of Scripture alone. Despite their desire for unity, the Restorationists soon dissolved into dozens of sects. Still, the movement left a lasting mark in at least one area: It weakened the grasp of older denominations and religious

*Nineteenth-century sod house in the American Midwest. During the Second Great Awakening, Methodists used "circuit-riding preachers" to minister here, along the sparsely populated American frontier.*

## Did You Know?

America's distaste for older religious traditions led some people away from Christianity. In Joseph Smith's Book of Mormon, America stood at the center of God's plans. Native Americans were, Smith claimed, displaced Israelites. Jesus would return to Independence, Missouri. In Nauvoo, Illinois, Smith declared himself "King of God's Kingdom." After a mob murdered Smith, Brigham Young led the so-called "Latter-Day Saints" to Utah.

## Think About It...

Do people in your church pray simply and spontaneously? Sponsor week-long revivals? Urge new converts to "walk the aisle?" If so, Finney's "New Measures" affect your church. What do you think of his "New Measures"? Is revival a human act or a divine act? Can Christians become perfect in this life?

## On The Web

Learn more about Finney's theology at . . .

*http://www.gty.org/~phil/articles/finney.htm*

traditions on American Christians. The Restorationist legacy lingers today in the Churches of Christ, Disciples of Christ, and Christian churches.

### God's Lawyer

One key figure in the Second Great Awakening was an aspiring lawyer named Charles G. Finney. A teenaged girl named Lydia Andrews met Charles in 1820. She quickly saw that he wasn't a Christian. So, she began to pray for his salvation. A year later, God answered Lydia's request. Finney decided one morning that he would find God's grace that day or die trying. Amid the autumn leaves of a New York forest, Charles G. Finney became a Christian. Little did Lydia know that the reply to her prayers would revolutionize American religion.

The day after he accepted Christ, Charles began preaching. As he left his law practice, he remarked to a client, "I have a retainer from the Lord Jesus Christ to plead his cause, and I cannot plead yours." Charles' high pressure performances soon erupted across America. Three years later, Lydia Andrews married Charles Finney. Lydia was shy. She struggled throughout her life with a poor self-image. Still, she traveled with Charles and led prayer vigils during his revivals.

Reason-centered optimism ruled Charles' theology. For him, revival wasn't a miracle. "Revival," he contended, "consists entirely in the right exercise of the powers of nature." Finney's so-called "New Measures" included pressuring people not to leave his meetings until they were sure of their salvation. Seekers walked the aisles and sought salvation on "anxious benches" (areas near the platform set aside for prayer and counseling). So optimistic were Finney's beliefs that he taught that Christians could become morally perfect in this life.

Many of Finney's beliefs contradict historic Christian theology. Still, some of his practices can be respected. For example, Finney never divorced evangelism from social reform. Many churches charged "pew rent" (yearly fees for attending church). Finney openly embraced all people, rich and poor. When Finney was president of Oberlin College, African-Americans and women attended the same classes as white males. The college later became a station on the Underground Railroad.

## MODERN OPTIMISM AND THE RISE OF MODERN THEOLOGY

### A Boring Book and a New Theology

Do you suffer from insomnia? I possess the perfect panacea—the *Critique of Pure Reason*, by Immanuel Kant. Try to read the German philosopher's *Critique* and you will sleep—guaranteed.

If you aren't an insomniac, let me summarize Kant's *Critique* in two sentences: Reason can grasp anything within space and time. Beyond space and time, reason is useless. What's wrong with Kant's ideas? God surpasses space and time. So, if Kant was correct, reason would be unrelated to Christian faith. Christianity would affect only what we do and feel—not what we think.

A few years after the *Critique* was published, another thinker echoed Kant—Friedrich Schleiermacher [SHLI-err-MAW-kerr]. Schleiermacher argued that the core of Christian faith is not any historical event, such as Jesus' resurrection. It is, instead, an awareness of one's dependence on God; this awareness leads a person to imitate Jesus' good deeds. "The true nature of religion is," Schleiermacher claimed, "immediate consciousness of the Deity as found in ourselves and in the world." The resulting vision of God was closer to the Force of *Star Wars* than to the God of the Bible. Schleiermacher's new focus earned him the title "the father of modern theology."

Today, the idea that religion is primarily a matter of feelings still affects churches—even conservative churches. You don't believe me? Let's take a field trip into the present. A few years ago, my brother-in-law served as the pastor of a rural congregation in Elm, Missouri. Even in Elm, you can find traces of Schleiermacher and Kant in things as simple as Gothic windows, emotional hymns, and the proportion of women to men.

### A Field Trip into the Present

Look at the windows of Elm Spring Baptist Church. The sides curve inward to form points at the top. They are *Gothic windows*. Gothic designs first appeared in medieval cathedrals in the 1100s. In the 1800s, Gothic motifs became popular again, especially in church buildings, replacing the "classical" architectural styles of the Renaissance era. When the people at Elm, Missouri, designed their church building in the late 1800s, they followed a popular trend.

Why did medieval designs become popular in the 1800s? Nineteenth-century folk wanted feelings to fuel their Christian faith. Many people viewed the Middle Ages as a romantic era of pure feelings. So, they revived designs and motifs from the Middle Ages.

Follow me through the front doors of Elm Spring Baptist Church. Do you hear the congregation singing a nineteenth century hymn? "The great Physician now is near, the sympathizing Jesus;/He speaks the drooping heart to cheer, Oh! hear the voice of Jesus." Do you hear the echoes of Schleiermacher? Do you hear the emphasis on feeling God?

Look at the congregation. There are more women than men. Why? I really don't know—but it could be because of a nineteenth-century assumption. In the 1800s, many people assumed that women were more emotional than men. If religion was an emotional matter, religion must be the woman's realm. The result was a double standard. Society winked at men behaving badly and expected women to remain pure-minded and religious. Today, women still outnumber men in many churches.

## Think About It...

Are religious emotions wrong? No, not as long as Christians balance their emotional experiences with solid, biblical theology.

*Nineteenth century church buildings, like Elm Spring Baptist Church, revived Gothic motifs.*

## In Case You're Confused

The barbarian Goths migrated into the Roman Empire in the early Middle Ages. Late medieval cathedrals were called "Gothic" because they blended barbarian ideals with classical Roman designs. The nineteenth-century "Gothic Revival" (also known as "Romanticism") popularized Gothic designs again.

## Did You Know?

"A.W. Pugin claimed that you could not convert England to Christianity with pagan, by which he meant classical, architecture. For the Houses of Parliament he designed Gothic inkwells, thus encouraging parliamentarians to write their letters in a Christian frame of mind, or at least a Christian frame of ink. There were Gothic railway stations, Gothic prisons, Gothic bakeries and Gothic horse troughs, though no Gothic horses."
*From Gavin White,* How the Churches Got to Be the Way They Are *(Philadelphia: Trinity Press, 1990) 13-14.*

## MODERN OPTIMISM AND THE QUEST FOR THE HISTORICAL JESUS

Friedrich Schleiermacher, the father of modern theology

Schleiermacher's new focus also encouraged *higher criticism.* Higher critics tried to reconstruct the various sources that biblical authors might have used. In the process, many higher critics began to question the Bible's accuracy. After all, if faith was—as Kant and Schleiermacher implied—only a matter for people's emotions, couldn't the Bible be merely a record of ancient people's feelings about God?

Some higher critics became convinced that the Gospel-writers didn't write about the real, flesh-and-blood Jesus Christ (the "historical Jesus"). Instead, the Gospel-writers described how the stories of Jesus transformed the early Christians' lives. According to these critics, Jesus' miracles were legends, not historical events. Jesus' death was an example, not a sacrifice. What was revived on Easter was the disciples' love for Jesus, not Jesus himself.

For these critics, all that mattered were Jesus' teachings about divine love and social reform. The essence of Christianity was, one liberal theologian claimed, "the universal fatherhood of God, the brotherhood of man, and the infinite worth of the human soul." The higher critics' search became known as "the quest for the historical Jesus." In the 1990s several liberal scholars formed the "Jesus Seminar" and revived the nineteenth-century quest for the historical Jesus.

## MODERN OPTIMISM AND SOCIAL REFORM

### The Era of Reform

A very contemporary world usually surrounds my writing. Today, however, I am surrounded by a 1562 edition of Calvin's *Institutes,* an original Geneva Bible and an 1856 printing of *Pilgrim's Progress.* What encompasses me is the library of a nineteenth-century English pastor named Charles H. Spurgeon.

It was in Spurgeon's era that many postmillennial Christians began to ask, "How can we create God's millennium when workers are exploited and Africans are enslaved? How can Christ's kingdom come while orphans roam the streets?" Those questions, asked in the midst of the Industrial Revolution, turned the 1800s into an era of social reform.

In the late 1700s Robert Raikes had started Sunday schools to educate urban children in Britain. In the 1800s the concept of Sunday schools spread to the United States. Charles Sheldon's book *In His Steps* urged Christians to express their faith through social action. Angelina and Sarah Grimke crusaded for women's rights. William Wilberforce, an evangelical Anglican and a member of Parliament, worked to outlaw slavery in Britan. Catherine and William Booth organized the Salvation Army. Wealthy British evangelicals founded the YMCA. In the process, some church

Charles H. Spurgeon (1834-1892) became a pastor at age 17 and in 1854 was called to New Park Baptist Church in London. His Metropolitan Tabernacle became one of the largest houses of worship in Europe, seating 6,000 people.

### On The Web

Take a virtual tour of Spurgeon's library at . . .

*http://www.spurgeon.org/ fsl.htm*

members allowed their emphasis on social reforms to overwhelm their concern for evangelism. This tendency became known as the "Social Gospel."

Charles H. Spurgeon, pastor of the Metropolitan Tabernacle in London, was one preacher who balanced social reform with an emphasis on evangelism. He was a postmillennialist. He denounced American slavery. He founded schools, orphanages, and nursing homes. During a strike, Spurgeon took the workers' side.

At the same time, Spurgeon never believed that social reforms were enough. For Spurgeon, social reform was meaningless without sound theology and a personal relationship with Christ. Every Sunday, more than 6,000 people packed the London Metropolitan Tabernacle to hear Spurgeon's homespun metaphors and his passionate pleas for persons to accept Christ.

### The Scratch of Slavery

An African-American Christian named Isabella became a resounding voice for social reform in the United States. Isabella had been a slave in the southern United States. She gained her freedom around 1843. Afterward, she became convinced that Christ was calling her to "travel up and down the land, showing the people their sins." She changed her name to fit her mission. Throughout the northern United States, "Sojourner Truth" preached about slavery and salvation. In one city, a man snarled, "I don't care any more for your talk than I do for the bite of a flea." "Perhaps not," Sojourner replied, "but, Lord willing, I'll keep you scratching."

Sojourner's messages were so well-crafted that some people denied she was a woman. Others doubted that she had ever been a slave. Still, she kept Americans "scratching"—chafing at the sins of sexism and slavery.

## MODERN OPTIMISM AND THE COMING KINGDOM

### Miller's Mixed-Up Mathematics

While Sojourner kept America scratching, other preachers kept America unstrung. William Miller, a self-proclaimed biblical scholar from Vermont, claimed Christ would return by March 21, 1844. Spring, 1844, passed without a peep from Gabriel's trumpet. Miller decided he had made a mathematical mistake. Christ would return, Miller claimed, on October 22, 1844. Again, nothing happened. (A New York farmer did later claim that he saw a vision of the Second Coming on October 22.)

Even after this double disappointment, a few people remained convinced by Miller's math. One of them was a nineteen-year-old woman named Ellen G. H. White. Ellen prophesied that one reason Christ hadn't returned was because Christians were not obeying God's Old Testament laws. Her Sabbath-keeping followers became known as "Seventh-Day Adventists."

## In Case You're Confused

In the 1800s most Christians were postmillennialists. They believed Jesus would return after (post-) God's people initiated God's kingdom. Premillennialists believe Jesus will return before (pre-) the kingdom begins. Some premillennialists believe God will "rapture" Christians out of the world before a time of tribulation. Amillennialists believe the kingdom exists here and now, among God's people.

*Read one of Sojourner Truth's sermons at. . .*

*http://eserver.org/race/ aint-i-a-woman.txt*

*(Courtesy of Leib Image Archives)*

## Did You Know?

William Miller wasn't the only one who expressed his optimism through bizarre prophecies. Charles Taze Russell claimed that Jesus returned spiritually in 1872. Russell's followers (now known as "Jehovah's Witnesses") revived the Arian heresy. Mary Baker Eddy claimed that Christ returned around 1875, through her Gnostic-flavored writings. She founded the Christian Scientists.

## The American Civil War

After a stock market crash in 1857, a Third Great Awakening began in Canada and swept England and America. Prayer revivals, led by a Methodist laywoman named Phoebe Palmer, became popular in the northeastern United States. Yet nothing could divert the coming conflict over American slavery. On the eve of the war, Methodists, Presbyterians, and Baptists all suffered internal splits over the slavery issue.

Throughout the Civil War, Americans on both sides assumed that God supported their cause. A southern pastor claimed, "The Confederacy will be the Lord's peculiar people." A Union victory, a northern writer contended, would unleash the "millennial glory."

Few Americans realized that God's kingdom does not depend on human triumphs or defeats. One of them was an unbaptized politician who never joined a church. "Each party claims to act in accordance with the will of God," he noted. "Both may be, and one must be, wrong. . . . It is quite possible that God's purpose is something different from the purpose of either party." The politician's name? Abraham Lincoln.

After the Civil War southern farmers freed four million slaves. This newfound freedom could not, however, erase centuries of racism. Slavery lingered for over a century under new names—names like "sharecropper," "slums," and "Jim Crow laws."

## THE OPTIMISM UNRAVELS

In the late 1800s the optimism that had marked the Modern Age began to unravel. Liberal churches had reduced the Christian faith to a "Social Gospel." Conservative church members saw that social reforms were not enough. Yet they couldn't agree on an alternative. Some church leaders, like D.L. Moody and Pope Pius IX, tried to resist and reject the modern world. Others, like B.B. Warfield, tried to express their faith in ways that a modern world could understand.

### Resisting the Modern Age—Pope Pius IX

By the middle of the nineteenth century, modern people's mistrust of ancient powers had sapped the pope's religious and political powers. Pope Pius IX was slow to accept such changes. He denounced the idea that "the Roman pontiff should harmonize himself . . . with recent civilization."

In 1854 Pius IX defied attempts to limit his authority in doctrinal matters. He decreed the doctrine of the Immaculate Conception—the tradition that Mary was free from original sin. Many Catholics questioned the new dogma. They were not protesting the doctrine itself. What they questioned was whether a pope could define a doctrine without a church council's consent. In other words, was the pope infallible when he defined a doctrine? Or, could only a council claim that the Holy Spirit preserved its decrees from error?

*Americans on both sides of the Civil War assumed that God supported their cause.*

### Did You Know?

Lyman Beecher, a Congregational pastor, sent rifles to anti-slavery forces in the Midwestern United States. The weapons were shipped in crates marked "Bibles;" so, the rifles became known as "Beecher's Bibles." Beecher's daughter wrote the book *Uncle Tom's Cabin*.

### Did You Know?

In 1847 Missouri outlawed African-American schools inside the state's borders. John Berry Meachum, a Black Baptist, conducted Sunday school on a steamboat, in the Mississippi River near St. Louis. For nearly 20 years, Black children learned to read on Meachum's "Steamboat Sunday School."

The pope convened a council to answer the question. In 1869 more than 500 bishops gathered at the Vatican. The First Vatican Council lasted nearly a year. Near the end, Pope Pius IX joked, "If the council lasts much longer, I shall doubtless be infallible, but I shall also be bankrupt!"

In the end, the doctrine of the Immaculate Conception was confirmed, and the bishop of Rome was declared infallible—but only when he "defines a doctrine . . . by the Divine assistance promised to him in the blessed Peter." Even with the power of infallibility, a pope can only redefine the *outward expressions* of the Catholic Church's faith. No pope or council has the power to change any essential doctrine of the Church.

### Rejecting the Modern Age—Dwight L. Moody

Dwight L. Moody arrived in Chicago as a teenaged shoe salesman with a very modern goal—making money. He was a backwoods bumpkin with a fifth grade education and lots of energy. He had been a Christian less than a year. In only five years, he saved $7,000. Then, a financial panic rocked his plans. Moody went from selling shoe soles to winning people's souls. He began to witness full-time.

In 1871 a fire destroyed large portions of Chicago, including Moody's home. Instead of lamenting his loss, D.L. Moody headed across the Atlantic Ocean, to preach in Britain. There, another preacher remarked, "The world has yet to see what God can do with a man fully consecrated to him." Those words lit a blaze in Moody's soul.

The next year, Ira Sankey, a singer and composer, joined Moody for a revival tour. Moody aimed his simple sermons at the middle class—a class that also enjoyed Sankey's singing. In Great Britain alone, four million people flocked to the Moody-Sankey revivals.

D.L. Moody ignored modern scholarship and rejected theological studies. "Except to go in one door and out the other," he once boasted, "I've never been to seminary." For Moody, the Bible was a source of simple quotes, treated without reference to their contexts. He traded the optimistic post-millennialism of previous generations for a more pessimistic view of the world. His sole focus was soul-winning. "The world [is] a wrecked vessel," he once said, "God has given me a lifeboat and said, 'Moody, save all you can.'"

### Redeeming the Modern Age—*The Fundamentals*

One of the wisest responses to the Modern Age arose at a Bible conference in Niagara, New York. There, several conservative Christians listed five truths that they believed were basic (or, "fundamental") to the Christian faith. The five truths were: (1) Jesus was uniquely divine, (2) born of a virgin, (3) died as a sacrifice for sin, and (4) will come again. And, (5) the Scriptures contain no errors; the Bible is "inerrant."

*Some members of the Women's Christian Temperance Union, including Carrie Nation, were known to burst into saloons with hatchets, attempting to rid their communities of alcoholism.*

### Did You Know?

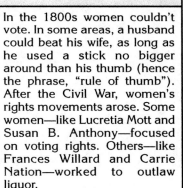

In the 1800s women couldn't vote. In some areas, a husband could beat his wife, as long as he used a stick no bigger around than his thumb (hence the phrase, "rule of thumb"). After the Civil War, women's rights movements arose. Some women—like Lucretia Mott and Susan B. Anthony—focused on voting rights. Others—like Frances Willard and Carrie Nation—worked to outlaw liquor.

### Did You Know?

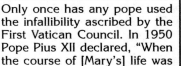

Only once has any pope used the infallibility ascribed by the First Vatican Council. In 1950 Pope Pius XII declared, "When the course of [Mary's] life was finished, she was taken up body and soul into glory."

*Dwight L. Moody*
*(Courtesy of Billy Graham Center Archives)*

*During the American Civil War, Moody worked as a chaplain. After battles, Moody wandered the fields, witnessing to wounded soldiers on both sides who had not accepted Christ.*

## Did You Know?

Ira Sankey popularized a blind poet's hymns. The poet's name? Fanny Crosby. Locate several songs in your church's hymnal that were written by Crosby or Sankey. Imagine how each song might have been used in Moody's crusades.

## On The Web

Study *The Fundamentals* for yourself at . . .

*http://www.xmission.com/ ~fidelis*

After the conference, a Christian entrepreneur financed a series of pamphlets that defended the five basic beliefs. The pamphlets contained articles written by prominent Christian scholars. The pamphlets were called *The Fundamentals.* Persons who accepted the five basic beliefs became known as "fundamentalists." Like Moody, the authors of these pamphlets believed in the absolute authority of Scripture. Unlike Moody, they believed that faith in the accuracy of Scripture could go hand-in-hand with serious theological scholarship.

The pamphlets did not try to fight against every aspect of the Modern Age. Some of the writers were post-millennialists; others were pre-millennialists. Three authors in the first volume of *The Fundamentals* believed that God created the earth through evolution. B.B. Warfield, a major contributor to the pamphlets, declared, "I do not think that there is any general statement in the Bible . . . that need be opposed to evolution." Most of the authors even embraced the modern world's optimistic confidence in human reason and progress. It would take an economic depression and two world wars to shake that confidence.

## CHAPTER ELEVEN LEARNING ACTIVITY

This quiz will help you review what you read in Chapter Eleven. Fill in the blanks.

1. List two words that describe the 1800's:
   (a) _____ (b) _____

2. How does Matthew 28:19-20 relate to William Carey?
   _____
   _____

3. How does 1 Corinthians 9:20-23 relate to Hudson and Maria Taylor? _____
   _____

4. How does John 17:20-21 relate to the Stone-Campbell Restoration Movement?_____
   _____

5. How does James 5:16 relate to Lydia Andrews and Charles Finney? _____
   _____

6. List one word that describes the teachings of Kant and Schleiermacher. _____
   _____

7. How does Mark 13:30-32 relate to William Miller and Ellen G. H. White? _____
   _____

8. List the five fundamental beliefs that were affirmed at the 1895 Bible conference. Locate a Bible verse that relates to each one. (a) _____
   (b) _____ (c) _____
   (d) _____ (e) _____

Special thanks to the Partee Center for Baptist Historical Studies and the Spurgeon Library at William Jewell College for providing lodging, research facilities, and access to Spurgeon's archives while I completed this chapter.

# WHAT YOU SHOULD KNOW ABOUT CHRISTIAN HISTORY
## AD 1906—1999

### Four Events You Should Know

1. *Azusa Street Revival* (1906): William Seymour, a Black Holiness preacher, founded a mission on Azusa Street in Los Angeles. There, many people began to speak in "unknown tongues." The Pentecostal movement is still growing today.
2. *Edinburgh Conference* (1910): More than 1,200 delegates gathered for this missions conference. The gathering helped trigger the modern ecumenical movement.
3. *Wycliffe Bible Translators Organized* (1934): Cam Townsend founded this organization to translate the Bible into other languages. By 1980, the Bible was translated into more than 1,600 languages. Translation continues.
4. *Dead Sea Scrolls Discovered* (1947): A shepherd-boy found the earliest known copies of the Jewish Scriptures at Qumran, near the Dead Sea. The scrolls verified that modern copies of the Hebrew Bible were nearly identical to ancient copies. Take a virtual tour of Qumran at <http://www.mustardseed.net/html/pqumrand.html>.

### Seven Names You Should Know

1. *Charles Fox Parham* (1873-1929): Holiness preacher. Taught that speaking in "unknown tongues" was the sign of the "second blessing." One of his students was William Seymour.
2. *Teilhard de Chardin* (1881-1955): Controversial Catholic theologian and scientist. Taught that all life is a process that will eventually be drawn into God's being. For Teilhard, God is both the goal of this process and the power within the process. Teilhard influenced the beliefs that became known as "process theology."
3. *Albert Schweitzer* (1875-1965): Theologian, musician, and missionary doctor. Schweitzer criticized the "quest for the historical Jesus." At the same time, he argued that Jesus mistakenly expected the immediate end of the world.
4. *Paul Tillich* (1886-1965): Liberal Lutheran theologian. Tried to bridge the gap between modern culture and Christianity by adapting the Christian faith to modern people's questions.
5. *Harry Emerson Fosdick* (1878-1969): Liberal Baptist pastor. His sermon "Shall the Fundamentalists Win?" questioned the inerrancy of Scripture and the Virgin Birth.
6. *Bob Pierce* (1914-1978): Evangelical leader. Founder of World Vision and Samaritan's Purse.
7. *Hans Kung* (1928-): Controversial Catholic theologian. In the late 1960s he questioned the extent of the pope's power. His license to teach as a Catholic theologian was withdrawn in 1979.

### Four Terms You Should Know

1. *Fundamentalists*: Originally referred to people who accepted the five fundamental beliefs (see Chapter Eleven). By the 1950s the term referred to conservative Christians who focused on precise personal standards and on separation from every hint of liberalism.
2. *Theological Liberals*: Persons who altered Christian theology to fit the outlook of the Modern Age by separating Christian theology from traditional doctrines and biblical texts.
3. *Evangelicals*: Originally synonymous with "fundamentalists." During the 1950s the term "evangelical" replaced "new [or, neo-] evangelical" as a description of believers who emphasized Christian unity, the unique authority of Scripture, salvation by grace through faith, and evangelism.
4. *Post-Modernity*: The world-view that arose at the end of the Modern Age. The Modern Age lasted from the late 1700s until the mid-1900s. Modernity stressed words, reason, and the material world. Post-modernity emphasizes personal experiences and the spiritual realm.

# Chapter Twelve

## FROM MODERN TO POST-MODERN AND BEYOND

You can approach twentieth-century church history in one of two ways: Read a drawn-out history text and—if you're still awake—try to fit your faith into its framework. Or, follow me on a typical Wednesday. The people you meet (and the ones you don't) will teach you a lot about Christianity in the twentieth century.

When I served as a pastor in rural Missouri, several local pastors gathered every Wednesday morning to study Scripture. Follow me into one of those Bible studies, and we'll learn about our contemporary Christian heritage together. Trinity Lutheran Church is hosting today's study. Soon, an Episcopalian, a Disciple of Christ, a Roman Catholic, and a Baptist join me and the Lutheran pastor. Jeff, the Presbyterian pastor, is predestined always to arrive late. Sometimes, some Methodists show up. But, lately, their free wills have kept them home. It's a fairly diverse group. Still, some people are missing. Believe it or not, church history can help you understand the people you meet as well as the ones you don't.

### THE ORTHODOX CHRISTIANS

Worldwide, 140 million people belong to Orthodox churches, but most of them live in Russia and eastern Europe. The closest Orthodox church to my home in central Missouri was two hours away. That may be why no Orthodox priest has ever attended Wednesday Bible study.

Why hasn't Orthodoxy flourished outside its native lands? A quick look at a map partly answers the question. For 500 years, Muslims controlled the lands where Orthodoxy thrived. The influence of Islam limited the Orthodox Church's chances to expand beyond eastern Europe and Asia Minor.

### The Rise of Communism

The Russian Orthodox Church remained untouched by Islam. However, in the early twentieth century a new form of religious oppression arose in Russia, further limiting the church's opportunities to expand. Between 1917 and 1922, Russia became a Communist country. Vladimir Lenin was the first dictator of Communist Russia. Lenin's theology was simple, "Even flirting with the idea of God is unutterable vileness." Under Lenin, Russian Orthodoxy lost its status in Russian society. Tikhon, the Orthodox patriarch of Moscow, denounced Lenin's policies. In the fury that followed, Lenin's followers executed 28 patriarchs and 1,000 priests. The persecution worsened under the next dictator, Josef Stalin.

| In This Chapter |
| --- |
| AD 1906—AD 1999 |

Karl Barth
C. S. Lewis
Charles Fox Parham
Dietrich Bonhoeffer
Second Vatican Council
Mother Teresa
Billy Graham

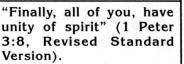

**Key Concept**

"Finally, all of you, have unity of spirit" (1 Peter 3:8, Revised Standard Version).

## On The Web

Does Russian Orthodoxy intrigue you? Check out the Russian Orthodox Church's web-site,

*http://www.russian-orthodox-church.org.ru/en.htm*

*The Church of the Resurrection of Christ, a Russian Orthodox Church in St. Petersburg, Russia.*

## Words: From The Ones Who Were There

*H. Richard Niebuhr, American theologian*
Describing nineteenth century liberal theology . . .
"A God without wrath brought men without sin into a kingdom without judgment through . . . a Christ without a cross."
*The Kingdom of God in America, 193.*

Later, Communist officials forced Christian families to live in low-quality housing. Children of Christians were often placed in low-quality schools. Churches that weren't native to Russia, such as Baptists and Pentecostals, endured even harsher persecution. To survive the Communist onslaught, the Russian Orthodox Church appointed leaders who were willing to work with the Communist government. Not until the fall of Russian Communism in the early 1990s could Christianity grow freely in Russia. Even after the fall of Communism, government leaders have attempted to limit the expansion of Christianity in Russia, especially among evangelical believers.

### Russian Orthodoxy After the Fall of Communism

Yesterday morning, I ate breakfast with a Baptist pastor from Belarus. I asked Aleksandr about the Russian Orthodox Church. His reply echoed the feelings of many Russian Protestants: "For hundreds of years, the Orthodox Church was part of the government. Russia's spiritual emptiness led to atheism. There are true Christians in the Orthodox Church. But, in Russia, Orthodoxy is fading. The future of Russian Christianity is with the evangelical churches."

Despite Aleksandr's analysis, at the close of the 1990s, the Orthodox Church is expanding. Perhaps, in the 2000s, Orthodoxy will find a renewed future beyond its ancient borders. And maybe, one day, an Orthodox priest will find a place in our Bible study.

### "HOW DOES THE TEXT APPLY TO YOU?" WHY?

Wednesday morning Bible study followed a fairly standard pattern. One pastor had been chosen to study the weekly Scripture passages. That person shared the context and the historical background with the rest of us. Then, we talked about how each text pertained to our parishioners' lives. We tried very hard to blend the application of the text with its historical context. Even if we didn't realize it, we weree partly indebted for this pattern to a twentieth-century pastor named Karl Barth [BART].

### How Barth's Teachers Got Bombed

When World War I erupted, Karl Barth was the pastor of a small church in Safenwil, Switzerland. Karl Barth's professors, well schooled in nineteenth century theological liberalism, had trained Barth how to dissect Bible verses and find their historical contexts. What they never taught him was how God's Word could touch ordinary people's lives. They had divorced the Bible's historical context from its significance in people's lives.

As a pastor, Barth became frustrated with his professors' methods. He struggled to prepare sermons that addressed his people's spiritual needs. He complained that it was difficult for graduates of liberal schools "to undertake activity in the pulpit or at the sick-bed."

In 1914 a statement that supported Germany's war policy surfaced in Switzerland. Nearly all of Barth's professors had signed the statement. Barth was appalled. "Nineteenth-century theology," Barth later recalled, "no longer held any future for me." In despair, Barth turned to the Bible. In the past, he had read the Bible as a human religious record. Now, he read the Bible as God's Word, addressed to himself. He tried to blend the historical context of each Scripture with its application in his own life.

In 1919 Barth's *Romerbrief* (commentary on Romans) introduced his new approach to pastors throughout Europe. Among pastors willing to forsake theological liberalism, the result was a renewed focus on God's power and grace.

In his zeal to abandon theological liberalism, Barth argued that nothing within creation reveals God. (Remember, nineteenth century liberal theology had urged people to find God within creation and in their own feelings.) Alone, even the words of Scripture are not God's Word. Why? According to Barth, God's Word isn't a concept that human words can convey or control. God's Word is a living event, expressed supremely in Jesus Christ. Barth believed that the Bible *becomes* God's Word when the Holy Spirit reveals Jesus through Scripture.

Barth's emphasis on Scripture and on God's sovereignty echoed the sixteenth century reformers. At the same time, some aspects of Barth's thinking differed from historic Christian theology. So, his approach became known as "neo-Reformation" or "neo-orthodox" theology.

In the late 1800s and early 1900s, liberal theologians, intoxicated by the optimism of the Modern Age, had stressed humanity's ability to create a perfect world. During World War I, the same progress that had created new medicines and motor-cars also mass-produced mustard gas and machine guns. Ten million soldiers died on the battlefields of Europe. Europe's modern optimism died there too.

## DEFENDING THE FUNDAMENTALS

More than a few ministers near my central Missouri home described themselves as "fundamentalists." Yet none of them ever showed up at Wednesday morning Bible study. A glance at America in the 1920s may help you understand why.

For liberal Americans, the World War I had been a chance to "make the world safe for democracy." For many conservative Americans, the war had been a crusade against liberal German theology. Yet World War I didn't destroy liberal theology, and the world became less safe instead of more. Still, the carnage never touched North America. So, fragments of modern optimism remained in the United States.

## Words: From The Ones Who Were There

*Karl Barth*
Criticizing the "God" of nineteenth-century theology . . .
"[This deity] isn't even righteous. He cannot prevent his worshipers, . . . , from falling upon one another with fire and sword . . . It is time for us to confess openly and gladly that this god, to whom we have built the tower of Babel, is not God. He is an idol. He is dead."
*Das Wort Gottes und die Theologie*, 22.

## Did You Know?

Fragments of modern optimism persisted in the United States until the Great Depression began in 1929. During the Depression, an American pastor named Reinhold Niebuhr employed Barth's theology to find a halfway point between liberalism and fundamentalism. Niebuhr also wrote the famous Serenity Prayer: "Lord, give us serenity to accept what cannot be changed, courage to change what should be changed, and wisdom to distinguish the one from the other."

*Parsonage where Richard and Reinhold Niebuhr were born in Wright City, Missouri.*

## In Case You're Confused

"Fundamentalist" originally referred to anyone who accepted the five fundamental beliefs. After World War I, many conservative Christians added other beliefs, such as premillennialism and a rejection of evolution, to the five fundamentals.

After World War I, The fragments of optimism drove some Americans toward a frenzied pursuit of pleasure. This was the era of jazz and flappers, of short skirts and speakeasies. Many women adopted the same relaxed sexual standards as men. Other Americans immersed themselves in moral crusades to recognize women's right to vote and to outlaw alcoholic beverages. When Prohibition was approved, Billy Sunday, a fundamentalist evangelist, preached a public funeral for "John Barleycorn" (his name for drunkenness). Yet Prohibition couldn't keep John Barleycorn in the grave. And, in 1920, women and men alike chose one of America's most corrupt leaders as president. Something was seriously wrong in America.

## Looking for the Problem

If something is wrong, people naturally look for the problem. Usually, it's easier to locate one problem than to admit there might be several problems. During the 1920s many conservative Christians became convinced that liberalism was *the* problem in America. These "fundamentalists" separated themselves from every notion that had any links with liberalism.

Liberals had been postmillennialists; fundamentalists were premillennialists. Liberals tended to be educated; fundamentalists rejected theological training. (Billy Sunday boasted, "I don't know any more about theology than a jack-rabbit knows about ping-pong!") Liberals relished Darwin's theories; fundamentalists rejected all forms of evolution—even though several authors of *The Fundamentals* pamphlets had accepted God-guided evolution. (If you don't recall *The Fundamentals*, glance back at Chapter Eleven.) In 1925 fundamentalists in Tennessee convinced their state legislature to pass the Butler Act, "prohibiting the teaching of the Evolution Theory in all public schools of Tennessee."

## "The Monkey Trial"

That summer, the evolution debate became a nationwide media melee. John Scopes was a first-year football coach in Dayton, a small town in rural Tennessee. Occasionally, Scopes taught freshman biology. After the Butler Act passed, a few citizens in Dayton wanted to make their town famous. They convinced Scopes to say he might have taught that apes and people sprang from a common ancestor. He was charged with violating the Butler Act. In July, 1925, his case went to trial.

The trial should have been open-and-shut; Scopes himself said he had violated the Butler Act. But Clarence Darrow, a well-known liberal lawyer, became Scopes' attorney. Three-time presidential candidate William Jennings Bryan offered to prosecute Scopes. The presence of two famous lawyers drew more than 1,000 spectators into the sweltering courthouse. It was a made-for-TV trial. (Unfortunately, TV hadn't been invented yet. So, folk settled for a radio broadcast.)

*In the 1920s, fundamentalism thrived in the churches in Midwestern and Southern United States.*

On day five, Darrow placed Bryan on the witness stand. Darrow asked, "Do you claim that everything in the Bible should be literally interpreted?" Bryan replied, "I believe everything in the Bible should be interpreted as given there. Some of the Bible is given illustratively."

Darrow began to prod Bryan about the earth's age. "Does the statement 'The morning and the evening were the first day' mean anything to you?" Bryan said, "I do not think it necessarily means a 24-hour day. . . . My impression is that they were periods." Darrow tried to force Bryan to state the length of the "periods." Finally, Bryan bellowed, "The only purpose Mr. Darrow has is to slur the Bible!" Darrow retorted, "I object! I am examining you on your fool ideas that no intelligent Christian on earth believes!"

Clarence Darrow didn't want Bryan to deliver a closing statement. So, Darrow himself asked that Scopes be found guilty. Eight minutes later, the trial was over. John Scopes was convicted of violating the Butler Act. William Jennings Bryan offered to pay the football coach's $100 fine.

After the trial, many fundamentalists forsook Bryan. Why? They believed that creation had occurred in six 24-hour days. Bryan took Scripture seriously, but during the trial he had stated that the "days" of creation were probably long time-periods. Five days after Scopes' conviction, William Jennings Bryan died.

Fundamentalist tensions soon split both the Northern Baptist Convention and the Northern Presbyterian Church. Many fundamentalists formed their own denominations and organizations, separate from other Christians.

## Fundamentalism Does the Splits

In the 1940s some fundamentalists began to question fundamentalism's focus on total separation from the modern world. These fundamentalists would become known as the "new evangelicals" (or, "neo-evangelicals") and eventually, simply as "evangelicals." (Before this time, "fundamentalism" and "evangelicalism" had referred to the same group.)

In October, 1941, several new evangelicals gathered at Moody Bible Institute to form the National Association of Evangelicals (NAE). "We will not be," the chairperson declared, "negative or destructive." And they weren't. Fundamentalism had focused on separation and precise personal standards. The NAE was willing to listen to anyone who embraced salvation by grace through faith in Christ.

The new evangelicals soon realized that their evangelical ties meant more than their denominational titles. So, they formed interdenominational fellowships, like Youth for Christ, InterVarsity Christian Fellowship, and Campus Crusade for Christ. The writings of C.S. Lewis, a British Christian, encouraged many new evangelicals to think deeply about their faith.

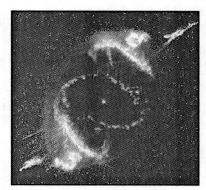

*Seventy-five years after the "Monkey Trial," how God created the world is still a weighty issue for Christians.*

### Words: From The Ones Who Were There

"At the best, Mr. Darrow's agnostic views completely disqualify him to represent any but the most extreme antagonists of the Bible. . . . There is a convincing argument for the conservative position, but Mr. Brady . . . has neither the mind nor the temper for the task."
*The Christian Century*, Editorial on the Scopes trial, 1925.

### Think About It...

To learn more about C.S. Lewis, watch the movie *Shadowlands*. Then, check out the Internet links at . . .

*http://www.scriptorum.org/1/links.html*

## Words: From The Ones Who Were There

*Billy Graham*
Reflecting in 1998 on his early ministry . . .
"I preached Americanism too much. . . I began to realize we are not the kingdom of God. . . The real kingdom is the kingdom of believers."
"People were ready for a message that pointed them to stability and lasting values. In the providence of God, we were able to take advantage of the spiritual hunger."
*"Withholding judgment." USA Today. (2/5/1998): D-1.*
*Just As I Am, 729.*

An evangelistic meeting in Los Angeles in 1949 catapulted new evangelicalism into international renown. The speaker was a 31-year-old college president named William F. Graham. Few non-Christians attended the meetings at first. Then, a popular radio host interviewed Graham. By the campaign's final night eight weeks later, 11,000 people packed the tent. Billy Graham was a celebrity.

Some fundamentalists criticized Graham's willingness to work with Roman Catholics and liberal Protestants. Strong fundamentalists like John R. Rice and Bob Jones soon separated from the "neo-evangelicals."

An emphasis on separation still characterizes fundamentalism today. Still, many Christians—both fundamentalists and non-fundamentalists—look forward to the day when all Christians "reach unity in the faith and in the knowledge of the Son of God" (Ephesians 4:13).

## THE PENTECOSTAL POWER

Each Sunday more than 240,000 people attend Yoido Full Gospel Church in Seoul, South Korea, the world's largest church. Their congregation is part of a movement that involves more than 100 million people worldwide. They are the Pentecostals.

### From Topeka to Azusa Street and Throughout the World

Modern Pentecostalism arose within the Holiness branch of American Methodism. Holiness Christians had emphasized a spiritual experience—a "second blessing"—that led to "Christian perfection."

In 1900 Charles Fox Parham, a Holiness evangelist, who earlier had been miraculosly healed, founded a Bible college in Topeka, Kansas. Parham taught his students that "speaking with other tongues" should accompany the second blessing. He based his belief on what happened to early Christians on Pentecost (Acts 2:1-20).

After searching the scriptures independently, all forty students concluded they had been missing the complete power of the Holy Spirit. On January 1, 1901, one of Parham's students began to speak in a language unknown to them. (One linguistics expert later said that the language sounded similar to Mandarin Chinese.) Eventually nearly all the students received other languages and many went as missionaries to other countries.

Five years later, Parham's views weren't just in Kansas. William Seymour, a Black Holiness preacher who had been a student of Parham's, preached the Pentecostal message at the Apostolic Faith Gospel Mission on Azusa Street in Los Angeles. Many of his hearers also began to speak in unknown tongues.

Soon, hundreds of Holiness Christians were flocking to Azusa Street to experience "baptism with the Holy Ghost." Many of them returned to their churches with the message that speaking

*Charles Fox Parham*
*(Courtesy of Mrs. Les Hromas)*

in tongues should accompany the second blessing. In 1914 the Assemblies of God, the first Pentecostal denomination, merged several Pentecostal groups.

How did other Christians respond to the Pentecostals? Throughout the 1910s and 1920s, people in both groups hurled thoughtless criticisms at one another. Some non-Pentecostal Christians called Pentecostal worship "hell hatched free lovism." They ridiculed Pentecostals who were poor and uneducated. A few Pentecostals seemed to think that their "Holy Ghost baptism" placed them above other believers. These attitudes led to mutual mistrust between some Pentecostals and non-Pentecostals.

Despite criticisms from non-Pentecostals, Pentecostal churches grew. The greatest expansion didn't occur near the movement's birthplace, though. Pentecostalism has expanded most rapidly in Africa, Asia, and Latin America.

*The modern Pentecostal movement began here, at the Apostolic Faith Gospel Mission.*

### Christian Faith Beyond Europe and North America

In Africa in 1915 Simon Kimbangu became a popular healer and preacher. Six months after his ministry began in Zaire, he was imprisoned on false charges of treason. Even though Kimbangu died in prison, his African Independent Church became one of the world's fastest growing Christian denominations. By 1990 Kimbangu's followers numbered more than seven million.

In China, "Watchman" Nee Duosheng emphasized miraculous healings. In India, Sundar Singh's ministry began with a dazzling vision. Singh's wealthy father disowned him. So, Singh became a *sadhu*—a wandering preacher—in southern Asia.

In Latin America, Pentecostalism grew swiftly among lower-class Latinos. Today, the two largest Latino congregations in the world are both Pentecostal.

**Did You Know?**

Several women, including Aimee Semple McPherson and Kathryn Kuhlman, earned prominent places in Pentecostal pulpits. McPherson popularized the "Foursquare Gospel": Jesus is the Savior, Healer, Baptizer, and Bridegroom.

## LUTHERANS AND CATHOLICS TOGETHER! HOW?

### Bill and Ken's Ecumenical Adventure

Bill was a Roman Catholic priest. Ken was a Lutheran pastor. For many years after Martin Luther nailed his theses to the Wittenberg chapel door, Lutherans and Catholics didn't play well together. Yet, every week, Bill and Ken studied the Bible together at our Wednesday Bible study.

Obviously, something significant happened between the Reformation and Wednesday Bible study. Part of that "something" was the ecumenical movement—a movement within the church that sought to unite all Christians in a spirit of unity. The ecumenical movement tried to take seriously Jesus' plea, "I pray . . . for those who will believe in me . . . , that all of them may be one" (John 17:20, 21).

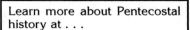

**On The Web**

Learn more about Pentecostal history at . . .

*http://www.oru.edu/ university/library/holyspirit/ pentorg1.html*

## On The Web

Read about the World Council of Church's contribution to the ecumenical movement at. . .

*http://www.wcc-coe.org/ wcc/who/histor-e.html*

*Dietrich Bonhoeffer*
(Beverly Hall, Artist)

## On The Web

Learn more about Bonhoeffer's life and beliefs at . . .

*http://www.dbonhoeffer.org*

## Words: From The Ones Who Were There

*The Confessing Church*
"Jesus Christ, as he is testified to us in Holy Scripture, is the one Word of God, whom we are to hear and whom we are to trust and obey in life and death. We deny the false teaching that the church can . . . recognize any . . . truths as divine revelation alongside this one Word of God."
*The Barmen Confession.*

## Trying to Be One

The contemporary ecumenical movement began in 1910 at a missions conference in Edinburgh, Great Britain. After the conference, an Anglican invited "all churches which accept Jesus Christ as God and Savior to join . . . for the consideration of all questions pertaining to Faith and Order." When the "Faith and Order" Conference met after World War I, delegates claimed that they achieved 85 percent agreement on doctrinal issues.

In 1925 ninety-one liberal groups took a different approach. Their "Life and Work" Conference focused on social reform. "Maybe," they seem to have thought, "if we downplay doctrine, we can achieve complete unity." In 1938 the "Faith and Order" and "Life and Work" Conferences merged to form a provisional World Council of Churches (WCC). Their plans for union were suspended the next year when World War II erupted in Europe.

## To Identify With the Oppressed

A famous politician campaigned for family values in the 1930s. He condemned homosexuality, pornography, and Communism. Baptist World Alliance delegates declared, "He gives to the temperance movement the prestige of his personal example since he neither uses intoxicants nor smokes." German Protestants formed a Christian coalition to support him. The politician's name? Adolf Hitler. Hitler planned to turn Europe into an invincible empire, ruled by a race of physically flawless Germans ("Aryans"). In the process, he helped to trigger World War II. Few Christians resisted Hitler at the time. One resister was a young Lutheran named Dietrich Bonhoeffer [BONN-hoh-ferr].

As a seminary student in Berlin, Bonhoeffer had been deeply influenced by Karl Barth, who was now a theology professor in Germany. As a student pastor, Bonhoeffer involved himself in the growing ecumenical movement. In 1928 he moved to New York to attend Union Theological Seminary. At first, American preaching disgusted Bonhoeffer. "One may," he wrote, "hear sermons . . . on almost any subject; only one is never handled: . . . the gospel of Jesus Christ." Then, Bonhoeffer went to an African-American church in Harlem. Amid people depressed by poverty and prejudice, he heard the gospel that he hadn't heard from upper-class pulpits. He also realized that to be like Jesus was to identify with the oppressed (Isaiah 53:3-5). A year later he wrote, "I became a Christian."

## The Struggle for Costly Grace

While Bonhoeffer was in New York, Hitler tried to merge all German Protestants into one pro-Nazi denomination. However, in 1934, five thousand Christians, including Karl Barth, gathered in Barmen, Germany, to protest the denomination's Nazi policies.

Their Barmen Confession promised total obedience to God's Word, even if it meant disobeying Hitler. The signers became known as the "Confessing Church."

When he returned to Germany, Bonhoeffer founded a seminary for the Confessing Church. There, he wrote *The Cost of Discipleship*, a bold attempt to apply the Sermon on the Mount to the twentieth century.

By the mid-1930s Hitler's claws had begun to clench the Confessing Church. The state commanded professors to pledge allegiance to Hitler. Karl Barth balked. The Nazis deported him. Next, the state required pastors to pledge allegiance to Hitler. Despite Bonhoeffer's objections, even the Confessing Church did not protest this requirement.

In 1938 a 17-year-old Jewish boy shot a minor German official. It was the excuse that Hitler was awaiting. In one night, the Nazis killed or imprisoned more than 30,000 Jews. Hundreds of homes and synagogues were destroyed. Bonhoeffer was the only Christian who publicly protested the massacre. Bonhoeffer declared, "Only the one who protests on the Jews' behalf has a right to sing [Christian hymns]!"

A few Christians—including Magda and Andre Trocme and Corrie ten Boom—risked their lives to rescue Jews during World War II. Pope Pius XI's letter "With Burning Sorrow" protested some of Hitler's crimes. A Catholic document entitled "The Ten Commandments as Laws of Life" indirectly criticized the Holocaust. Pope Pius XII also sheltered Jewish refugees in the Vatican. Yet most church members, Protestant and Catholic, ignored Hitler's atrocities.

### The Cost of Discipleship

To protect Bonhoeffer, an American theologian named Reinhold Niebuhr secured a teaching post for him in the United States. Bonhoeffer accepted the position, but he couldn't escape what he had learned in Harlem: To be a Christian was to identify with the oppressed. Bonhoeffer wrote to Niebuhr, "I shall have no right to participate in the reconstruction of Christian life in Germany after the war if I do not share the trials of this time with my people."

When he returned to Germany, Bonhoeffer involved himself in a plot to assassinate Adolf Hitler. In 1943 the Gestapo jailed Bonhoeffer for smuggling Jews out of Germany. The next year, the assassination plot failed. The Gestapo found Bonhoeffer's name in the plans to kill Hitler. Bonhoeffer was placed in the Flossenberg concentration camp. On April 5, 1945, Hitler decreed his death.

Three days later, Bonhoeffer preached a short sermon to his fellow prisoners. Gestapo agents burst through the doors before the service ended. "Bonhoeffer!" they barked. "Come with us!" Bonhoeffer whispered, "This is the end—for me, the beginning—of life."

### Words: From The Ones Who Were There

*Dietrich Bonhoeffer*
"Cheap grace is our church's deadly enemy. . . Costly grace is the gospel which must be sought again and again . . .. Such grace is costly because it costs one's life; it is grace because it leads to the only true life. . . Above all, it is costly because it cost God his Son's life. . . Above all, it is grace because God did not reckon his Son to be too dear a price to pay for our life."
*Nachfolge*.

### In Case You're Confused

In 1965 Time magazine asked, "Is God dead?" What prompted such a bizarre cover story? In a few letters, Bonhoeffer had mentioned the "death of God." What he meant was that— because modern science can explain many mysteries that earlier people ascribed to God— *the concept of God as nothing more than an explanation for the universe's mysteries* was "dead." The death of that concept should (Bonhoeffer argued) free people to pursue a real relationship with God. In the 1960s several theologians distorted Bonhoeffer's words and argued that *the biblical concept of God* was "dead."

## Words: From The Ones Who Were There

*Martin Niemoller,*
*Confessing Church leader*
Admitting his failure to resist the Nazis adequately . . .
"First, they came for the socialists, and I did not speak out because I was not a socialist. . . . Then, they came for the Jews, and I did not speak out because I was not a Jew. Then they came for me, and there was no one left to speak for me."

## Did You Know?

Here are some key results of Vatican II:

*Session One*: Allowed translation of Mass into native languages. Urged laypeople to study Scripture. Stated that Scripture is the primary source of divine truth. Declared that all Christians—not just priests, monks, and nuns—are called by God to be God's people.

*Session Two*: Created a college of bishops to assist the pope.

*Session Three*: Non-Catholics "are not deprived of significance ... in the mystery of salvation." Mary must "never take away from... Christ the One Mediator." Discouraged praying to saints.

*Session Four*: "In matters religious no one is to be forced [by one's government] to act in a manner contrary to one's own beliefs."

The next morning, Dietrich Bonhoeffer knelt and prayed beside the gallows. The camp doctor commented, "I have hardly ever seen a man die so entirely submissive to God's will." Four weeks later, the Allied forces were victorious. Three months after Hitler's defeat, the atomic bomb ended the war and hurled humanity into the nuclear age.

## A New Beginning: The Ecumenical Movement After World War II

Throughout the war, members of the German Confessing Church had supported the ecumenical movement. After World War II, the leaders of the Confessing Church met with the provisional World Council of Churches. Their purpose? To admit their failures during the war and to be reunited with their fellow Christians. "We blame ourselves," the Confessing Church declared, "that we didn't witness more courageously, pray more faithfully, believe more joyously, love more ardently. . . . We rejoice deeply in this new beginning, in which we know ourselves to be warmly tied to the other churches of the ecumenical fellowship."

Three years later, Orthodox, Anglican, and other Protestant delegates gathered in Amsterdam to form the World Council of Churches. At first, some Orthodox Christians refused to join the WCC because the council did not require belief in the Trinity. In 1961, the WCC redefined itself as "a fellowship of churches which . . . seek to fulfil together their common calling to the glory of one God, Father, Son, and Holy Spirit." This change brought more than 30 million Orthodox Christians into the ecumenical movement.

## The Updating: Roman Catholics at the End of the Twentieth Century

For most of the twentieth century, Roman Catholics remained outside the ecumenical movement. In 1958 John XXIII became pope. Most people did not expect the 76-year-old to live long or do much. Pope John XXIII didn't live long, but he did a lot.

Previous popes had condemned all Protestants; John XXIII called Protestants "separated brothers." He sent observers to the World Council of Churches. He was responsive to how the world had changed in the past century. His linguists received requests that no previous pope had even imagined—like finding a Latin word that means "rotor-blade." (The pope wanted to bless a helicopter.)

Many Catholics assumed that, because the First Vatican Council had ascribed infallibility to the pope, there would never be another church council. Pope John XXIII disagreed. In 1962 he gathered more than 2,500 cardinals, bishops, and abbots for the Second Vatican Council. Over 500 of the delegates were Africans and Asians. The key word at the Vatican II was *aggiornamento*—"updating the outward forms." John XXIII died after the first session. The next pope, Paul VI, continued the council. Between 1962 and 1965 the council gathered four times.

The council's final declaration was a joint statement from Pope Paul VI and Patriarch Athenagoras of Constantinople. The Roman Catholic Church and the Orthodox Church finally forgave each other for the schism of 1054, when each church had condemned the other. The two leaders declared that they "regret the offensive words [that] . . . accompanied the sad events of this period. They likewise . . . remove . . . the sentences of excommunication."

*Saint Peter's Basilica at the Vatican*

In 1978 Pope John Paul II became the first non-Italian pope in 456 years. He was from Poland. John Paul II described himself as the "universal pastor." He lived up to his title by traveling throughout the world. In 1979 he visited eastern Europe, his homeland. "Holy Spirit," he prayed, "renew this land." Ten years later, the Roman bishop's prayer was answered. The destruction of the Berlin Wall marked the collapse of Communism in eastern Europe. In 1997 Pope John Paul II officially apologized for his church's "lack of moral leadership" during the Holocaust.

In the 1990s, Pope John Paul II declared his determination to lead the Roman Catholic Church beyond the year 2000. "If the Lord were to call him home now," one Catholic leader quipped in 1999, "he'd have one upset man on his doorstep." Despite failing health, John Paul II did continue to guide Roman Catholics into the third millennium.

Despite the changes made by Vatican II, many aspects of Catholic teaching remained untouched at the end of the twentieth century. An emphasis on righteous works as part of salvation lingered. Pope John Paul II has repeated his church's bans on women priests, married priests, and artificial forms of birth control. Nevertheless, a fresh wave of openness continues to sweep the Roman Catholic Church. That's why a Lutheran and a Catholic can study Scripture together today.

## EVANGELICALISM TODAY

After Wednesday Bible study ended each week, we discussed the day's most pressing theological issue: Where should we eat lunch? Our eating preferences differed sharply—but that was okay because, when it came to issues that really mattered, we usually agreed. ... One word that united most of us was "evangelical." Despite our differences, nearly all of us called ourselves "evangelical Christians."

## Did You Know?

Two twentieth-century Catholics inspired the world with their passion for the poor. Dorothy Day founded the Catholic Worker farm communes. Mother Teresa, an Albanian nun, devoted her life to the and poor lepers of India.

## On The Web

To understand the Evangelicals and Catholics Together controversy, browse this site—
*http://www.leaderu.com/ect/*

## Evangelicalism—From 2:00 a.m. to *Christianity Today*

Around 2:00 a.m. one morning in 1953 Billy Graham had a great idea. His idea would help draw together English-speaking evangelicals throughout the world. "I wish we could," he commented, "start a magazine . . . from an evangelical viewpoint . . . [that would] avoid extremes." Three years later, the magazine *Christianity Today* rolled off the presses. Nearly 50 years later, *Christianity Today* continues to provide a forum for thoughtful, evangelical dialogue.

In 1974, Graham chaired the International Congress on World Evangelization in Lausanne, Switzerland. In the Lausanne Covenant, evangelical Christians affirmed that "evangelism . . . summons us to unity" and urged Christian missionaries to respect native cultures.

As evangelicalism grew, so did the differences between fundamentalism and evangelicalism. Some fundamentalists focused their efforts on fighting new versions of the Bible, rock music, and contemporary fashions. Others tried to balance faithfulness to Scripture with openness to fresh ideas. Some of these new ideas included easy-to-read Bibles, contemporary Christian music, and—in the mid-1990s—a willingness to dialogue with Roman Catholics.

### Evangelicals and Catholics Together

In 1994 forty Catholic and evangelical leaders signed a statement entitled, "Evangelicals and Catholics Together: The Christian Mission in the Third Millennium" (ECT). The ECT statement called for Catholics and evangelicals to cooperate on social issues. The statement also emphasized the beliefs that evangelicals and Catholics share, such as the Apostles' Creed and "justification by grace through faith because of Christ."

Supporters of the ECT statement included Charles Colson, Bill Bright, J.I. Packer, Elizabeth Achtemeier, and Richard John Neuhaus. Several respected evangelicals—including R.C. Sproul, John MacArthur and D. James Kennedy—criticized the statement. Critics of the ECT statement argued that the statement ignored the Protestant belief in "justification by grace alone through faith alone."

Three years later, the supporters of the ECT statement issued a second statement, "The Gift of Salvation." This statement dealt directly with the issue of justification. In "The Gift of Salvation," a group of evangelical and Roman Catholic theologians agreed that "justification is not earned by any good works or merits of our own; it is entirely God's gift . . . . The gift of justification is received through faith." The same year, several Lutheran groups officially approved a Joint Declaration on the Doctrine of Justification. According to the Joint Declaration, "By grace alone, in faith in Christ's saving work and not because of any merit on our part, we are accepted by God."

*In 1973 Billy Graham preached to 1.1 million Koreans, the largest crowd in history.*

(Courtesy of Billy Graham Center Archives)

## Words: From The Ones Who Were There

Timothy George,
*Evangelical leader*
Supporting the statement "The Gift of Salvation" . . .
"We sense the urgency in our Lord's high-priestly prayer for all his disciples—'that they may all be one . . . so that the world may believe that Thou hast sent me' (John 17:21). True Christian unity, we believe, is not so much a goal to be achieved as a gift to be received."
*"Evangelicals and Catholics Together: A New Initiative."* Christianity Today (12/8/1997): 34-35.

## Key Concept

"Finally, all of you, have **unity of spirit**" (1 Peter 3:8, Revised Standard Version).

# THE DAWN OF POST-MODERNITY

How often have you heard the terms "Generation X" and "post-modern"? How often have you wondered, "What is 'Generation X,' anyway? And what does it mean to be 'post-modern'?" Near the end of the 1990s both terms have been commonly used and rarely understood. Yet post-modernity will profoundly affect the future of Christianity.

Between the 1950s and the 1990s it became clear that a new world view was emerging. The end of World War II had plunged America into an era of wealth. On the surface, America seemed wealthy and free. Yet, beneath the surface, America's past was catching up with the present. American soldiers from every race had experienced equal pay and equal pain during the war. At home, racism still reigned.

In the late 1950s, Martin Luther King, Jr., a Baptist pastor, inspired Black and White Americans to oppose America's prejudice peacefully. Soon, Baby Boomers were protesting racism, patriotism, clean clothes, and most other things that their parents accepted, including traditional views of God and the church.

What was happening? The Great Depression and two world wars had buried the optimism of the Modern Age. So, a new, narrower optimism had emerged. At first, people focused on themselves. They placed their faith in sexual freedom, and found AIDS. They placed their faith in mighty armies and found massive debt. They placed their faith in money and found that savings and loans sometimes loan more than they save. In this context, a new world view arose—*post-modernity.* "Generation X" was the first post-modern generation.

Positively, the post-modern world view prompts people to look at life from more than one angle. Negatively, the post-modern outlook encourages the notion that truth is relative.

Twenty-first century Christians must acknowledge that the post modern world-view is partly correct: Words and logic can't explain everything; feelings and personal experiences are important; and, sometimes, more than one view may be valid. At the same time, personal experiences and feelings must never overrule the eternal Word of God.

## Did You Know?

Christians who introduced Pentecostal ideas in non-Pentecostal churches became known as Charismatics (from *charisma*, the Greek word for spiritual gifts). The Charismatic Movement reflected many post-modern concerns. In post-modern thinking, words and institutions obstruct as much meaning as they convey. So, post-modern people welcomed worship that transcended words and logic. The "Jesus Movement" spread Charismatic ideas among youth.

## In Case You're Confused

Post-modernity is the world-view that arose at the end of the Modern Age. The Modern Age lasted from the late 1700s until the mid-1900s.

### Modern emphasis

One logical viewpoint
Words and reason
The individual mind
Progress toward the future

### Post-Modern emphasis

Many possible viewpoints
Personal experience
The whole self, in
  community with others
Satisfaction here and now

# CHAPTER TWELVE LEARNING ACTIVITY

This "Who Am I?" exercise will help you recall what you learned as you read Chapter Twelve.

1. When the Russian Revolution occurred, we lost our special status. Who are we? _____

2. When I saw my professors' names on a statement that supported World War I, I forsook liberal theology. Who am I? _____

3. I guided a seminary for the Confessing Church. Hitler himself decreed my death. Who am I? _____

4. I was a popular fundamentalist evangelist. When Congress prohibited alcoholic beverages, I preached a funeral for "John Barleycorn." Who am I? _____

5. I prosecuted John Scopes in the famous "Monkey Trial." Who am I? _____

6. Our movement began in Kansas and spread to Azusa Street in Los Angeles. Who are we?

   _____

7. I was a 76-year-old Italian cardinal when I became pope. I convened the Second Vatican Council in Rome. This council urged Roman Catholics to study the Bible. Who am I? _____

8. I asked God's Spirit to heal my homeland. Ten years later, Communism collapsed. Who am I? _____

9. Delegates from Orthodox, Anglican, and other Protestant churches joined to form our ecumenical group. Who are we?

   _____

10. I was a founder of *Christianity Today*. I have been called "the best-known and best-loved American Christian." Who am I?

    _____

11. Check out the movie *Inherit the Wind* from your library or video store. The movie depicts the "Monkey Trial" of 1925. The movie changes several key facts and scenes. (Bryan becomes "Brady"; Darrow becomes "Drummond"; Scopes becomes "Cates.") Still, it's a useful resource to help Christians think about their beliefs. If possible, download a review from <http://www.firstthings.com/ftissues/ft9702/iannone.html>. After watching the movie, reread the section entitled "The Monkey Trial." How did the movie help you understand American fundamentalism in the 1920s?

    _____

12. Define "post-modernity" in your own words:

    _____

# Epilogue

## FINAL REFLECTIONS

"After supper she got out her book and learned me about Moses and the Bulrushers," Huckleberry Finn recalled after his time with Widow Douglas, "and I was in a sweat to find out all about him; but by and by she let it out that Moses had been dead a considerable long time; so then I didn't care no more about him, because I don't take no stock in dead people."[1] Neither do most Christians. Yet "dead people" form the heart of Christian history. "We are," the author of Hebrews remarked, "surrounded by such a great cloud of witnesses" (Hebrews 12:1). The Apostles' Creed echoes, "I believe . . . in the communion of the saints." When Christians gather, it isn't only the living who are present. By some means that transcends human understanding, the saints of the past—Huck Finn's "dead people"—are present too. Like a cloud, Blandina and Athanasius, Francis of Assisi and Catherine of Sienna, Kaetie Luther and D.L. Moody surround us. Their presence points us toward Jesus Christ, "the author and perfecter of our faith" (Hebrews 12:2).

Together, the saints of the past and present form a living house for the living God (Hebrews 3:6). Christ is its unchanging cornerstone (1 Peter 2:5-7). Through their testimony about Jesus, the apostles supplied a foundation (Revelation 21:14). Yet the walls are still growing, and what Christians do today decides the shape of tomorrow's walls (1 Corinthians 3:9-17).

"In the history of the church the old may suddenly become new," Gavin White has noted, "and the new may suddenly become old. What seemed to be permanent often fades away, and what seems to have faded is there after all. The church is pushed this way and that by waves and by winds, and yet it never quite goes on the rocks. Henry Scott Holland described it in 1914 when the Bishop of Zanzibar wrote a pamphlet asking where the church stood. Scott Holland said it did not stand at all, but 'moves and pushes and slides and staggers and falls and gets up again, and stumbles on and presses forward and falls into the right position after all'. That is church history."[2]

## Words: From The Ones Who Were There

*J. I. Packer*
"It will be sad if zeal for inerrancy entrenches a wholly backward-looking bibliology. Fruitful questions thrown up in the liberal camp . . . await evangelical exploration . . . The battle for the Bible must continue as long as unbelieving babble about the Bible continues, but . . . the best defense of any doctrine is the creative exposition of it."
"Battling for the Bible." *Regent College Bulletin* 9 (Fall 1979).

## Think About It...

In the space below, list any significant events that have happened in Christian history since this book was written. Then, write your own ending to the church's story.

---

1. Mark Twain, *The Adventures of Huckleberry Finn* (New York:Grosset and Dunlap, [n.d.]) 2.

2. Gavin White, *How the Churches Got to Be the Way They Are* (Philadelphia: Trinity Press, 1990) 120.

# Leader's Guides

Group sessions are approximately 40-60 minutes long (90 minutes if you show a video). Suggested times are for a 6-12 person group. If you use a video, show only a 15-30 minute portion that clearly portrays a central point of the chapter.

## INTRODUCTORY SESSION OF CHRISTIAN HISTORY MADE EASY

### Session Goals
This session will help students:
• understand why Christians should study church history.
• recognize that this study will be taught on their level.
• recognize that this study will be applicable to their lives.

### Supplies
One large piece of poster-board or shelf paper for a sign

1. **Preparation**
   • Ask God to guide you throughout the session.
   • Have a textbook and a *Christian History Time Line* pamphlet for each student.
   • Carefully read "Why Does Church History Matter?" in the textbook.
   • Study Introductory Learning Activity.
   • Make a sign that reads: *CHURCH HISTORY IS YOUR FAMILY HISTORY.* Hang it wherever your group will meet.
   • Select songs for the session. Consider choosing a theme song for the entire study, such as, "O God, Our Help in Ages Past," "Word of God, Across the Ages," "Faith of Our Fathers," "For All the Saints," "God of Grace and God of Glory," or "The Church of God, in Every Age."

2. **Before the Session**
   • As students enter, hand out the textbooks and pamphlets.
   • Ask students to complete Introductory Learning Activity as other students arrive.

3. **Worship—*4-6 minutes***
   After everyone arrives, sing the theme song. Or, sing another appropriate song, such as, "The Church's One Foundation."

4. **Learning Activity—*12 minutes (or) 30-40 minutes***
   Have students locate Introductory Learning Activity. Tell them the answers to the questions. Discuss the answers. Never let them feel ignorant, even if their answers are incorrect.
   **ANSWERS: 1**-Peter, **2**-Houses, **3**-Constantine, **4**-Chrysostom, **5**-Hildegard, **6**-Wycliffe, **7**-Luther, **8**-Calvin, **9**-Simons, **10**-Las Casas, **11**-Wesley, **12**-Spurgeon, **13**-Barth, **14**-Bonhoeffer, **15**-Graham
   • [If you want to lecture or show a video, do so here.]

5. **Small Group Discussion—*10 minutes***
   Organize the class into several three- to five-person groups. Ask each group to select a discussion leader. Each group should discuss these questions:
   (1) What is "the church?"
   (2) Some Christians don't care about church history. Why?
   (3) Why should we study church history?

## 6. Large Group Discussion—*12 minutes*

Ask each group's discussion leader to respond to the four questions. The following answers are suggestions. Use them as you interact with the groups.

(1) What is "the church?"
- Have someone read Colossians 1:18; 1 Timothy 3:14-15.
- The church is a local, visible fellowship of baptized believers and the invisible fellowship of all God's people, living and dead.

(2) Some Christians don't care about church history. Why?
- Sometimes, church history isn't easy to understand.
- Church history is often difficult to apply to our lives.

(3) Why should we study church history?
- Church history deeply affects every Christian. It affects how we read Scripture. It affects how we view God. It affects our worship. If we are church members, the church's story is our family history.

- Point to the poster. Say: "*Every Christian is part of our family in the faith. So, church history is our family history. Christians of the past aren't dusty figures that contemporary church members can forget. They are our brothers and sisters, our mothers and fathers, our in-laws and (in some cases) our outlaws! In this study, we will explore church history from the time of the apostles to the present. We will learn about ordinary people that God used in extraordinary ways. We will also learn to apply this knowledge in our daily lives. From ancient saints and modern martyrs, we will understand even more deeply what it means to follow Christ.*"

## 7. Upcoming Assignment—*1 minute*

Say: "*Read the preface and first chapter of Christian History Made Easy, and, complete the Chapter One Learning Activity before our next group session. Be sure to bring a Bible to every group session!*"

## 8. Prayer—*9 minutes*

End the session by asking each group to spend some time praying. Encourage them to let this study draw them into a deeper relationship with God and into a deeper understanding of God's work.

---

## CHAPTER ONE—DISCUSSION AND REVIEW SESSION

### Session Goals

This session will help students:
- reinforce the knowledge they have gained by reading Chapter One.
- understand how God often uses human longings to accomplish God's work.

### Supplies
- Six 3 x 5 cards
- One large piece of poster-board or shelf paper

### 1. Preparation
- Ask God to guide you throughout the session.
- Read Chapter One in the textbook and complete the Chapter One Learning Activity.
- Post a sign: *GOD USES HUMAN FACTORS TO PRODUCE SPIRITUAL RESULTS.*

## Digging Deeper

If you live in the Midwestern United States, plan a group tour of the Missions Memorial and Bible Museum. Call (918) 459-0431 for details.

**Audio/Video**
*The Blood of the Martyrs*
Vision Video (#25027). 50 minutes. You can contact Vision Video at. . .(800) 523-0226 or visit their web-site at . . .
*http://www.gatewayfilms.com*

**Print**
*Christian History Time Line.* Pamphlet (Item #413X). Torrance, CA, Rose Publishing, 1997. Contact Rose Publishing at . . . (310) 370-7152.

*How We Got the Bible.* Pamphlet (#407X). Rose Publishing, 1995.

Maxwell-Stuart P., *Chronicle of the Popes.* New York: Thames and Hudson, 1997.

Sanders, Fred, *Dr. Doctrine's Christian Comix.* Downers Grove: IVP, 1999.

Spickard, P. and K. Cragg, eds., *God's Peoples.* Grand Rapids: Baker, 1994.

Tucker, R. and W. Liefeld, *Daughters of the Church.* Grand Rapids: Academie, 1987.

## Notes

## Digging Deeper

**Audio/Video**
"Foundations," "Spread," "Accusations," and "Persecutions." *The Trial and Testimony of the Early Church.* Vision Video (#4043). 30 minutes each.

**Print**
Frend, W.H.C., *The Rise of Christianity.* Philadelphia: Fortress, 1984. 1-244.

*New Testament Time Line.* Wall Chart (#402). Rose Publishing.

"Persecution in the Early Church." *Christian History* Issue 27. To order back issues of Christian History, call (800) 873-6986. Or, visit their web-site, at . . .

*http://www.christianhistory.net*

## Notes

- On each 3 x 5 card, write one of the following Scripture references: (1) Acts 18:12-15; (2) 1 Corinthians 10:23-25; (3) 1 Timothy 2:5; (4) 2 Timothy 4:16-18; (5) Jude 1:12.
- Select songs for the session. "God Moves in a Mysterious Way," "For All the Saints," or "Must Jesus Bear the Cross Alone" would be appropriate.

**2. Before the Session**
As students enter, hand the cards to persons who can read well publicly.

**3. Worship—5-7 minutes**
Sing two or more songs.

**4. Learning Activity—*12 minutes (or) 30-40 minutes.***
Ask the students to locate the Chapter One Learning Activity. Tell them the answers to questions 1-11. State that you will discuss question number 12 later.

> **ANSWERS: 1**-TRUE; **2**-FALSE: The fire probably began by accident in an oil warehouse; **3**-TRUE; **4**-FALSE: Romans preferred old, proven products; **5**-FALSE: Christians wouldn't let unbelievers observe the Lord's Supper; **6**-TRUE; **7**-FALSE: Domitian demanded the title "Lord and God"; **8**-FALSE: The temple burned in 70; **9**-FALSE: After AD 70 Christians couldn't return to the Jewish faith; **10**-FALSE: Domitian persecuted Christians because they wouldn't worship him; **11**-Possible answers include: Christianity excluded other gods; Pagans did not understand Christian customs; Christianity challenged the social order.

As you discuss the answers, review the events described in Chapter One. If you have a chalkboard, write important facts on the board. Ask: *"What lessons did you learn as you studied the early churches? Allow two or three persons to respond. Don't let the discussion wander away from the question."*
- [If you want to lecture or show a video, do so here.]

**5. Large Group Discussion—*12-15 minutes***
- Ask students who received cards to find the verses indicated on the cards.
- Have someone read Acts 18:12-15. Ask the entire group: *"According to this passage, how did Roman rulers view the early church?"* (They treated Christianity as part of the Jewish faith.)
- Have someone read 2 Timothy 4:16-18. Ask: *"When was Paul probably arrested the second time? What was the outcome of Paul's trial?"* (Paul was arrested again during Nero's reign. Paul was beheaded.)
- Have someone read 1 Timothy 2:5. Say: *"This verse would have offended many Romans. Why?"* (This verse denies the presence of any gods besides the God of the Bible, as revealed in Jesus Christ.)
- Have persons read 1 Corinthians 11:23-25 and Jude 1:12. Ask: *"How did the Romans understand the church's references to "flesh," 'blood,' 'brothers,' 'sisters,' and 'love-feasts'?"* (Many Romans believed that Christians committed incest and cannibalism.)

**6. Life Application—*15 minutes***
- Review question 12. Possible answers include: Because of the tragedy in Jerusalem, Christianity became distinct; The ancient religions were no longer adequate; People wanted moral guidance. Ask: *"Do you think that early Christians saw how God would use these factors?"* Allow persons to respond briefly.

Say: *"Sometimes, the early church may have noticed how God was using social and political factors. At other times, God's work was unclear. Yet the people's longings became opportunities for God's work. What do people long for in your community? in your school? at your job? How can our church use these longings to help persons know God? Discuss three practical responses to these questions."*

**7. Upcoming Assignment—*1 minute***

Remind the students that, at the next meeting, they should be prepared to discuss Chapter Two.

**8. Prayer—*5 minutes***

Close with a benediction. This prayer, from the account of Polycarp's death, would be fitting: *"Good-bye, brothers and sisters. May the word of Jesus Christ give you life through God's good news. May we give glory, with Jesus Christ, to God the Father and to the Holy Spirit, until the salvation of God's chosen people. Amen."*

---

## CHAPTER TWO—DISCUSSION AND REVIEW SESSION

### Session Goals

This session will help students:
- reinforce the knowledge they have gained by reading Chapter Two.
- consider how they can balance past truths with their present circumstances.

### Supplies

- A piece of paper and a pencil for each student
- One large piece of poster-board or shelf paper

**1. Preparation**
- Ask God to guide you throughout the session.
- Study Chapter Two and the Chapter Two Learning Activity.
- Use the poster-board to post a sign that reads: *WHAT IS ESSENTIAL?*
- Have a piece of paper and a sharpened pencil for each student.
- Select appropriate songs, such as, "Great Creator of the Worlds" (from the "Words from the Ones Who Were There" box page 18) or "We Are God's People," "The Church of Christ, in Every Age," and "Stir Your Church, O God."

**2. Before the Session**
- As students enter, be sure they have completed the Chapter Two Learning Activity.
- Give each person a piece of paper and a pencil.

**3. Worship—*4-6 minutes***
- Sing the theme song and one or two other songs.

**4. Learning Activity—*8 minutes***

Work as a class through the Chapter Two Learning Activity.
**ANSWERS: 1**-A; **2**-B; **3**-C; **4**-A; **5**-C; **6**-A; **7**-C; **8**-B; **9**-A; **10**-B

**5. Large Group Discussion and Review—*15 minutes (or) 30-40 minutes***

After finishing the learning activity, ask students the following questions.

—*"Why did persecution decrease during the late second century?"* (The Roman government was in turmoil. So, most rulers ignored the churches.)

## References

***The church's attitude toward slaves and women:*** Everett Ferguson, *Backgrounds of Early Christianity* 2nd edition (Grand Rapids: Eerdmans, 1993) 556-564

***Why Christians were persecuted:*** Williston Walker. et al., *A History of the Christian Church* 4th edition (New York Scribner's) 50-53

***Jewish-Roman conflicts in the first century:*** Josephus, *Wars of the Jews*, Book II; Josephus. *Antiquities*, Books 19-20

***Curse against Nazarenes:*** F. F. Bruce, *The Gospel of John* (Grand Rapids: Eerdmans, 1983) 215

***Concerning Phoebe and Junias:*** F. F. Bruce, *Romans* rev. edition (Grand Rapids: Eerdmans, 1985) 252-253, 258-259; Craig S. Keener, *The IVP Bible Background Commentary: New Testament* (Downers Grove: IVP, 1993) 446-448; Ruth A. Tucker, et. al., *Daughters of the Church* (Grand Rapids: Academie, 1987) 72-74

***Status of first-century women and children:*** Ferguson, *Backgrounds of Early Christianity*, 70-74

## Digging Deeper

**Audio/Video**

Mullins, R. "Creed." *A Liturgy, A Legacy, and a Ragamuffin Band.* Word Records. Audio/video.

"Persecutions" *The Trial and Testimony of the Early Church.* Vision Video (#4043). 30 minutes each.

**Print**

*Christianity, Cults, and Religions.* Pamphlet (#404X). Rose Publishing.

"Heresy in the Early Church." *Christian History* Issue 51.

Hinson, E.G., *The Early Church.* Nashville: Abingdon, 1996

## References

*Marcion's background:* E. Glenn Hinson, "Patristic Views of the Church," in *The People of God* (Nashville: Broadman, 1991) 187-190

*The church's response to Gnosticism:* Roland Bainton, *Early Christianity* (New York: Van Nostrand-Reinhold, 1960) 35-46, Walker, *A History of the Christian Church,* 45-50, 72-77

*The shift toward a priesthood of overseers:* Polycarp, *To the Philippians,* 3:2-3; 9:1; Irenaeus, *Against Heresies,* 3:2-2

*Montanism:* Bainton, *Early Christianity,* 41-42

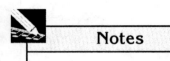

## Notes

—"*What did Marcion believe about Jesus Christ?*" (Jesus was an ordinary human being. At his baptism, a Christ-spirit descended on Jesus. On the cross, the Christ-spirit deserted him.)

—"*How did Christians decide which books God had inspired?*" (They asked: Was the book connected to an apostle? Do other churches use the book? Does the book agree with what we already know about God?)

—[If you want to lecture or to show a video, do so here.]

• Say: "*One of the church's responses to the Gnostic heresy was the Rule of Faith. The Rule listed several teachings that must never be compromised. These teachings were essential doctrines—teachings on which a Christian's salvation depends. The Bible lists many teachings that we can't compromise. Paul wrote:* [read 1 Cor. 12:3]. *Yet the Bible also lets us disagree peaceably about nonessential teachings:* [read Rom. 14:1-5] *At the top of your paper, write: ESSENTIAL, NONESSENTIAL, and UNSURE. As we discuss essential and nonessential beliefs, list beliefs on your papers, beneath the appropriate heading.*"

6. **Individual Life Application—***12-15 minutes*
   • If you have a chalkboard, write ESSENTIAL and NONESSENTIAL at the top of the chalkboard. Discuss as a group what doctrines might belong in each list. *Christianity, Cults, and Religions* (see Digging Deeper) outlines several essential beliefs. Here are some suggestions to start the discussion:

| ESSENTIAL | NONESSENTIAL |
|---|---|
| Salvation is by grace through faith. | How we understand predestination. |
| Jesus Christ is Lord. | Whether women should be ordained. |

   • Ask students to use their list of essential beliefs to write their own Rule of Faith on the back of their paper. After 8 minutes, ask if anyone would like to share his or her Rule. Allow several persons to share their Rule.
   • Ask: "*How can we embrace Christians who hold different nonessential beliefs?*" Try to come up with four practical responses to the question.

7. **Upcoming Assignment—***1 minute*
   Remind the students that, before the next meeting, they should study Chapter Three.

8. **Benediction—***5 minutes*
   Close the session by singing a chorus that emphasizes Christian unity.

---

**CHAPTER THREE—DISCUSSION AND REVIEW SESSION**

**Session Goals**
This session will help students:
• reinforce the knowledge they have gained by reading Chapter Three.
• see how churches can avoid responding to growth in unhealthy ways.

**Supplies**
- Four 3 x 5 cards
- A copy of "Of the Father's Love Begotten" and "Glory Be to the Father" for each student. (You may photocopy the songs from this page.)
- One large piece of poster-board or shelf paper

1. **Preparation**
   - Ask God to guide you throughout the session.
   - Study Chapter Three and Chapter Three Learning Activity.
   - Post a sign: *GROWTH! HOW SHOULD THE CHURCH RESPOND?*
   - On each 3 x 5 card, write one of the following titles:
     (1) "Of the Father's Love Begotten," verse 1;
     (2) "Of the Father's Love Begotten," verse 2;
     (3) "Of the Father's Love Begotten," verse 3;
     (4) "Glory Be to the Father."
   - Select songs. "Of the Father's Love Begotten" and "Glory Be to the Father" would be appropriate.

2. **Before the Session**
   As students enter, ask them to complete Chapter Three Learning Activity while other persons arrive if they haven't already done so.

3. **Worship**—*7 minutes*
   Sing "Of the Father's Love . . ." and "Glory Be to the Father."

4. **Learning Activity**—*15 minutes*
   Ask the students to look at Learning Activity #3. Place A-J in the correct order. If possible, write the events in the correct order on a chalkboard.
   **ANSWERS: A-6; B-3; C-4; D-9; E-8; F-1; G-7; H-10; I-2; J-5**
   Ask students to answer K-N aloud.
   - **K** - (1) Answers include: The phrase isn't in the Bible; The phrase could imply that the Trinity is not made up of three distinct persons. (2) and (3): Answers may vary.
   - **L** - Answers include: Many Christians didn't embrace the church's new-found acceptance.
   - **M** - Answers include: The Great Cappadocians founded communities in cities, rejected extreme self-denial, and involved themselves in social ministries.
   - **N** - Answers include: Christians still treat the Trinity as an essential doctrine; Christians still recite the Nicene Creed, which is based on the Creed of Nicaea.

5. **Small Group Discussion and Review**—*12-20 minutes (or) 30-40 min.*
   - [If you want to lecture or show a video, do so here.]
   - Hand a copy of the songs to each student. Organize the class into four groups. Give each group a card. Say: "*Read the song or verse indicated on your group's card.*"
     —"Glory Be to the Father" was written during or shortly before the controversy about Arius.
     —"Of the Father's Love Begotten" was written soon after the Council of Nicaea, to affirm the Creed of Nicaea.
   - Say: "*Find one phrase in your verse or song that denies Arius' teachings. Explain how the phrase challenged Arius.*"

---

## Of The Father's Love Begotten

*by Aurelius Clemens Prudentius, AD 348-413. Translated by John Mason Neale and Henry W. Baker*

*Verse 1*
Of the Father's love begotten,
Ere the worlds began to be,

He is Alpha and Omega,
He the source, the ending He,

Of the things that are,
that have been,
And that future years shall see,

Evermore and evermore!

*Verse 2*
O ye heights of heav'n adore Him:
Angel hosts, His praises sing;

Pow'rs, dominions,
bow before Him,
And extol our God and King;

Let no tongue on earth be silent,
Ev'ry voice in concert ring,

Evermore and evermore!

*Verse 3*
Christ, to Thee with
God the Father,
And, O Holy Ghost, to Thee,

Hymn and chant and
high thanksgiving
And unwearied praises be:

Honor, glory, and dominion,
And eternal victory,

Evermore and evermore!

---

## Glory Be To The Father

*Author unknown—Fourth century AD, perhaps earlier*

Glory be to the Father, and to the Son, and to the Holy Ghost;

As it was in the beginning,

Is now, and ever shall be,
world without end.

Amen, Amen.

## Digging Deeper

**Audio/Video**

"Beginnings." *History and Holy Sacraments of Orthodox Christianity.* Vision Video (#4095). 30 minutes.

"Persecutions," "Testimony," and "Transition." *The Trial and Testimony of the Early Church.* Vision Video (#4043). 30 minutes each.

**Print**

"Converting the Empire." *Christian History* Issue 57.

*The Trinity.* Pamphlet (#410X). Rose Publishing.

Grant, M., *Constantine the Great.* New York: Scribner's, 1993.

## References

*Constantine's initial prayer to the Sun-God:* Paul R. Spickard, et al., *God's Peoples* (Grand Rapids: Baker, 1994) 55; See also, Eusebius, *Life of Constantine,* 1:28:1

*Constantine's continuing identification of Jesus with the Sun-God:* W. H. C. Frend, *The Rise of Christianity* (Philadelphia: Fortress, 1984) 484, 488; Justo Gonzalez, *The Story of Christianity* Volume 1 (San Francisco: Harper, 1984) 122-123; Michael Grant, *Constantine the Great* (New York: Scribner's, 1993) 135; Walker, *A History of the Christian Church,* 129.

*The AD 362 assembly in Alexandria:* Frend, *The Rise of Christianity,* 604-606

*Jerome as the first defender of Mary's perpetual virginity:* Frend, *The Rise of Christianity,* 717; Walker, *A History of the Christian Church,* 197; See also, Jerome, *Against Helvidius,* 5.

- After nine minutes, ask each group, "*What phrase challenged Arius? How?*" These are suggested answers:
  "Of the Father's Love Begotten," verse 1
  —Jesus is the "source" of everything; so, he can't be created.
  "Of the Father's Love Begotten," verse 2
    —This verse calls Jesus "God."
  "Of the Father's Love Begotten," verse 3
    —Christ, the Father, and the Holy Ghost are worshiped as one.
  "Glory Be to the Father"
    —This song ascribes equal glory to the Father, Son, and Holy Ghost.

6. **Large Group Discussion—*12-14 minutes***
   Ask: "*When someone says, 'God is blessing our church,' what is usually happening?* [Allow persons to respond until numerical growth is mentioned.] *We assume that growing churches are always 'being blessed.' Often, that's true.* [read Acts 2:41-42] *But, sometimes, God's people may proclaim the truth about God with negative results.* [read 1 John 2:19] *What was happening in John's church?* [The church was losing members who weren't true Christians.] *A growing church isn't always a healthy church. In God's kingdom, quality matters more than quantity. During Constantine's reign, churches grew, but God's message became diluted. How might some of today's churches trade purity for numeric or financial growth? How might our church be diluting God's message for the sake of growth?*" [Allow students to respond until they come up with three specific answers. For each answer, come up with one specific way that your church can avoid that pitfall.]

7. **Upcoming Assignment—*1 minute***
   Remind the students: "*Before the next session, each of us will read Chapter Four. Please complete the Chapter Four Learning Activity before coming to the group meeting. Be sure to bring a Bible to every session!*"

8. **Prayer—*3 minutes***
   Close the session with a prayer like this one: "*Lord, we have seen how past Christians misunderstood and misused your message. We admit that we also are guilty. We also dilute your message to gain human approval. You know our foolishness. Our wrongs are not hidden from you. Forgive us. Purify us. Love us. Amen.*"

---

### CHAPTER FOUR—DISCUSSION AND REVIEW SESSION

**Session Goals**
This session will help students:
- reinforce the knowledge they have gained by reading Chapter Four.
- consider how Christians today can be responsible servant-leaders.

**Supplies**
- One large piece of poster-board or shelf paper
- A chalkboard (or) another large piece of poster-board or shelf paper
- A three-by-five card and a pencil for each student

1. **Preparation**
   - Ask God to guide you throughout the session.
   - Study Chapter Four and the Chapter Four Learning Activity.

- Use one piece of poster-board to post a sign that reads: *HOW'S YOUR SERVE?*
- At the top of the other piece of poster-board (or) chalk-board, write: *SERVANT-LEADERS OR LEADERS OF SERVANTS?* Beneath the heading, write: *AMBROSE, CYRIL, GREGORY, JOHN CHRYSOSTOM, HILDA, JUSTINIAN, OLYMPIAS,* and *THEODOSIUS.* Post the sign in a prominent place.
- Prepare a brief (10-12 minute) lecture, based on the contents of Chapter Four. Study an encyclopedia article or Internet site about Augustine of Hippo, Benedict of Nursia, or Pope Gregory.
- Select at least three of the ancient songs that appear in the margins throughout the Leader Guides. Other appropriate songs might include, "Let All Mortal Flesh Keep Silent" (a hymn from around AD 400), "Be Thou My Vision" (an Irish hymn from the fifth century or earlier), "Make Me a Servant," or "The City of God."

2. **Worship—*10 minutes***
   Sing the theme song and three or four other appropriate songs.

3. **Learning Activity—*4 minutes***
   Review the answers to the Chapter Four Learning Activity:
   **ANSWERS: 1**-Jovinian; **2**-Ambrose; **3**-Olympias; **4**-Augustine **5**-Nestorius; **6**-Leo; **7**-Chalcedon; **8**-Justinian; **9**-Scholastica; **10**-Hilda; **11**-pope; **12**-Answers will vary.

4. **Large Group Discussion and Review—*20 minutes (or) 35-45 minutes***
   - After finishing the learning activity, ask the following questions.
     —*"In AD 381, the First Council of Constantinople confirmed a creed. What do contemporary Christians call that creed?"* (Christians call it "the Nicene Creed," because it echoes the decisions of the Council of Nicaea.)
     —*"What did One-Nature Christians believe?"* (One-Nature Christians thought Jesus' deity absorbed his humanity.)
   - [If you want to show a video, do so here. 15-30 minutes.]
   - In your lecture: (1) Summarize the chapter in your words. Include any interesting facts that your research uncovered. (2) Select one major struggle that Christians faced between AD 370 and 664. Talk about a similar struggle that today's Christians face. (3) Discuss these questions: "How did the cleft between clergy and laypeople enter the churches? Does your church encourage every Christian to be a servant-leader?"

5. **Individual Life Application—*9 minutes***
   - Distribute the cards and pencils. Point to the list of names on the chalkboard. Say: *"On your card, write one name from this list. Beside the name, note whether that person was a "servant-leader" or a "leader of servants." Then, write one reason why you believe your assessment is correct. After 5 minutes, allow one person to respond to each name. State that each person may have exhibited both traits at different times in his/her life."*
   - Say: *"Jesus' disciples tried to be leaders instead of servants more than once: [read Mark 10:43-45] These words call us to ask ourselves, 'How's my serve? Do I expect church leaders to serve my church's needs? Or, have I accepted my God-given responsibility to be a servant-leader in my church?'"*

6. **Benediction—*2 minutes***
   To end the session, read Philippians 2:5-8 and lead a brief prayer.

## Savior of All Peoples

*by Ambrose, Bishop of Milan*

Savior of all peoples, come,
Virgin's Son,
make here your home.
Be amazed, O sky and earth,
That our Lord chose such a birth.
Christ, the Father's only Son,
Through his cross
our life has won.
Endless will his kingdom be;
When will we its splendor see?

Sing to the tune of "Holy Bible, Book Divine" or "Holy Spirit, Truth Divine."

## O Splendor of God's Glory Bright

*by Ambrose, Bishop of Milan*

O splendor of God's glory bright,
From light eternal bringing light;
O Light of lights,
life's living spring
True day, all days illumining.
Amen.

Sing to the tune of "Doxology" (Old 100th, Altered).

## References

*The Cappadocians' response to Apollinarius:* Gregory of Nazianzus, *To Cledonius,* Epistle 101

*Christian History Made Easy*

149

## Digging Deeper

**Audio/Video**
"Augustine of Hippo." *Pioneers of the Spirit.* Vision Video (#4255).

*Chant.* Angel Records, 1994. 57 minutes. Audio.

**Print**
"John Chrysostom." *Christian History* Issue 47.

Augustine. *Confessions.*

## I Sing As I Arise Today

*by Patrick of Ireland*

I sing as I arise today;
I call upon my Father's might;
The will of God to be my guide,
the eye of God to be my sight.

The Word of God to be my
speech, the hand of God
to be my stay,

The shield of God to be my
strength, the path of God
to light my way.

Sing to the tune of "I Heard the Bells on Christmas Day" (Waltham).

## Digging Deeper

**Audio/Video**
"Byzantium." *History and Holy Sacraments of Orthodox Christianity* Vision Video (#4095). 30 minutes.

**Print**
"Eastern Orthodoxy." *Christian History* Issue 54.

Queller, D., et al., *The Fourth Crusade.* Philadelphia: Penn, 1997.

## CHAPTER FIVE—DISCUSSION AND REVIEW SESSION

**Session Goals**
This session will help students:
• reinforce the knowledge they have gained by reading Chapter Five.
• be encouraged to understand others before criticizing them.

**Supplies**
• A half-sheet of paper and a pencil for each student
• A timer
• One large piece of poster-board or shelf paper

1. **Preparation**
   • Ask God to guide you throughout the session.
   • Select songs, such as "All Glory, Laud, and Honor," (by Theodolf, one of Charlemagne's aides).
   • Study Chapter Five and the Chapter Five Learning Activity.
   • Use the poster-board to post a sign that reads: *CHRIST-LIKE CRITICISM=COMPASSION+COMPREHENSION+DESIRE TO HELP OTHERS KNOW CHRIST.*
2. **Before the Session**
   As students enter, give each one a piece of paper and a pencil.
3. **Worship—***5 minutes*
   Sing the theme song and/or another appropriate song.
4. **Learning Activity—***7 minutes*
   Discuss the Chapter Five Learning Activity.
   **ANSWERS: 1-B; 2-C; 3-A; 4-C; 5-A; 6-C; 7-C; 8-D; 9-C; 10-A; 11-B; 12-E**
5. **Large Group Discussion and Review—***20 minutes (or) 40-50 minutes*
   • [If you want to lecture or show a video, do so here. 15-30 minutes.]
   • Say: "*Glance at Chapter Five. Choose one person mentioned by name in the chapter. Write a series of Who Am I? statements about that person. Include at least three facts about the person.*"
   Here's a sample riddle:
   "*I seized the Eastern throne;*" "*Pope Leo III refused to appeal to me;*" "*I convened the Second Council of Nicaea to end the icon disputes.*" **ANSWER:** *Empress Irene*
   • Allow the students 9 minutes to write their "Who Am I?" riddles.
   • Have students wad up their "Who Am I?" riddles. Set the timer at 1 minute. Tell the students to toss around the paper wads until the timer goes off. At the end, each student should have one paper wad.
   • Ask each student to share the riddle on his/her paper wad. Urge the group to guess the answer to each riddle.
6. **Individual Life Application—***12 minutes*
   • **Read Acts 18:24-27.** Say: "*Christians must always be kind, but being kind does not necessarily mean being silent. Sometimes, Christians must point out the errors of other religious groups. Three attitudes should rule Christians when they criticize others: (1) Compassion; (2) Understanding; and (3) A desire to guide the offenders toward an accurate knowledge of God's nature. In the early Middle Ages, many Christians condemned Muslims, Jews, and other Christians. Did these three attitudes rule their criticisms?*"
   **[Allow several responses. Most persons will answer no.]**

"*Unfortunately, Christians today still criticize others without first trying to understand them. Name some religious groups with which you disagree.*" [Write the responses on a chalkboard. Here are some suggestions to guide your discussion: {a Christian denomination unlike your own}; Mormons; Jehovah's Witnesses; Muslims.]

- Say: "*The members of some of these groups are Christians. Others are not. Do you have compassion for the people in each of these groups? Do you understand their basic beliefs? Especially if they aren't Christians, could you guide them toward an accurate understanding of Christ? Peter said:* [read 1 Peter 3:15]."

- Say: "*On the back of your paper, list several groups or individuals that you either don't understand or don't feel compassion for. Your list may include family members, fellow-Christians, other races, or other religious groups. Choose to work to understand the people on your list. Then, ask God to help you love them with God's own love.*" Allow the students 4 minutes to finish their lists.

7. **Upcoming Assignment—*1 minute***
Remind students to study Chapter Six and to complete the Chapter Six Learning Activity before the next session.

8. **Closure—*5 minutes***
Close the session with a time of silent prayer. Urge students to pray for the people that they listed.

## References

***Pope Leo III's refusal to appeal to Empress Irene:*** John J. Norwich, *Byzantium: The Early Centuries* (New York: Knopf, 1989) 377-380

***The life of Marozia:*** Gonzalez, *The Story of Christianity* Volume 1, 274-276

***Photius and the addition to the Nicene Creed:*** Gonzalez, *The Story of Christianity* Volume 1, 262-265, Mark A. Noll, *Turning Points* (Grand Rapids: Baker, 1997) 134-141

***Pope Innocent III and the Sack of Constantinople:*** Donald E. Queller, *The Fourth Crusade* revised edition (Philadelphia: Penn, 1997) 89-92, 101-103, 172-192

---

## CHAPTER SIX—DISCUSSION AND REVIEW SESSION

**Session Goals**
This session will help students:
- reinforce the knowledge they have gained by reading Chapter Six.
- choose to join in God's work in their areas of influence.

**Supplies**
- Four pieces of paper and four pencils
- One large piece of poster-board or shelf paper
- One white robe, one brown robe, and one black robe

1. **Preparation**
   - Ask God to guide you as you prepare for the session.
   - Post a sign that reads: *WARNING! GOD IS WORKING HERE!*
   - Write one heading on each paper:
     (1) MISSIONARY MONKS; (2) MYSTICS;
     (3) MENDICANTS; (4) SCHOLASTICS.
   - Plan to sing some of the following songs: "All Creatures of Our God and King" (Francis of Assisi); "The Day of Resurrection" (John Damascus); "Jerusalem the Golden," (a monk from Cluny).
   - Study Chapter Six and the Chapter Six Learning Activity.
   - Ask three students to arrive at the discussion session early. Dress each one in one of the robes.

2. **Worship—*8 minutes***
Sing the theme song and some of the suggested hymns.

## O God, You Are the Father

*by Columba of Iona*

O God, you are the Father
of all who trust in you.
To mankind you have granted
faith, life, and power, too.
O God, you have created earth
full of living things.
You are the righteous Judge
and the holy King of kings.

Sing to the tune of "The Church's One Foundation" (Aurelia).

## Digging Deeper

**Audio/Video**
*Becket.* Vision Video (#7287). 150 minutes.

*Hildegard.* Vision Video (#9895). 52 minutes.

Sequentia. *Hildegard von Bingen: Symphoniae.* BMG Classics. 62 minutes. Audio.

**Print**
"Bernard of Clairvaux." *Christian History* Issue 24.

Flanagan, S. *Hildegard of Bingen.* London: Routledge, 1990.

"Francis of Assisi." *CH 42.*

## References

*The failures of Cyril and Methodious:* John J. Norwich, *Byzantium: The Apogee* (New York: Knopf, 1993) 71-79

*The betrayal of John of Damascus:* William R. Cannon, *History of Christianity in the Middle Ages* (Nashville: Abingdon, 1960) 106-114

*Bernard's influence on the veneration of Mary and of Jesus' humanity:* Spickard, *God's Peoples,* 89; Gonzalez, *The Story of Christianity* Volume 1, 282, 299

*Anselm and the cruel abbot:* Eadmer, *The Life and Conversation of St. Anselm,* 1:22

3. **Large Group Review—***7 minutes*
   - Ask the person wearing the white robe to stand. Ask: *"If (name) were a monk, to what order might (name) belong?"* [**Cistercian**] Ask: *"Why did Cistercians wear white?"* [**To avoid any appearance of wealth, they didn't dye their clothes.**]
   - Ask the person wearing the brown robe to stand. Ask: *"If (name) were a monk, to what order might (name) belong?"* [**Franciscan**] Ask: *"Why did Franciscans wear brown robes?"* [**When Francis first committed himself to Christ, that's what he put on.**]
   - Ask the person wearing the black robe to stand. Ask: *"If (name) were a monk, to what order might (name) belong?"* [**Dominican monks wore black robes over white robes.**] Ask: *"What Scholastic thinker was also a Dominican monk?"* [**Thomas Aquinas**].

4. **Learning Activity—***7 minutes*
   As a class, review the Chapter Six Learning Activity.
   **ANSWERS:** 1-Bernard; 2-Waldo; 3-Assisi; 4-Anselm; 5-Mendicant; 6-Mystics; 7-Damascus; 8-nuns; 9-Aquinas; 10-Lioba; 11-Bingen; 12-Francis; 13-Cluny; 14-Scholastic; 15-crops; 16-Ill; 17-God; 18-Cyril

5. **Small Group Life Application—***18 minutes (or) 40-50 minutes*
   - [If you want to lecture or to show a video, do so here. 15-30 min.]
   - Organize the class into four groups. Give each group a pencil and a piece of paper. Say: *"On each paper, you'll find the title of a type of Christian mentioned in Chapter Six. In your books, locate the section mentioned on your paper. Find two truths that Christians today can learn from that type of Christian. Write the truths on your group's paper."* Allow folk 9 minutes to complete the assignment.
   - Ask each group to share its list. Here are some suggestions: Missionary monks reminded Christians to reach out to unreached peoples. Mystics urged Christians to experience God with their emotions. Mendicants turned Christians' focus away from their possessions. Scholastics taught Christians to think deeply about their faith.
   - Say: *"In this chapter, you learned that despite the medieval church's failures God never stopped working. That shouldn't surprise us.* [**read John 5:17**] *God is always working! In one place, God may be preparing non-Christians to become followers of Christ. Somewhere else, God may be giving God's people a deep desire to encounter God anew. Never ask, 'God, are you working here?' God is always working! Ask, 'God, how are you working here? Please prepare me to join you in your work.'"*

6. **Closure—***5 minutes*
   Discuss how God might be working today in unexpected ways. Ask: *"How can you actively join in God's work where you are?"* Discuss three specific answers. Close the session with a brief prayer. Ask God to show the students where God is working in their lives.

---

### CHAPTER SEVEN—DISCUSSION AND REVIEW SESSION

**Session Goals**
This session will help students:
- reinforce the knowledge they have gained by reading Chapter Seven.
- look for opportunities to be voices of repentance and reform in their churches.

## Supplies
- Twelve balloons (six different colors, two balloons of each color)
- One small paper bag
- Six slips of paper
- One large piece of poster-board or shelf paper
- A chalkboard or overheard projector

1. **Preparation**
   - Ask God to guide you throughout the session. Is there someone in the study group who annoys you? Pray specifically for him/her. Send an encouraging note to that student, thanking him/her for attending the study.
   - Study Chapter Seven and the Chapter Seven Learning Activity.
   - On the poster-board, write in large letters: *ARE YOU THE ONE?* Post the sign wherever your group meets.
   - Put six balloons (one of each color, not inflated) in the paper bag.
   - On each slip of paper, write one of the following names: (1) CELESTINE V; (2) CATHERINE OF SIENNA; (3) JOHN WYCLIFFE; (4) JAN HUS; (5) THOMAS A'KEMPIS; (6) ERASMUS.
   - Place each slip of paper in one of the remaining balloons. Inflate and tie the balloons with the papers inside.
   - Place a chair near the front of the room.
   - Select several songs that focus on renewal and revival.

2. **Before the Session**
   As students enter, be certain they have completed the Chapter Seven Learning Activity.

3. **Worship—*4 minutes***
   Sing your theme song or another appropriate song.

4. **Learning Activity—*8 minutes***
   Ask students to locate Learning Activity #7. Talk about their answers.
   **ANSWERS: 1**-Answers will vary, elderly, humble; **2**-Avignon; **3**-Answers will vary, unbridled parties, penance parades; **4**-The Council of Constance deposed all three popes and elected a new pope; **5**-All Christians are equal members of God's church; **7**-Answers will vary, brave, innocent; **8**-They focused on practical, human ideas instead of abstract logic; **9**-Answers will vary, intelligent, humanist; **10**-Answers will vary.

5. **Large Group Discussion and Review—*20 minutes (or) 30-45 min.***
   - [If you want to lecture or show a video, do so here. 15-30 min.]
   - Set a timer for one minute. Have students bat the balloons among themselves until the timer beeps. Whoever is holding a balloon when the timer beeps must keep the balloon.
   - Say: "*If you're holding a balloon, pop it. Inside each balloon is a slip of paper. Read in your textbook about the person whose name is written on your paper. Do not show anyone your paper!*"
   - Allow students two minutes to refresh their memories. Say: "*If you got a balloon, you're so special that the class will now interview you! The class can ask you any question about the person whose name is written on your paper except the person's name. Everyone, even the person being interviewed, can use her or his textbook!*"
   - Randomly pull a balloon out of the paper bag. Ask: "*Who popped the (color) balloon?*" Ask the respondent to sit at the front of the room.

## Father, We Praise You

*by Gregory, Bishop of Rome*

*Verse:*

All holy Father,
Son, and equal Spirit,

Trinity blessed,
your salvation send.

Yours is the glory,
shining and resounding,

Through all creation,
your world without end.

*Chorus:*

Father, we praise you!
Father, we praise you!

Active and watchful,
we stand before you.

Singing, we offer
our prayers and devotion.

Thus we adore you,
our Savior and King.

Sing to the tune of "Great Is Thy Faithfulness" (Faithfulness).

## Digging Deeper

**Audio/Video**
*The Agony and the Ecstasy.* Vision Video (#2277). 139 minutes.

*Henry V.* Fox, 1989. 138 minutes. (or) *Henry V.* Paramount, 1944. 127 minutes.

*Joan of Arc.* Vision Video (#6212). 100 minutes (or) *Joan of Arc.* CBS, 1999 Approx. 150 minutes.

*John Hus.* Vision Video (#4133). 30 minutes.

*John Wycliffe.* Vision Video (#4053). 30 minutes.

**Print**
"John Wycliffe." *Christian History* Issue 3.

Tuchman, B. *A Distant Mirror.* New York: Ballantine, 1978.

### References

*The end of the imperial papacy and the transition to Avignon:* Cannon, *History of Christianity in the Middle Ages,* 250-251, 292

*Reactions to the Black Plague:* Norman Davies, *Europe* (Oxford: Oxford University, 1996) 409-412; Spickard, *God's Peoples,* 146-148; Tuchman, *A Distant Mirror,* 92-123

## King of the Earth

*by Gregory, Bishop of Rome*

King of the earth and ev'ry life,

Banish our weakness, hate, and sin.

Bring us to heav'n, to praise your name,

With joy and peace that ne'er shall end.

Sing to the tune of "When I Survey the Wondrous Cross" (Hamburg). Sung slowly *a capella* by a unison choir, this arrangement sounds similar to a Gregorian chant.

---

• Let students ask questions until someone guesses whose name was written on the paper. Give the person the balloon that you pulled from the bag as a "prize." Allow the person to return to his/her seat. Repeat the process until all six colors have been used.
• Say: *"We have talked about six ordinary Christians. Each one saw a problem in the church and called God's people to repent. Were they simply complaining? No. The problems they saw affected vital parts of Christian faith, such as the authority of Scripture and personal holiness. Name some similar problems that confront contemporary churches."*
• Write the students' responses on the chalkboard (or) transparency. After the list includes 12 items, ask: *"Which problems threaten vital parts of the Christian faith? Circle those problems."*
• Lead the class to select three circled items that specifically threaten their churches. Underline those problems.
• [Read I Corinthians 16:14; Ephesians 4:14-16] Point to the poster. Ask: *"Is God calling you to be the voice of repentance and reform in your church? How can you call your church to deal adequately with the problems we have underlined?* Allow students to respond until they think of three responses. Write the responses on the board.

6. **Small Group Life Application—7 *minutes***
   Organize the class into three groups. Assign one response to each group. Ask each group to pray about its assigned problem. After they've finished praying, students may leave.

7. **Upcoming Assignment—*1 minute***
   As students begin to leave, remind them to study Chapter Eight and to complete the Chapter Eight Learning Activity before the next session.

---

### CHAPTER EIGHT—DISCUSSION AND REVIEW SESSION

**Session Goals**
This session will help students:
• reinforce the knowledge they have gained by reading Chapter Eight.
• decide when Christians should and should not divide.

**Supplies**
• One sheet of paper and a pencil for each student
• Two large pieces of poster-board (or) shelf paper
• One large board (or) an old door (or) a bulletin board
• Two hammers
• One tack for each student

1. **Preparation**
   • Ask God to guide you throughout the session.
   • Study Chapter Eight and the Chapter Eight Learning Activity.
   • Post a sign that reads: *DIVISION IS NEVER DESIRABLE. WHEN IS IT NECESSARY?*

- On the other poster-board, write the following sentences: THEY DENY CHRIST'S DEITY; I DON'T KNOW THE SONGS THEY SING; THEY BAPTIZE BY IMMERSION; THEY DENY THE AUTHORITY OF SCRIPTURE; SOMEONE GOSSIPED ABOUT ME; THEIR SERVICES BORE ME; I DISAGREE WITH THEIR VIEW OF THE END-TIMES; THEY TEACH THAT WORKS ARE NECESSARY FOR SALVATION. Write the phrases in vivid colors. Hang the poster near the front of the classroom.
- At the top of each student's paper, write MY THESES. (If you have a photocopier, make a master and reproduce it.)
- Place the hammers, tacks, and board near the front of your classroom.
- Select songs to sing during the session, such as "A Mighty Fortress Is Our God" (Martin Luther).

2. **Before the Session**
As students enter, give each one a pencil and *My Theses* paper.

3. **Worship—*6 minutes***
Sing the theme song and another appropriate song.

4. **Learning Activity—*12 minutes***
Ask students to locate the Learning Activity. Read the suggested answers for each blank in the Chapter Eight Learning Activity. Have students share the words they added in the blanks.
   **SUGGESTED ANSWERS:** Other answers may also be suitable. 1-Spanish, Soldier, Jesuit, Catholic; 2-Studious, French, Fled, Institutes, Geneva; 3-English, Catherine; 4-Barrel, Nun, Wife; 5-German, Translator, Monk, Wittenberg, Theses; 6-Swiss, Anabaptist, Fled, Zurich, Drowned; 7-Dutch, Anabaptist, Priest, Fled; 8-Catholic, Council; 9-Studious, English, Translator, Priest, Fled, Cambridge, Strangled; 10-Swiss, Priest, Zurich

5. **Small Group Life Application—*10 minutes (or) 25-45 minutes***
   - [ If you want to lecture or show a video, do so here. 15-30 min.]
   - Say: "*Many people left the established church during the Reformation because they believed their church's teachings were no longer biblical. Others left because of the church's corruption. A few left because they disliked the church's moral standards. In this session, we'll discuss when Christians should divide from others who profess Christ.*"
   - Organize the class into three groups. Assign each group one of the following texts: 1 Cor. 5:9-13; Gal. 1:6-9; 1 John 2:18-23. Say to each group: "*Ask yourselves, 'According to this Scripture, when should Christians divide?'*" After 8 minutes, allow each group to respond. Here are the suggested responses:
     - *If someone who professes Christ defies God's moral precepts . . . (1 Corinthians 5:9-13).*
     - *If someone alters the plan of salvation . . . (Galatians 1:6-9).*
     - *If someone denies Jesus' identity as Messiah, God, and man . . . (1 John 2:18-23).*

6. **Individual Life Application—*14 minutes***
   - Say: "*In each situation, someone was endangering a vital part of the Christian faith. I've listed several reasons why people who profess Christ divide. Some endanger vital parts of the Christian faith. Others don't.*" [**Read each sentence from the poster.**]

## Digging Deeper

**Audio/Video**
King, Wes. "Martin Luther." *The Robe*. Reunion Records. Audio.

*A Man For All Seasons*. Vision Video (#9967). 120 minutes.

*Martin Luther: Heretic*. Family Films/Concordia Publishing. 75 minutes.

*Reformation Overview*. Vision Video (#4110). Six 30 minute programs.

Sproul, R.C. *Love God? Sometimes I Hate Him!* Ligonier Ministries. 50 minutes. Contact Ligonier Ministries at . . . (800) 753-8735. Or, visit their web-site . . . *http://www.gospelcom.net/ligonier*

**Print**
Bainton, Roland. *Here I Stand* [Various editions].

Bruster, Bill. "Is Your Church Free or Reformed?" For free copies of this pamphlet, call (888) 801-4223.

Estep, William. *Renaissance and Reformation*. Grand Rapids: Eerdmans, 1986.

Jones, Timothy Paul. "John Calvin and the Problem of Philosophical Apologetics." *Perspectives in Religious Studies*. Winter 1997-1998.

**8**
**Chapter 8**

## References

*The relationship of Martin and Kaetie Luther:* Bainton, *Here I Stand*, Chapter 17; Tucker *Daughters of the Church*, 180-181

**Menno Simons' early life:** C.D. Weaver, *A Cloud of Witnesses* (Macon, Georgia: Smyth and Helwys, 1994).

## Notes

- Say: "*On your "My Theses" papers, list several situations when Christians should divide from others who profess Christ. Your reasons don't necessarily need to come from my list.*" [Allow 5 minutes.] "*Look at each item on your list. Ask, "Is this difference essential to the Christian faith?" If it isn't essential, cross out the difference. If you're uncertain, circle the difference.*" [Allow 4 min.]
- Say: "*Let's spend some time praying. Reread your lists. As you read each crossed-out item, ask God to help you accept that difference in other Christians. As you read each circled item, ask God to give you wisdom to know if that is a vital part of the Christian faith. When you finish praying, nail your theses to the board at the front of the class. Let that be your commitment to follow God's leadership when you are faced with a division in the body of Christ.*" Nail your own paper on the board to show students what you want them to do. If possible, play meditative background music while students pray and nail their theses to the board.

7. **Upcoming Assignment and Closure—***3 minutes*
   Remind students to complete the Chapter Nine Learning Activity before the next session. Sing "In Christ, There Is No East or West" or another appropriate song.

---

### CHAPTER NINE—DISCUSSION AND REVIEW SESSION

**Session Goals**
- This session will help students reinforce the knowledge they have gained by reading Chapter Nine.
- recognize that lasting transformations among God's people must include both individual and institutional changes.

**Supplies**
- Four sheets of colored paper
- A slip of paper for each student
- One large piece of poster-board or shelf paper

1. **Preparation**
   - Ask God to guide you throughout the session.
   - Study Chapter Nine and the Chapter Nine Learning Activity.
   - Use the poster-board to post a sign that reads:
     *CHANGE! IT'S PERSONAL, TOO.*
   - On each sheet of paper, write one of these headings:
     (1) Does the sun move or does the earth? Joshua 10:12-13.
     (2) Did God ordain Europe's quest of distant coastlands? Isaiah 11:11-12.
     (3) Does God want Canaan's descendants to be slaves? Genesis 9:25.
     (4) Is it okay to use violence to compel people to become Christians? Luke 14:23.
   - Organize the slips of paper into four equal groups. Write one of the following texts on each group's slips of paper: Josh. 10:12-13; Isaiah 11:11-12; Genesis 9:25; Luke 14:23.
   - Hang one of the sheets of paper in each corner of the room. Prepare a circle of chairs beneath each sheet.
   - Prepare to sing the theme song and another appropriate song, such as the Bohemian Protestant hymn, "Sing Praise to God Who Reigns Above."

    

2. **Before the Session**
   As students enter, randomly hand out the slips of paper.
3. **Worship**—*5 minutes*
   Sing the theme song and/or another appropriate song.
4. **Learning Activity**—*5 minutes*
   Review the Chapter Nine Learning Activity as a group.
   **ANSWERS:** 1-B; 2-G; 3-L; 4-H; 5-J; 6-K; 7-F; 8-I;
   9-C; 10-D; 11-A; 12-Answers will vary.
5. **Small Group Life Application**—*15 minutes*
   • Say: *"Each of you should have a slip of paper. The Scripture on your paper matches one of the posters at the corners of the room. Someone in church history misused each of those Scriptures. Go sit beneath your assigned Scripture reference. Carefully study your assigned text as a group. Ask yourselves, 'How did past Christians misuse this text? What is its actual meaning?' Write your answers on the sheet of paper above your circle of chairs."*
   • Allow 12 minutes for discussion.
   • Reassemble the class. Allow each group to talk about its assigned text. Do not allow students to argue or to stray from the subject. Here are some suggested responses:
   (1) Galileo realized that the earth rotates around the sun. Church leaders used Joshua 10:12-13 to prove that the sun rotates around the earth. Yet the Bible portrays historical events from a human perspective. From Joshua's perspective, the sun seemed to stand still.
   (2) Columbus used Isaiah 11:11-12 to prove that God ordained his quest. Yet, in its context, the passage refers to Israel's return from exile.
   (3) Slave owners used Genesis 9:25 to prove that God wanted Africans to be slaves. Yet the Bible never clearly affirms that this text refers to Africans. Also, Noah (not God) is speaking here. The Bible never claims that God approved Noah's curse.
   (4) Settlers used Luke 14:23 to justify their wars against non-Christian natives. Jesus did compel people with convincing words. Yet he never approved violence.
   • **[Read Deuteronomy 18:20.]** Say: *"Today, God doesn't call Christ's people to kill false prophets. But it's still a serious matter to misapply God's words. How can Christians today avoid misusing biblical texts?"*
   • Allow several responses. If possible, use the article "What It Means to Me" (see Digging Deeper) to guide a discussion about misusing biblical texts.
6. **Large Group Life Application**—*10 minutes (or) 25-40 minutes*
   • [If you want to lecture or show a video, do so here. 15-30 minutes.]
   • Say: *"Christianity changed radically in the Reformation. Most of the changes were needed, and the changes did solve some of the church's problems. Yet the changes failed to solve all the church's problems. Many church members continued to kill and exploit other human beings for religious reasons. What people failed to see was that change can't be confined to institutions. Real change must begin with the individual. How do Christians today try to transform institutions and fail to see changes that are needed in individual lives?"*

## Notes

## References

**The Puritans:** Spickard, *God's Peoples*, 222-227

**Columbus' claims that he was fulfilling Scripture:** "Columbus and Christianity" *Christian History* Issue 35; Mark A. Noll, *A History of Christianity in the United States and Canada* (Grand Rapids: Eerdmans, 1992) 12

**Settlers' actions toward Native Americans:** Gonzalez, *The Story of Christianity,* 382-284, 409-411; Stephen Keillor, *This Rebellious House* (Downer's Grove InterVarsity, 1996) 26-27, 37; Spickard, *God's Peoples,* 216-217

**The life of Pedro Claver:** Gonzalez, *The Story of Christianity,* 392-394

## Notes

---

- Repeat the question. Allow students to respond until they come up with three specific answers. Here are some suggested responses: When a church doesn't grow, members criticize the pastor instead of making certain that they're right with God; When God's presence seems absent, churches try new programs instead of seeking spiritual awakening.

7. **Individual Life Application—*5 minutes***
   Urge students to ask themselves, How do I fail to see areas in my life that need to change? Spend a few moments in silent prayer. If possible, play a meditative song as people pray. End the time of meditation with an appropriate prayer, such as: *Lord, we also have misused your words. We have expected institutions to change when, in truth, it is we ourselves who need to change. Show us our sins. Cleanse our sins. Give us strength to turn from them. Amen.*

8. **Closure—*2 minutes***
   Sing "Spirit of the Living God" or another appropriate song. Remind students that, before the next group meeting, they should complete the Chapter Ten Learning Activity.

---

### CHAPTER TEN—DISCUSSION AND REVIEW SESSION

**Session Goals**
This session will help students:
- reinforce the knowledge they have gained by reading Chapter Ten.
- see when and how the Christian faith can answer the questions of its culture.

**Supplies**
- Eight overhead transparencies (or) a hymnal for each student
- Eight three-by-five-inch cards
- One large piece of poster-board or shelf paper

1. **Preparation**
   - Ask God to guide you throughout the session.
   - Use the poster-board, to post a sign: *HOW CAN CHRISTIANS ADAPT TO THEIR CULTURE WITHOUT COMPROMISING THEIR FAITH?*
   - On each card, write one of these statements. *Include the numbers 1-8!*
     1. Before the 1700s most Christians sang only psalms, like "Lift Up Your Heads," a paraphrase of Psalm 24:7-10.
     2. In the 1700s Pietists, like the Moravians, wrote songs that focused on their relationship with Jesus. Nikolaus Zinzendorf, a Pietist, wrote "Christian Hearts, in Love United" and "Jesus, Lead the Way."
     3. Through the Moravians, God drew John and Charles Wesley to Christ. "And Can It Be" captures the heart of the Wesleys' faith.
     4. For a few years, George Whitefield and the Wesleys split over predestination. Had they not reunited, you might never have sung, "Hark! The Herald Angels Sing." Charles Wesley wrote the song. But you sing Whitefield's altered version.
     5. Isaac Watts was another Pietist hymn-writer. Isaac Watts wrote "I'll Praise My Maker." Around 1737 John Wesley modified Watts' original words.

6. Deism focused people on God's creation. In "I Sing the Mighty Power of God," Watts praised God as Creator.
7. Unlike Deists, Watts and other Pietists went beyond praising God as the Creator. In "When I Survey the Wondrous Cross," Watts worshiped Christ as his Redeemer and God.
8. John Wesley and other Great Awakening preachers spoke against slavery. In 1764 a slave trader named John Newton became a Christian. He rejected his old ways and wrote "Amazing Grace."

- Locate these hymns: "Amazing Grace" (Newton); "And Can It Be" (Wesley); "Christian Hearts, in Love United" or, "Jesus, Lead the Way" (Zinzendorf); "Hark! The Herald Angels Sing" (Wesley/[Whitefield]); "I Sing the Mighty Power of God" (Watts); "I'll Praise My Maker" (Watts/Wesley); "Lift Up Your Heads" (Weissel); "When I Survey the Wondrous Cross" (Watts). If your church's hymnal does not include these songs, you can write the lyrics of public-domain hymns on transparencies. Each hymn except "I Sing . . ." is public domain.
- Enlist a pianist and song leader to direct the hymns.
- Study Chapter Ten and the Chapter Ten Learning Activity.

2. **Before the Session**
   - As students arrive, disburse the cards to students who can read well publicly. Comment that the cards are numbered. The first card will be read after the opening song. The second card will be read after "Lift Up Your Heads," and so on.

3. **Worship—*30 minutes***
   - Sing the theme song or another appropriate song, such as, "O For a Thousand Tongues to Sing" (Wesley).
   - [Read Psalm 78:12-23] Say: "*The ancient Hebrews reviewed their history through this psalm. Let's follow their example. Let's review our Christian heritage through God's gift of music. So . . .* " [Read Psalm 78:1-8]
   - Ask the student who received the first card to read his/her card. After each reading, the song leader should immediately lead everyone in singing the first verse of the suggested hymn. Continue until all eight cards have been read and the group has sung all eight hymns.

4. **Large Group Review—*7 minutes (or) 20-35 minutes***
   - [If you want to lecture or show a video, do so here. 15-30 minutes.]
   - Quickly review the Chapter Ten Learning Activity.
     **ANSWERS: 1**-Roger Williams; **2**-Anne Hutchinson; **3**-Jonathan Edwards; **4**-Nikolaus Zinzendorf; **5**-Susanna Wesley; **6**-George Whitefield; **7**-John Wesley; **8**-Sarah Crosby; **9**-Answers will vary **10**-Answers will vary.
   Use the definitions of Deism and the Enlightenment listed at the beginning of Chapter Ten to help students answer these questions.

5. **Life Application—*12 minutes***
   - Say: "*In the 1700's, Deism threatened Christianity. According to Deists, God was the Creator—but nothing more. Many people who called themselves Christians embraced Deism. By the late 1700's and early 1800's, many churches had abandoned the Bible's depiction of God. They had adapted their beliefs to their culture until they had nothing left to believe in. What false religious ideas are popular in our culture?*" [Allow students to respond until they

## Digging Deeper

**Audio/Video**
*First Fruits: Zinzendorf and the Moravians.* Vision Video (#4009). 70 minutes.

*Gospel of Liberty.* Vision Video (#4213). 37 minutes.

"Hans Egede." *Children's Heroes.* Part 2. Vision Video (#4206). 9 minutes.

*Baptists in America.* Southern Baptist Historical Society (#VA9999). Six 29 minute programs. Call (800) 966-BAPT to order SBHS resources.

**Print**
"George Whitefield." *Christian History* Issue 38.

Keillor, S. *This Rebellious House.* Downer's Grove: InterVarsity, 1996.

## Notes

## References

*Roger Williams and the Puritans:* Keillor, *This Rebellious House*, 70; Leon McBeth, *The Baptist Heritage* (Nashville: Broadman, 1987) 124-136

*Edwards, Whitefield, Wesley, and the Great Awakening:* Keillor, *This Rebellious House*, 74-80; Noll, *A History of Christianity in the United States and Canada*, 91-92, 109

*Religious opposition to the American Revolution:* "The American Revolution" *Christian History* Issue 50

*Religious beliefs of Founding Fathers:* "The American Revolution" *Christian History* Issue 50; Keillor, *This Rebellious House*, 84-86, 90-91, 101-102; Noll, *A History of Christianity in the United States and Canada*, 132-136

## Notes

come up with five ideas. The ideas may be perversions of Christian truth (like the denial that Jesus is the only way of salvation) or of Christian practice (like changing the Christian faith to appeal to non-believers). List the ideas on a chalkboard or transparency.]

- Say: "*Like many false ideas, Deism arose from a good desire—a longing for tolerance and peace. Why did the false ideas that we've listed arise?*" [As students respond, try to help them see that false ideas usually arise from good desires. The problem is that people fail to locate the right response to their desires.]
- Say: "*Christians must never adapt their faith to false beliefs. But Christians can let non-believers' longings help them understand how to respond to false ideas in their culture. Name some correct responses to the desires that led to these false beliefs.*" [Allow students to respond until at least three specific responses surface.]

6. **Upcoming Assignment and Closure—*3 minutes***
   - Lead a brief prayer. Ask God to help your students respond appropriately to false beliefs.
   - Remind the students to complete the Chapter Eleven Learning Activity before the next session.

## CHAPTER ELEVEN—DISCUSSION AND REVIEW SESSION

**Session Goals**
This session will help students:
- reinforce the knowledge they have gained by reading Chapter Eleven.
- refuse to try to limit God's work in their lives.

**Supplies**
- Christmas decorations (e.g., a small tree, tinsel, lights, etc.)
- A piece of paper and pencil for each student
- A photocopy of the essay "Christmas Wasn't Born Here" (see Digging Deeper) for each student. Your local library should be able to locate the essay.
- Articles about five of these people—William Carey, Amy Carmichael, Fanny Crosby, Sarah Grimke, Ann H. Judson, Lottie Moon, C. H. Spurgeon, Hudson Taylor, Sojourner Truth, William Wilberforce. You can find articles through:
   —The Internet
      *http://www.christianhistory.net*
      *http://www.gty.org/~phil/menu.htm*
      *http://gospelcom.net/chi/glimpses/indexpage.htm*
      *http://christianhistorymadeeasy.homepage.com*
   —Your local library (*Oxford Dictionary of the Christian Church* and encyclopedias)
- A chalkboard
- One large piece of poster-board or shelf paper

1. **Preparation**
   - Ask God to guide you throughout the session.
   - Study Chapter Eleven and the Chapter Eleven Learning Activity.
   - Post a sign that reads: LET GOD GO OUT OF BOUNDS!
   - Trim the classroom with the Christmas decorations.
   - Arrange the articles, papers, and pencils on tables.

- On the board, write the names of people about whom you found articles.
- Select two or three songs to sing during the session, such as "It Came Upon a Midnight Clear" (a nineteenth-century Christmas song), "Faith is the Victory" (one of Ira Sankey's hymns), "Mine Eyes Have Seen the Glory" (a song from the Civil War), or some of Fanny Crosby's hymns.

2. **Before the Session**
   As students enter, be certain they have completed the Chapter Eleven Learning Activity. Give each student a copy of "Christmas Wasn't Born Here" to read while other students arrive.

3. **Worship**—*10 minutes*
   Sing the theme song and two or three nineteenth-century hymns.

4. **Learning Activity**—*12 minutes*
   Review Chapter Eleven Learning Activity. Answers will vary. These answers are suggestions:
   **ANSWERS: 1**-modern, optimism, progress; **2**-Carey challenged his church's refusal to obey this text; **3**-To reach the Chinese, the Taylors adopted Chinese culture; **4**-The Restorationists wanted Christians to forsake denominations so that they could obey this text; **5**-God used Lydia's prayers to bring Charles to salvation; **6**-feelings; **7**-Both White and Miller believed persons could predict Christ's return; **8**-(a) Jesus is God, John 1:1; (b) Jesus was virgin-born, Matthew 1:18; (c) Jesus died as a sacrifice for sinners, 1 John 2:2; (d) Jesus arose from the dead and will come again, Acts 1:3-11; (e) The Bible contains no errors, 2 Timothy 3:16-17.

5. **Large Group Reflection and Review**—*5 minutes*
   - Say: "*In the 1600s and 1700s, few Christians in England or the Americas observed Christmas. When Christmas was celebrated, it was—in a nineteenth century bishop's words—'a day of worldly festivity, shooting, and swearing.' In the 1800s, Clement Moore published a poem titled 'Twas the Night Before Christmas.' According to a Dutch legend, St. Nicholas dropped dowries down chimneys for poor girls. Moore's poem popularized the legend of St. Nicholas in America and England. By 1843, Christmas was a time to stay home with one's family. Yet the new Christmas focused on human reason and human goodness. In Charles Dickens' A Christmas Carol, the spirit of Christmas, not Christ, is what transforms Scrooge. People had placed human boundaries—boundaries like faith in human reason, human goodness, and human progress—around God's boundless work until they no longer felt a need for a personal relationship with Christ. Today, Christians still try to limit God's work. They try to restrict the Spirit's movements to their denomination, their race, or their traditions. They forget that God's only limit is God's own nature, as expressed in Scripture.*"

6. **Research and Sharing**—*20 minutes*
   - Say: "*On the board, I've listed five names. Each of these people allowed God to break human boundaries—to go 'out of bounds'—in his or her life. Use the resources on the tables to research one of these Christians. On your paper, list (1) an intriguing fact about the person, (2) one way that the person broke human boundaries, and, (3) how Christians today can break the same boundary.*"

## Digging Deeper

**Audio/Video**
"Damien," "Robert Raikes," "William Carey," "William Wilberforce." *Children's Heroes.* Vision Video (#4208). 9 minutes each.

Eagles. "The Last Resort." *Hell Freezes Over.* Audio and video. How can a pop song teach history? This song captures the 1800's optimism and its tragic results. The lyrics even grasp the shift from postmillennialism (at first, the focus is an earthly paradise) to premillennialism (the focus shifts to "what it's like up there").

*Hudson Taylor.* Vision Video (#99733). 85 minutes.

*Midnight Cry!* [William Miller.] Vision Video (#31253). 102 minutes.

*William Wilberforce.* Vision Video (#4070). 35 minutes.

*Wrestling with God.* [Alexander Campbell.] Vision Video (#3950). 72 minutes.

**Print**
For pamphlets about nineteenth-century frontier missions, contact the Partee Center, 816/781-7700. Ask for these pamphlets—*John Berry Meachum, John Mason Peck, James E. Welch,* and *Old Bethel Church.* The Partee Center can also arrange tours of C.H. Spurgeon's library in Liberty, Missouri.

*Baptist Heritage Series.* Pamphlets. Southern Baptist Historical Society (#PH9999).

Noll, M. *Scandal of the Evangelical Mind.* Grand Rapids: Eerdmans, 1993.

Woodward, K. L. "Christmas Wasn't Born Here." *Newsweek* (12/16/96): 71.

## References

*Charles G. Finney's teachings:* "Charles G. Finney," *Christian History* Issue 20; Noll, *A History of Christianity in the United States and Canada,* 176

*Gothic architecture in the 1800s:* White, *How the Churches Got to Be the Way They Are,* 13-16

*Sojourner Truth:* Bill Leonard, *Word of God Across the Ages* (Greenville: Smyth and Helwys, 1991) 68-71

*Religious responses to the American Civil War:* Noll, *A History of Christianity in the United States and Canada,* 317-318, 322-323

**The Fundamentals** *and the theory of evolution:* Noll, *A History of Christianity in the United States and Canada,* 370-372; White, *How the Churches Got to Be the Way They Are,* 69-71

## Notes

- Allow students 12-15 minutes for research.
- Organize the class into three roughly equal groups. Have students share their lists with their group. Each group should select the most interesting list from among its members.
- Ask each group to share its chosen list with the entire class. On the chalkboard, list the ways that Christians today can break human boundaries.

7. **Closure and Upcoming Assignment—8 minutes**
   - Lead the class in prayer. Ask God to guide each student to let God go "out of bounds" in their lives. Tell students to study Chapter Twelve and complete the Chapter Twelve Learning Activity before the next meeting.

---

## CHAPTER TWELVE—REVIEW AND CLOSURE SESSION

### Session Goals
This session will help students:
- reinforce the knowledge they have gained by reading Chapter Twelve.
- decide how to use the knowledge they have gained from their study of church history.

### Supplies
- Black bread (such as pumpernickel), Swiss cheese, sauerkraut, ice cream and sundae toppings, bananas, sunflower seeds, tortilla chips, Italian-flavored snacks or pizza, Polish sausages, trail mix, Graham crackers (If you do not want to eat during the final session, cut out a picture of each food from magazines.)
- One of the videos suggested in Digging Deeper. (I have placed asterisks beside videos available at most video stores.)
- One large piece of poster-board

1. **Preparation**
   - Ask God to guide you throughout the session.
   - Post a sign that reads: *HOW DID YOU GET TO BE THE WAY YOU ARE?*
   - Ready the video and VCR.
   - Prepare food, flatware, plates, and drinks.
   - Enlist an accompanist and song-leader.
   - Study Chapter Twelve and the Chapter Twelve Learning Activity.
2. **Before the Session**
   - As members enter, make certain they have finished the Chapter Twelve Learning Activity.
   - Ask some members, "*Is there a song or Scripture that has become more meaningful to you because of this study?*" Compile three songs and three Scriptures.
3. **Worship—12 minutes**
   Sing the theme song and the songs suggested by class members. Read the three Scriptures. Ask the class: "*How have these songs and Scriptures become more meaningful to you through this study?*" Let several students respond.
4. **Large Group Review—Time will vary**
   - Ask members to locate the Chapter Twelve Learning Activity. Say: Each of the first ten answers relates to one of the foods on the table. Randomly point at foods and ask: *What question and answer does* [**food**] *suggest?*

**ANSWERS: 1**-Russian Orthodox Church (Black bread is a Russian staple); **2**-Karl Barth (He was Swiss.); **3**-Dietrich Bonhoeffer (Sauerkraut is German.); **4**-Sunday (ice cream sundae); **5**-William Bryan (Monkeys eat bananas.); **6**-Pentecostals (Sunflower seeds are often associated with Kansas.); **7**-John XXIII (Italian snacks or pizza.); **8**-John Paul II (Polish sausages—He's Polish.); **9**-World Council of Churches (Trail mix—The WCC is a mixture of various groups.); **10**-Billy Graham (Graham crackers).

- Share your answers for question 11. Use the definition at the beginning of Chapter Twelve to answer question 12.
- Begin the video. Members can eat as they watch the video. After the video, read aloud a segment of Chapter 12 that relates to the video. Briefly discuss the video.

**5. Life Application—*12 minutes***
- Ask: *To what areas of your Christian life can you apply what you have learned through these studies?* Let students respond until three specific responses surface. Write the responses on a chalkboard.
- Read aloud the quote from Gavin White in "Final Reflections." Lead the class in prayer. Ask God to help members use their knowledge of their Christian heritage in their daily lives.

## Digging Deeper

**Audio/Video**
*Dietrich Bonhoeffer*. Vision Video (#4137). 60 minutes.

"A Hidden Treasure." *History and Holy Sacraments of Orthodox Christianity* Part 3. Vision Video (#4094). 30 minutes.

*\*The Hiding Place*. Vision Video (#8024). 145 minutes.

*\*Inherit the Wind*.

*\*Shadowlands*. Vision Video (#4054). 73 minutes.

"Sundar Singh." *Children's Heroes*. Vision Video (#4206). 9 minutes.

**Print**
Grenz, S. *A Primer on Post-modernism*. Grand Rapids: Eerdmans, 1996.

"The Monkey Trial and the Rise of Fundamentalism." *Christian History* issue 55.

Oden, T. *After Modernity. What?* Grand Rapids: Zondervan, 1991.

Wells, D. *No Place for Truth*. Grand Rapids: Eerdmans, 1993.

# Index

Allen, Richard: 112
Ambrose of Milan: 39
Anabaptists: 80, 85-87, 90, 93
Anglican Church (Church of England): 88-89, 92-93, 104, 110, 134,137
Anselm: 66-67
Apologists: 6, 12
Apostles' Creed, the: 21-23
Arius of Alexandria, Arianism: 26, 30-31, 38
Arminianism: 94, 111
Assemblies of God: 133
Athanasius of Alexandria: 26, 30-32
Augustine of Hippo: 36, 40-42, 45
Baptists: 97-98, 106, 122
Barbarians: 37-38, 40, 42, 44, 45, 65
Barth, Karl: 128-129, 134-135
Bible: see Scripture, Canon of
Bishops (overseers): 17, 21-22
Bonhoeffer, Dietrich: 134-136
Bubonic Plague (Black Death): 72-73
Bulls, papal: 54, 82
Bunyan, John: 97-98
Calvin, John: 80, 84-86
Calvinism: 85, 93-95, 111
Campbell, Alexander: 117
Canon: 19-21
Cappadocians, Great: 26, 33, 34, 38
Carey, William and Dorothy: 115-116
Catholicism, Roman: 55-58, 90, 92, 95, 96, 136-138
Chalcedon, Council of: 36, 43
Charismatic Movement: 139
Charlemagne: 51-52
Christian Scientism: 121
Cluny: 61-62
Columbus, Christopher (Cristobal Colon): 99
Conciliarism: 70
Constantine the Great, Emperor: 26, 28-31
Constantinople, First Council

of: 36, 38
Crusades: 55-57, 60, 99
Cyril of Alexandria: 42-43
Cyril of Moravia: 62-63
Day, Dorothy: 137
Dead Sea Scrolls: 9, 126
Deism: 104, 108, 109
Docetism: 16, 18
Donation of Constantine, The: 48, 51, 71
Donatism: 26, 30
Easter, date of: 22
Ecumenicalism: 131-134, 136
Edwards, Jonathan: 109, 111
Enlightenment, the: 104, 108
Episcopalianism: 112
Erasmus of Rotterdam: 70, 78, 81, 84, 86
Evangelicalism: 126, 131, 138-139
Finney, Charles G.: 118
Foursquare Gospel: 133
Francis of Assisi: 60, 66
Fundamentalism: 123-124, 126, 129-132, 138
Galileo, Galilei: 95
Gnosticism (Secret Knowledge Movement): 16-21
Gothic architecture: 68, 119-120
Graham, Billy: 132, 138
Great Awakening, the: 104, 109-112
Gregory the Great, Pope: 36, 44-45
Gutenberg, Johann: 77
Hildegard of Bingen: 64
Hutchinson, Anne: 106
Hus, Jan: 70, 74-75, 83
Icons, iconoclasm: 50-51, 62
Inquisition: 56, 70, 77
Islam: 55-56
Jehovah's Witnesses: 121
Jerome: 26, 33
Jesuits: 89, 92, 101
Joan of Arc: 76
John XXIII, Pope: 136-137
John Chrysostom: 39-40
John of Damascus: 62
John Paul II, Pope: 137

Kant, Immanuel: 118-120
Kimbangu, Simon: 133
King James Version: 97
Leo, Pope: 43-44
Lewis, C.S.: 132
Liberalism: 118-120, 126, 129-132
Loyola, Ignatius: 89
Luther, Martin and Kaetie: 81-84
Lutheranism: 84, 89, 90, 93
Marcion of Pontus: 16, 18-20
Masada: 11
Mennonites: 87
Methodism: 104, 110-111
Middle Ages (medieval era): 49
Moody, D.L.: 123-124
Monks and nuns: 32-34, 44-45,
    60-62, 64, 92
Montanism (New Prophecy
    Movement): 16, 23-24
Mormons: 118
Mother Teresa: 137
Muslims: 50, 55-56, 62, 77
Nero, Emperor: 7-8, 11
Nicaea, First Council of: 26,
    30-32, 38
Nicene Creed: 39
Origen: 16,19
Orthodoxy, Eastern: 54, 56-58,
    76-77, 104, 127-128
Parham, Charles Fox: 132
Patrick of Ireland: 46
Paul of Tarsus: 6-9, 13, 18
Paula: 33
Pentecostalism: 127, 132-134,
Peter: 6, 8
Photius, Photian Schism: 52-53
Polycarp of Smyrna: 6, 12, 19,
    21-22
Popes, papacy: 21, 44-45,
    54, 58, 122, 123, 136-137
Presbyterianism: 80, 89, 92
Process theology: 126
Puritanism: 92, 96-97, 105-107
Quakers (Society of Friends):
    104, 106
Renaissance humanism: 70,
    77-78
Rule of Faith (The Apostles'
    Creed): 16, 21, 23

Schleiermacher, Friedrich Daniel
    Ernst: 118-120
Scholasticism: 60, 66-68,
    75, 78
Scripture, Canon of: 20
Seventh-Day Adventists: 121
Slavery: 100-101, 121-122
Spurgeon, Charles H.: 120-121
Stone, Barton W.: 117
Taylor, Hudson: 116
Tyndale, William: 80, 87-89
Thomas A'Kempis: 76, 89
Thomas Aquinas: 60, 67-68
Thomas Becket: 67
Transubstantiation: 48, 56, 84
Vatican, First Council of the:
    123
Vatican, Second Council of
    the: 136-137
Waldo (Valdes), Waldensians:
    60, 65
Wesley, Susanna, Charles, and
    John: 104, 110-111
Whitefield, George: 111
Williams, Roger: 104-106
Wycliffe, John: 74-75
Zwingli, Ulrich: 83-85

# About the Author

Nearly one million people have studied Timothy Paul Jones's lessons in the popular *Family Bible Series* booklets, published by Lifeway Christian Resources. Thousands more have read his articles and sermons in *Preaching, Proclaim, Biblical Illustrator, The Door,* and *Perspectives in Religious Studies.* He is also the author of *Prayers Jesus Prayed* (Servant Publications) and of more than 200 articles and entries in *Nelson's New Christian Dictionary* (Thomas Nelson).

Timothy has earned the Bachelor of Arts in biblical studies from Manhattan Christian College, the Master of Divinity from Midwestern Baptist Theological Seminary, and the Doctor of Education from The Southern Baptist Theological Seminary. His doctoral dissertation focused on the relationship between Christian faith and the faith that is present in other religious faiths. In 1996, the faculty of Midwestern Baptist Theological Seminary awarded Timothy the Baker Book House Award for outstanding work in theology. *Christian History Made Easy* emerged from Timothy's "Church History 101" workshops, through which laypeople learn about their Christian heritage in an enjoyable, interactive format.

Timothy has served in churches throughout Kansas, Missouri, and Oklahoma as a pastor and a ministerial staff member. He is currently the pastor of First Baptist Church of Rolling Hills, in Tulsa, Oklahoma. Timothy and his wife, Rayann, live in Catoosa, Oklahoma, in a house owned by a mean-eyed cat named Martin Luther.

*Author, Timothy Paul Jones*

Printed in the United States
16770LVS00002B/89-510

9 781890 947101